BRAHMAN AND PERSON

Essays by Richard De Smet

BRAHMAN AND PERSON

Essays by Richard De Smet

Edited by

IVO COELHO

MOTILAL BANARSIDASS PUBLISHERS
PRIVATE LIMITED • DELHI

First Edition : Delhi, 2010

ISBN : 978-81-208-3459-0

MOTILAL BANARSIDASS
41 U.A. Bungalow Road, Jawahar Nagar, Delhi 110 007
8 Mahalaxmi Chamber, 22 Bhulabhai Desai Road, Mumbai 400 026
203 Royapettah High Road, Mylapore, Chennai 600 004
236, 9th Main III Block, Jayanagar, Bangalore 560 011
Sanas Plaza, 1302 Baji Rao Road, Pune 411 002
8 Camac Street, Kolkata 700 017
Ashok Rajpath, Patna 800 004
Chowk, Varanasi 221 001

Printed in India

By Jainendra Prakash Jain at Shri Jainendra Press,
A-45, Naraina, Phase-I, New Delhi 110 028
and Published by Narendra Prakash Jain for
Motilal Banarsidass Publishers Private Limited,
Bungalow Road, Delhi 110 007

CONTENTS

PREFACE

I count Fr Richard V. De Smet, SJ, as one of my great teachers and also a good friend. In 1988, he had requested my services for a year, to help him put his papers in order and move towards publication. Unfortunately I was not able to oblige him at the time. The present work may therefore be regarded not only as an act of *pietas* but also as an attempt to make up; and I hope it will not be the end, for there is much that still remains to be done to make Fr De Smet's work available to a larger public and to give it the attention it deserves.

A very large number of people have collaborated in the present work, and I am happy to acknowledge their help:

Banzelão Teixeira, Rolvin D'Mello, Peter Gonsalves, Cyril De Souza, Mayank Parmar, Tino Fernandes, Savio D'Souza, Jr., Lourdes Bravo da Costa, Julian Rodrigues, Valentine Coelho, Sahayadas Fernando, Jose Maliekal, Felix Fernandes, S. Panneerselvam, C.M. Paul, George Thadathil, Magdalena Strauch, A. Kunstmann, Crescens Lemos, J. Velinkar, and J. Saldanha for help with bibliographical research.

The Librarians of Jnana Deepa Vidyapeeth, Pune; De Nobili College, Pune; Ramakrishna Mission Institute of Culture, Kolkata; Goethals Library, Kolkata.

Nelson Falcao, Robert Pen, Tony George, Daniel D'Souza and Mylin Noronha for help with the Marathi translations.

Bernard Britto, Edward Pereira, Nazareth Denis and Shyju Babykutty for invaluable help with secretarial work.

Banzelão Teixeira and Joel D'Souza for proof-reading.

Michael Fernandes, Provincial of the Salesians of Don Bosco, Mumbai, and the staff and students of Divyadaan for the support and the space I have enjoyed while engaged in this work.

On all of them, blessings and peace!

Ivo Coelho, SDB
31 January 2009
Divyadaan: Salesian Institute of Philosophy, Nashik

Acknowledgements
The use of the following materials is gratefully acknowledged: "*Persona, Anima, Ātman*," which appeared in *The Philosophical Quarterly* (Amalner) **30**/4 (January 1958) 251-260. "Zum indischen Menschenbild," which appeared in *Kairos: Zeitschrift für Religionswissenschaft und Theologie* (Salzburg) **8**/3-4 (1966) 179-202, published with permission from De Nobili College, Pune; "The Discovery of the Person," "The Loss of the Person," "The Rediscovery of the Person," and "The Aristotelian-Thomist Conception of Man," which appeared in the *Indian Philosophical Quarterly* **4** (1976-77) 1-9, 10-23, 413-426; and **2**/4 (July 1975) 307-318. "The Open Person vs. The Closed Individual," "Early Trends in the Indian Understanding of Man," "Is the Concept of 'Person' Congenial to Śaṅkara Vedānta?" and "The Concept of Man in Thomism and Neo-Thomism," which appeared in *Indian Ecclesiastical Studies* **9**/3 (1970) 161-171; **10**/3 (1971) 169-178; **12**/3 (1973) 155-162; and in *Indian Theological Studies* **26**/4 (1989) 336-372. "*Ātmavada*," "*Ātmā – Ihetara Jīvana*," "*Jīva (Jīvātman)*," "*Mānavavāda*," "*Vyakti*," "*Vyaktitattva*," "*Vyaktivāda*," which appeared in the *Marāṭhi Tattvajñāna Mahākoṣa*, ed. D.D. Vadekar (Poona: Marathi Tattvajnana Mahakosa Mandala, 1974-75) **1**:69-70, 71-73, 262-263; **2**:436-437; **3**:97-98, 98-99, 99; published here with permission of Geeta Dharma Mandal, Pune, present copyright holder. "The Christian Conception of Man," which first appeared in *Southern Chronicle* **8**/1 (1982) 21-27 and was reprinted in two parts under the titles "The Biblical Concept of a Human Person," and "The Christian Concept of a Human Person," *Ignis* **19** (1990) 59-64, 127-130. "Materials Toward an Indo-Western Understanding of the Dignity of the Human Person," which appeared in the *Journal of Dharma* **21** (1996) 39-46.

INTRODUCTION

Indian scholars and religious personalities are prone to speak about the 'impersonal' Absolute *Brahman* of the Upaniṣads and the Vedānta, in contrast to the 'personal' God of the Christians, where impersonal and personal are translations of *nirguṇa* and *saguṇa* respectively. Under the influence perhaps of New Age, it is not unusual to find also a section of the Christian clergy and theologians adopting this usage.[1] It therefore comes as a surprise to read that, way back in 1973, at a seminar convened at the University of Madras on the topic of the person, the revered scholar and Vedāntin Prof. T.M.P. Mahadevan declared that the *Brahman* of Śaṅkara was, if anything, surely not impersonal.[2] Fr Richard V. De Smet, SJ, who reports this development, modestly calls this "an important linguistic change," and attributes it with even greater modesty to the participation by Christian scholars at various meetings of Indian philosophers in the previous twenty years. The twenty years in question, however, coincide roughly with the completion of De Smet's doctorate on the theological method of Śaṅkara in 1953 and his own active involvement with the Indian Philosophical Congress and other such associations, and we would not be far off the mark if we were to attribute the lion's share of the credit for this development to De Smet himself.[3] Further, Prof. Mahadevan's declaration is surely more than a mere linguistic change. It is an important moment in Indological scholarship and in interreligious and intercultural dialogue. Clearly, it has not yet received the attention it deserves. Studies about the person in Indian and Western thought continue to be ignorant of this development and of the contributions of De Smet that led up to it.[4] One of the reasons for this state of affairs is that De Smet's production was mostly in the form of articles scattered over a large number of relatively unknown Indian journals and publications. The present collection attempts to address this problem by bringing together De Smet's contributions on the topic of the person.[5]

In his introduction to *New Perspectives on Advaita Vedānta*, Bradley J. Malkovsky has already given us a life sketch of Fr De Smet.[6] Let me recall, however, at least the basic facts. Richard Vital De Smet was born in Belgium in 1916, joined the novitiate of the Society of Jesus in 1934, and came to India as a young student of Catholic theology in 1946. After completing the usual course of theological studies, he was asked to specialize in Indology, which, as he himself reports, had been an early interest.[7] By 1953 he had earned a Ph.D. from the Gregorian University, Rome, for his thesis on the theological method of Śaṅkara.[8] Against the prevailing current of opinion that would have Śaṅkara a philosopher, he showed how the great Vedāntin was a *śrutivādin*, a theologian who applied reason and available cultural resources to the sacred texts accepted as authoritative.[9] Back in India, he launched himself with vigour into his new field of competence, thus joining an impressive rank of Jesuit Indologists that included Roberto de Nobili in the seventeenth century and G. Dandoy, P. Johanns, R. Antoine and P. Fallon in the twentieth. For many years, however, De Smet taught not only Indian philosophy but also 'Western courses' such as metaphysics and philosophy of God; this accounts for his extraordinary familiarity with the Western and especially Christian metaphysical tradition.[10] As I have already noted, one of De Smet's great merits was to have immediately established contact with Indian philosophers in secular universities. The story of the impact of his contributions in the area of Indology has still to be written, but I allow myself to report here an extraordinary remark of Prof. S. Panneerselvam, Head of the Department of Philosophy at the University of Madras, to the effect that De Smet was one of the Vedāntins of India.[11] Besides his membership in the Indian Philosophical Congress and the Indian Philosophical Association, De Smet was also the founder and long time President of the Association of Christian Philosophers of India. In these various capacities, and through his work as professor at Jnana Deepa Vidyapeeth, Pune, he became mentor, guide and friend to countless scholars, young and old.[12]

De Smet's writings contain a veritable campaign on the notion of the person, beginning in 1957, barely three years after the completion of his doctorate, with the lecture "*Persona, Anima, Ātman.*"[13] Presented at the Indian Philosophical Congress and published subsequently both in the Proceedings of the Congress and *The Philosophical Quarterly* (Amalner), the lecture is a substantial clarification of the term 'person' in the West, with shorter notes on *anima* / soul and *ātman*; however, the history of the person ends with the Scholastics, and the note on *ātman* tends to remain within the dominant Upaniṣadic and Vedāntic trends. An article of 1966, "Zum indischen Menschenbild" (Concerning the Indian View of Man), tries to complete the picture with matter from non-Upaniṣadic and non-Vedāntic trends, but was published in a German language journal.[14] The campaign peaks in 1970 with a flurry of lectures. Three lectures delivered at the University of Madras but published in the *Indian Philosophical Quarterly* (University of Poona) and subsequently circulated in an offprinted booklet, contain an elaborate history of the person in the West, though not without forays into the East: "The Discovery of the Person," "The Loss of the Person," and "The Rediscovery of the Person."[15] "The Open Person vs the Closed Individual" of the same year, delivered as the Presidential Address of the Indian Philosophical Association, expands upon the shift from the organic notion of person achieved in high scholasticism to the atomic and isolated individual of the modern and contemporary period.[16] Another lecture of 1970 returns instead to the Indian understanding of man, outlining the contributions of the sacrificers (the Vedic period), the renouncers (both orthodox and heterodox), and the devotees (*bhaktas* of various sects); this lecture, first delivered at the 1970 session of the Indian Philosophical Congress, was published at least five times.[17] The fruits of the efforts of 1970 are reaped in an article of 1972 which proposes that the concept of person can be applied both to the Absolute *Brahman* and to the *jīvātman* of Śaṅkara Vedānta,[18] and in a rather extensive study of 1974 that works out an Indian view of the person.[19] Already in the latter, barely seventeen years after "*Persona, Anima, Ātman,*" De Smet is able to report Mahadevan's comment about the personal nature of *Brahman*. The work of this period is carried over into the entries contributed to the *Marāṭhi Tattvajñāna Mahākoṣa* (1974). These do not really bring in anything new, but are certainly a sign of the measure of the esteem in which De Smet was held.[20]

In 1975 De Smet returns once again to the Western idea of the person, but this time he focuses on the human person, and specifically on Christian thinking in this area.[21] The more substantial pieces—"The Aristotelian-Thomist Conception of Man" of 1975 and "The Concept of Man in Thomism and Neo-Thomism" of 1982-83—both seem to have been intended for a non-Christian readership, the former being published in the *Indian Philosophical Quarterly* (University of Poona) and the latter in the *Indian Philosophical Annual* (University of Madras).[22] The paper of 1975 is a presentation of the method devised by Aristotle for investigating the phenomenon of the human soul: unlike the Indian tradition in which *viveka* predominates, this is a method in which analysis is followed by synthesis, so that the 'field-unitariness' of the phenomenon is never lost sight of. The 1982-83 article complements the teaching of Aquinas with the thinking of the Neo-Thomists J. Maritain, J. Maréchal, É. Gilson, and Karol Wojtyła (Pope John Paul II). "The Christian Conception of Man" of 1982 seems instead to have been intended for a Christian readership, having been published in a Christian journal, the *Southern Chronicle*, and later reprinted in the Jesuit journal *Ignis* in two parts under the titles "The Biblical Concept of a Human Person" and "The Christian Concept of a Human Person."[23] This article begins with notes on the concept of man in the Old and New Testaments and then integrates earlier matter on the human person, before going on to new reading in the contemporary area, as evidenced by a series of unintegrated quotations from Max Scheler. In 1996, finally, we have a little note, published in the *Journal of Dharma* (Dharmaram College, Bangalore), concentrating on the *dignity* of the human person.[24]

1. Divine Personality

De Smet makes two major contributions on the topic of the person: he shows how the *Brahman* of Śaṅkara Vedānta must be acknowledged as personal, and he works out an Indian view of the person and even an Indian humanism.

In "*Persona, Anima, Ātman*" and more extensively in "The Discovery of the Person," De Smet outlines the origin of the term 'person' in the Greek *prosôpon* and the Latin *persona* and shows how it was transferred from its stage meaning of mask, character, role to the world stage, where it came to mean the God-given nature or role played by each individual in the drama of life. The Roman jurists took an extremely important step when they began using *persona* to indicate the citizen as subject of rights and duties, for now the term was predicated not merely of the nature of the individual but of its complete being. The term was then ready for use by the Christian theologians who were searching for ways to express adequately the revealed mysteries of Christ and God. At the end of a long, complex and much controverted development—largely because of the unequal pace of evolution between Greek and Latin Christians—it was agreed to say that Christ was one person in two natures, divine and human, and that God was a Trinity of persons subsisting equally in the perfect unity of the divine nature.[25] This precise application of *persona* to Christ and to God, De Smet notes, had the effect of clarifying its application to the human being and opening up the field to Christian humanism. *Genesis* teaches that all human beings are created in the image of God; it follows that, like God, all human beings, and not only Roman citizens, are persons. De Smet does not hesitate to declare: "The proclamation of this dignity was to have great consequences for the emancipation of man from all kinds of oppressions and for the whole development of Western culture and even for the destiny of all mankind."[26]

Subsequent clarifications of 'person' are not less significant. De Smet begins with Boethius' influential definition of the term: "Person, properly speaking, is an individual substance endowed with a rational nature." Already in "*Persona, Anima, Ātman,*" and with great wealth of detail in "The Loss of the Person," De Smet shows how the terms of this definition underwent a profound transformation at the hands of the scholastics and especially of Thomas Aquinas. Thus 'substance' was replaced by 'subsistent' to avoid any possibility of pantheism; 'individual' was replaced by 'singular' or 'distinct,' for among the different types of singularity, individuality is the lowest type, applicable only to material beings; the completeness of the person was insisted on, so that in the case of human beings it is not the soul that is the person, despite its subsistence, but rather the unity of body and soul; 'rational' was replaced by 'intellectual,' since rationality is but the lowest form of intellect; and finally, the person was affirmed to be an ultimate subject of intellectual, free activity and rights.[27] Clearly, such transformation and refinement of the definition of person was made with the intention of safeguarding its application to both God and the human being. In De Smet's words:

> '[P]erson' is a holistic concept, it refers to the whole, to the integrality of the agent, whether the latter is pure spirit like God or rational animal like man. It is, however, immaterial whether the personal agent is in itself simple, partless, absolute spiritual substance without accidents and thus pure Consciousness, or whether it is a complex subsistent comprising parts and functions, spiritual and also corporeal. What matters is that its integrality be predominantly spiritual, i.e., intellectually conscious. This, indeed, is required to make it a subject of attribution ultimate, freely responsible and an end in itself.[28]

A difficulty is perhaps presented by the fact that persons characteristically enter into interpersonal relationships, for how can God be related to finite persons? De Smet explains that Thomas' theory of relation enables the elimination of this difficulty. The truth of a relation depends on its foundation or ground. If this ground is intrinsic to the subject of the relation, that relation is not only true but real. If the ground is extrinsic to the subject but intrinsic to the term of the relation, the relation is regarded as true but merely logical in the subject, and the correlation as true but real in the term. Thus love, creatorship, lordship, etc. are logical relations, but being loved by God, creaturehood, dependence, etc. are real relations. God can, therefore, be related to finite persons without violation of his transcendence and simplicity.[29]

If De Smet's outline of the discovery of the person is important for understanding that the Christian meaning of the term person took shape in an effort to give expression to the mystery of God, his history of the loss of the person is important for an understanding of the reception of the term in India. Aquinas' person, he points out, was an organic, unified and intrinsically social being; this conception soon degenerated into atomic individualism. Duns Scotus stands at the head of this development, but the modern problematic was set by Descartes' option to regard the human being as two substances which are united neither substantially nor necessarily but only by the will of God. Spinoza abolishes the body-mind problem by opting for a monism of the divine substance, with man as merely a peculiar mode of God. Leibniz attempts to overcome both dualism and monism by positing an infinity of spiritual monads which, while retaining some traits of the person, jeopardize freedom, interpersonal relationships, society, as well as the transcendence of God. Hobbes inaugurates a new kind of dualism between the natural and the social states of man: since man is essentially individual, society is a construct and the state a despot. Locke modifies this despotism by positing a political contract based on trust. Hume regards the ego as merely a series of felt phenomena, and proposes that moral and social life is founded neither in God nor in reason, but in instinct, feeling and habit. Rousseau adopts Hobbesian individualism, only to end with the anti-individualist demand for the alienation of all rights to the state.[30]

It was in the context of such rationalistic individualism that the Protestant German philosopher F.H. Jacobi proposed that the term 'person' be restricted only to human beings, on the grounds that it necessarily implies limitation and relational dependence:

> [T]he rather obscure German philosopher, H. Jacobi, introduced an innovation which has not ceased to play havoc in the field of Indology and comparative religion. He said that to be a person one has to *have* qualities, relations, etc.; hence, only a limited being could be personal. Whereas the classical definition transcended the distinction between having and being, Jacobi's definition so linked personality with having, that it could henceforth be said of finite beings only.[31]

The trend inaugurated by Jacobi was followed by a small number of Protestant thinkers, chiefly Germans, but these influenced the great translators of Sanskrit works towards the end of the nineteenth century, who rendered *saguṇa* as 'personal' and *nirguṇa* as 'impersonal.' It is this that has led to the widespread Hindu conviction that the Christians have a lower, anthropomorphic conception of God equivalent to *īśvara* rather than to the Absolute *Brahman*.[32] Against the background of his history of the person, however, De Smet is able to conclude that none of the conditions for being a person prevent *Brahman* from being considered personal in the proper sense of the term:

> The concept of person transcends the opposition between *nirguṇa* and *saguṇa*, unqualified and qualified or rather incomplex and complex. Indeed, 'person' like 'being,' 'spirit,' 'bliss' (*sat, cit, ānanda*), etc. is not a predicamental but transcendental term whose highest range reaches the Absolute not only metaphorically but properly.[33]

De Smet adds immediately that not even transcendental terms apply univocally to God and creatures, and that in order to apply to God they must be de-finitized and elevated. Here he brings to bear another of his important discoveries: that Śaṅkara was familiar with and used the method of *jahad-ajahal-lakṣaṇā*, which is roughly equivalent to the analogy of intrinsic attribution of Thomas.[34] Thus the term 'person' is, in a first *ajahat* moment, applied to God; in a second, *jahat*, moment it is denied of God, for God is not person in the same sense that human beings are; these two moments, taken together, throw up the third or *arthāpatti* moment, when one realizes that God is person only in an eminent sense. De Smet concludes that the *Brahman* of Śāṅkara Vedānta is most properly and eminently personal, and that this supreme *Ātman* who is pure consciousness and absolute freedom is indeed the Super-person. In fact, as he points out very acutely, personhood is not a merely pedagogical device or a first deficient approach like *saguṇa*; it is instead "an enrichment of the proper and correct (though ever inadequate) understanding of the Absolute according to the Upaniṣads."[35]

De Smet does admit that "that the Indian conception of *nirguṇa Brahman* does not clearly connote the possibility of an interpersonal exchange between that pure Absolute and man"; however, he insists that "what it directly denotes is identical with the personal God as defined by the great councils, excepting, of course, his trinitarian aspect."[36]

We might add that, in the light of the personhood of *Brahman*, the mysterious pointings in the Indian tradition to love and grace do not have to be explained away or regarded with condescension as a lower form of religion: the discovery in the late Upaniṣads that the *Ātman* must not only be loved above all, but that this love is reciprocated;[37] the "highest word" entrusted by Kṛṣṇa to Arjuna, "I love thee well, thou art dear to Me";[38] the

Bodhisattva as a hero of charity, morality, and wisdom, a merciful saviour, an ideal to be emulated;[39] the great movement of *bhakti*. We might note also, with Malkovsky, how closely De Smet's assertion about the personality of *Brahman* is linked to his championing of a non-illusionistic interpretation of Śaṅkara.[40]

The assertion of the personhood of the *Brahman* does not in itself solve the problem of finding an Indian equivalent for the term 'person.' De Smet points out that concepts like *ātman*, *puruṣa*, *jīva*, and *vyakti* are not really able to carry the holistic meaning of person. In a piece of 1961 published in German, he observes:

> The idea of person is nowhere conceived clearly in the Indian tradition and neither is there any Sanskrit term which translates it exactly. Vyakti implies the idea of modal manifestation or emanation. Puruṣa... conveys primarily the idea of 'male being', but the ācāryas have linked it to the idea of pervading and thus to the idea of the universal Ātmā. The Sāṃkhyas have given it as name to their pure principle of awareness, but we know that they unfortunately exaggerate the scope of the principle of viveka and thus split every being into a puruṣa and prakṛti. The same difficulty is met in the Vedānta conception of ātmā: this also is but an inner principle and not the complete being which we affirm, since it does not really synthesize with its upādhis; only when applied to Brahma does it signify the integrality of a subsistent being and, therefore, the personality of the nirguṇa Brahma.[41]

In an article of 1965 he is somewhat more optimistic:

> India does not afford any such elaboration of the notion of person, yet this notion is not unknown to it. It is signified either by personal pronouns and proper names or by such terms as *jana*, *puruṣa*, *vyakti* and sometimes *ātman*. However, *ātman* is more generally used... in senses which do not coincide with the meaning of person. As to *vyakti*, either it denotes individuals within a class (*jāti*) and is therefore unsuited to designate the divine Persons who transcend all classes, or it only means a special manifestation or impersonation... and would thus give rise to a modalist brand of theology. On the other hand, *puruṣa*... has generally been used in the general sense of person (man or god) and, in philosophy, to designate either the conscious entity as opposed to *Prakṛti* (*Sāṃkhya*) or even the supreme Being (Upanishads, *Gītā*, Vedānta), seems to translate sufficiently well the term 'person'. However, *jana* which designates beings that are born (from root *jan-*), creatures, individual human beings (male or female), or also peoples, nations, is philosophically weak (inasmuch as it is not technically connected with any of the *darśanas*) and

therefore innocuous enough to have been preferred by translators in several Indian languages. I am inclined to agree with them.[42]

By 1974, De Smet and the editors of the *Marāthi Tattvajñāna Mahākoṣa* seem to have opted for the term *vyakti*, despite possible confusions with 'individual' and the risk of modalism. The fact is that meanings evolve, and that they are defined and become somewhat definite only through efforts at systematization, and so we might hope for an evolution and definition of the meaning of person in the East as in the West, this time perhaps through interreligious and dialogical efforts involving scholars and religious persons across the board.[43]

2. Human Personality

The articles of 1957 and 1966 contain precious clarifications about the meaning of *ātman* and how it relates to the Western terms soul and self, but also take note of alternative views of the human being in the non-Upaniṣadic traditions.[44] The article of 1972 upholds the personhood not only of Śaṅkara's *Brahman*, but also, surprisingly, of his conception of the *jīvātman*. The essay of 1974 then begins working towards an Indian conception of person in general.[45] Integrating matter found in "Early Trends in the Indian Understanding of Man" (1970), it adds notes on Jainism, Sāṁkhya, Early Buddhism, the *Gītā* and later Buddhism, culminating with the 'Śaṅkarian' view of the human person worked out in 1972.

Thanks to an equation between being and stability, and the consequent tendency to analyse in order to find the most stable and enduring element in man,[46] the holistic Vedic conception of man was torn apart in the Brāhmaṇas and the Upaniṣads, Jainism and Buddhism, Sāṁkhya and Nyāya-Vaiśeṣika.[47] However, there were also gains. The Upaniṣads rooted man in the divine Absolute and establish the creaturely dimension of his personality.[48] Jainism and Sāṁkhya obeyed the urge to reach man's spiritual core with "dangerous fearlessness," but the former at least insisted on the real connection of its naturally eternal *jīvas* with bodies of non-living matter, resulting in qualities that make them "very similar to the Aristotelian souls."[49] In addition, the prescription of *ahiṁsā* seems to imply the consubstantiality of the *jīvas* and their bodies: violence against the latter also disturbs the former.[50] Early Buddhism rejects the Jaina and Sāṁkhya tendency to solidify abstractions and takes analysis to a new extreme, but interestingly enough gives rise to a new ideal of personality centred around a set of attractive virtues exemplified by the Buddha: non-violent morality, selflessness, devotion to wisdom.[51]

The tension between the Vedic ideal of man, embodied in the caste-system in the age of the *dharmaśāstras*, and the challenge of the renouncers, orthodox and heterodox, was met in a brilliant way by the *Gītā* which inserted renunciation within the structure of duty itself through the concept of disinterested action. Further, the dualism of Sāṁkhya was overcome through a highly personalistic conception of the human being as well as of God. When the Absolute is not only the object of love, as in the Upaniṣads, but also Lover, and when the human beloved is marked by freedom, then both Lover and beloved are personal. The Mahāyāna Buddhists responded with an apophatic monism which, despite its *śūnyavāda*, was able to give birth to the conception of the Bodhisattva as a hero of charity, morality, and wisdom, as well as a merciful saviour, an ideal to be emulated. But it is in Śaṅkara's idea of the *jīvātman* as a reflection of the *Ātman* in the ego-sense that De Smet finds the most adequate conception of the human person available in India.[52] This ego is a contingent, dependent reality; it is not merely the only door by which to pass from the ordinary to the other meaning of I or Thou, but also the key to any correct anthropology. Here the human person is internally unified by the *Ātman* through the reflection-like *jīvātman*. In this way, says De Smet, Śaṅkara is able to integrate the *mahāvākyas* of the Upaniṣads without consenting either to pantheism or acosmism. Unfortunately, De Smet continues, his anthropology did not gain the attention it deserved.[53]

The *Gītā*, Mahāyāna and Śaṅkara represent attempts to transcend the transcendence of the renouncers in favour of an Absolute, whether conceived of as *Brahman* or as the Buddhist *Dharmakāya*, giving rise in the process to anthropologies that are less cut off from the world. In this sense, says De Smet, there is a remarkable affinity between the three: their focusing on the Absolute allows them to turn compassionate eyes to the world, and to adopt a humanistic perspective, though this is somewhat less obvious in the case of Śaṅkara. De Smet concludes with the interesting observation that an Indian personalism is bound to be meagre unless lit up by a religion of the Absolute.[54]

Interestingly, De Smet is also able to say that contemporary India itself has a concept of the human being that is congenial to the development of persons:

> This conception is made of various elements: the old hierarchical casteic conception of society, which provides the roots and ligaments that prevent Indian citizens from ever being isolated individuals; the modern conception, which sanctions the basic rights and freedoms of each man and abolishes excessive privileges or disabilities; the philosophy of Neo-Hinduism, which mingles the lofty transcendentalism of the Upaniṣads with the humanism of the Sermon on the Mount and the self-sufficiency of Hinduism with the universal openness of religious and cultural pluralism. The conjunction of these three has opened India to all the chief dimensions of the human person.[55]

So the Vedic conception of man, persisting today in the caste system and in the worship of the *devas*, brings in the note of wholeness as well as many-sided sociality and relatedness, and has the merit of being akin to the organic conception of the human person rather than to the atomic concept of individuality.[56] The Jaina conception brings in the element of consubstantiality between *jīva* and body. The Buddhist tradition brings in an exalted and attractive ideal of personality. The Upaniṣadic conception, incorporated later by Śaṅkara, insists on human dignity flowing from creaturehood. The *Gītā* implies the dignity of the human being as beloved of God called upon to respond freely in love, taking up the themes of grace and love from the late Upaniṣads as well as the Śaiva tradition, and opening the way for the great current of *bhakti* in India. Śaṅkara's conception of the *jīvātman* as reflection of the *Ātman* brings many of these qualities together: integrity, wholeness, subsistence; it is weak perhaps only in its social aspect. So, despite the fact that 'person' does not exist in Sanskrit, in De Smet's opinion there are enough materials for an Indian recognition of person.[57] The outstanding problem, perhaps, is that of rebirth, which prevents the choice of a term like 'person' for the human being. 'Person' covers the entire human aggregate, soul and body, but, at least in a popular understanding, rebirth involves belief "in the possibility of the same soul being reborn in all sorts of bodies."[58] In point of fact, there is no unanimity about that which migrates, which tends to be understood in widely differing ways: as the *liṅgaśarīra*, or the *jīvātman*, or the *manomaya* (the soul-body unity), or the mind, or the *ahaṁkāra*, or the *jīva* or the *liṅga*, or the *ātman* understood in different ways, or just plain action as in Buddhism which upholds Anātmavāda.[59]

3. Dialogue and Theology

De Smet's deeply sympathetic approach to Hinduism is in abundant evidence in the articles of the present collection. His reading of Indian texts is rich, sympathetic, nuanced and generous. Yet he remained a deeply committed Christian and Catholic: not for him the currently fashionable and antiseptic tactic of excising beforehand anything that might give offence to the partner in dialogue. He was convinced that true dialogue presupposed a strong and clear identity, not a lack of it, and that it was far more honest to state clearly one's convictions rather than hide them or bracket them in an attempt that was meant to be charitable but was in fact merely condescending. Of course these identities have to be clarified, of course they can be developed in new and unforeseen directions; but without a clear identity, there is no point, really, in dialogue.

In my opinion, De Smet's great advantage in dialogue and in his work of interpretation was the extent of his familiarity with both his own faith tradition and the Indian tradition. Because of this, he was in a position to achieve in himself the fusion of horizons that Gadamer talks of as the locus of adequate interpretation.[60] De Smet had, therefore, no need to engage in attacks on the Greco-Roman inculturation of the Christian faith, what John Paul II has called the 'first great inculturation' of the Christian faith.[61]

Apart from contributing to better understanding between traditions, De Smet's work on the person is also a contribution to a new way of doing Christian theology in India. This new way will consist of appropriating the faith and passing it on to future generations, in categories drawn from the cultures and religions of India. His work will certainly bear supplementing with more adequate attention to subaltern perspectives; nevertheless, his writings do bear witness to his sensitivity to the fact that life and praxis must also be appropriated in the effort of mining the past in order to speak to the present and to the future.[62]

Notes

[1] Already in 1963 De Smet had made a similar complaint: the traditional Christian definition of person, he said, had dominated all the great theological debates in Christendom "like a four-cornered tower," but it has since been so undermined by modern philosophers "that today even [Christian] theologians sometimes fail to claim it in its integrity." Cf. R. De Smet, "Categories of Indian Philosophy and Communication of the Gospel," *Religion and Society* **10**/3 (1963) 22.

[2] R. De Smet, "Towards an Indian View of the Person" 118 below.

[3] In "Forward Steps in Śaṅkara Research," *Darshana International* **26**/3 (1987) 33, De Smet reports that he first attended a session of the Indian Philosophical Congress in 1950 in Calcutta and that he became a life member soon after the Kandy session in 1954.

[4] De Smet's work is completely absent, for example, in Scaria Thuruthiyil's recent *Persona nella tradizione Indiana: I più importanti protagonisti del ventesimo secolo* (Rome: Bulzoni Editore, 2006). A start has been made, however, by Bradley J. Malkovsky who identifies the doctrines of non-dualist realism and the personhood of the *para Brahman* as some of De Smet's greatest contributions to the encounter between Christian theology and Śaṅkara's Vedānta. Cf. his "Introduction: The Life and Work of Richard V. De Smet, S.J.," *New Perspectives on Advaita Vedānta: Essays in Commemoration of Professor Richard De Smet, S.J.*, ed. Bradley J. Malkovsky (Leiden / Boston / Köln: Brill, 2000) 13, and also "The Personhood of Śaṃkara's *Para Brahman*," *The Journal of Religion* **77** (1997) 541-562.

[5] If we regard the contributions to the *Marāṭhi Tattvajñāna Mahākoṣa* as a single item, there are 15 items in all. Of these, I have been unable to trace "Contemporary Philosophical Anthropology" which, according to the bibliographies of both Kozhamthadam and Malkovsky, was published in a journal called *New Consciousness* **1**/3 (1973). Cf. J. Kozhamthadam, "Writings of Richard De Smet, S.J.: A Select Bibliography," *Interrelations and Interpretation: Philosophical Reflections on Science, Religion and Hermeneutics in Honour of Richard De Smet, S.J. and Jean de Marneffe, S.J.*, ed. Job Kozhamthadam (New Delhi: Intercultural Publications, 1997) 265-284; and B. Malkovksy, "A Bibliography of the Publications of Richard V. De Smet, S.J.," *New Perspectives in Advaita Vedānta: Essays in Commemoration of Professor Richard De Smet, SJ*, 165-178. The present collection therefore brings together 14 of De Smet's contributions on the topic of the person.

[6] Cf. above, note 4. Cf. also J. Lipner, "Richard V. De Smet, S.J.—An Appreciation by Julius Lipner," *Hindu-Christian Studies Bulletin* **11** (1998) 51, which Malkovsky draws on, and I. Coelho, "Fr. Richard V. De Smet (1916-97): Reminiscences," *Divyadaan: Journal of Philosophy and Education* **8/1** (1997) 3-15, which he does not.

[7] Cf. De Smet, "Forward Steps in Śaṅkara Research" 33, where he speaks about his chancing upon a French article on *advaita* as a 16 year-old schoolboy.

[8] R. De Smet, *The Theological Method of Śaṃkara* (Rome: Pontifical Gregorian University, 1953). This thesis, as Malkovsky reports, has had a long 'underground' history. De Smet never got round to publishing it, but that did not prevent it from being circulated in 'roneotyped' form among students and scholars East and West. (Malkovsky, "Introduction" 5) Malkovsky also indicates that the thesis is due to be published by The Council for Research in Values and Philosophy, Washington D.C. (ibid. 8, note 11). The publication is still awaited.

[9] Malkovsky reports that, as a result of the circulation of De Smet's doctoral thesis, many have been persuaded that Śaṅkara is a *śrutivādin* rather than a pure philosopher. See his "Introduction," *New Perspectives in Advaita Vedānta* 5. Among these may be counted F.X. Clooney, K. Ṣatchidananda Murty and Anantanand Rambachan.

[10] I have it on the authority of De Smet himself that the metaphysics notes of Fr Jean de Marneffe, SJ, used in Jnana Deepa Vidyapeeth, Pune in the 1970s and 1980s, were largely based on De Smet's own Latin notes, and this is also acknowledged by Fr de Marneffe: "I gladly acknowledge that these pages use freely material previously contained in the Latin Course of General Metaphysics which Father R.V. De Smet S.J. had prepared earlier and which each of us have been using for several years while teaching Metaphysics at the Pontifical Athenaeum of Poona." See "Preface," General Metaphysics: Study Guidelines Prepared by J. de Marneffe, S.J. (Pune: Pontifical Athenaeum, 1966). I have been unable to trace the Latin course in question.

[11] Prof. Paneerselvam wrote this to me in an e-mail which, unfortunately, I cannot trace anymore. Curiously, however, I came across a similar remark in a tribute to De Smet by Patrick Vincent: "Fr Richard De Smet was one of the foremost Vedantins in India." See P. Vincent, "Friend, Scholar and Man of Dialogue: Father Richard De Smet, SJ. 14 April 1916 – 2 March 1997," *Jivan: Jesuits of South Asia: Views and News* **18/5** (May-June 1997) 24.

[12] Two of these deserve mention: Sara Grant and Joseph Satyanand. Grant's thesis agreed largely with De Smet's own teaching about the non-reciprocal nature of the relation between *Brahman* and the world in Śaṅkara, while deepening it with solid scholarship: cf. S. Grant, *Śaṅkarācārya's Concept of Relation* (Delhi: Motilal Banarsidass, 1999). Satyanand's thesis showed that Nimbārka was a predecessor of Śaṅkara and one of the *pūrvapaksins* that he opposes: cf. J. Satyanand, *Nimbārka: A Pre-Śaṃkara Vedāntin and His Philosophy* (Varanasi: Vishwa Jyoti Gurukul, 1994).

[13] Chapter 1 below.

[14] Chapter 2 below.

[15] Chapters 3-5 below.
[16] Chapter 6 below.
[17] Chapter 7 below: "Early Trends in the Indian Understanding of Man."
[18] Chapter 8 below: "Is the Concept of 'Person' Congenial to Śāṅkara Vedānta?"
[19] Chapter 9 below: "Towards an Indian View of the Person."
[20] Chapter 10 below. De Smet was not only a member of the editorial board, but also had the distinction of being the most prolific contributor to the Encyclopedia, with more than 68 entries to his credit.
[21] Chapter 11 below: "The Aristotelian-Thomist Conception of Man." The missing "Contemporary Philosophical Anthropology" of 1973 is also probably part of this period.
[22] Chapters 11 and 13 below.
[23] Cf. chapter 12 below.
[24] Chapter 14 below: "Materials toward an Indo-Western Understanding of the Dignity of the Human Person."
[25] De Smet, "*Persona*, *Anima*, *Ātman*" 25-26 below, and "The Discovery of the Person" 45-47, 51-52 below. Cf. also "Towards an Indian View of the Person" 119-120.
[26] De Smet, "The Discovery of the Person" 52 below.
[27] All this is explained at length in "*Persona*, *Anima*, *Ātman*" 26-29 below, "The Loss of the Person" 55-60 below, and "Towards an Indian View of the Person" 120 below. Cf. also De Smet, "Indiens Beitrag zur allgemeine Metaphysik," *Kairos* 3/4 (1961) 180: "The supposite [sic] is correctly defined as 'any single, complete, subsistent being, of any nature whatsoever.' And the person is consequently 'a supposite endowed with an intellectual nature'. / The main property which follows necessarily from this definition of 'person' is that any person is capable of establishing through its intellect and will spiritual relationships with any being, especially with other persons, and above all with God, the supreme personal being." (The text cited here is the English original: "Indian Contribution to General Metaphysics," [1961], Collected Papers B, 356 = Collected Papers D, 22.)
[28] De Smet, "Is the Concept of 'Person' Congenial to Śāṅkara Vedānta?" 111 below. Encyclopedia articles on the 'person' are almost unanimous in acknowledging that Greek antiquity did not have the concept of person, and that this concept was hammered out in the process of expressing the Christian mysteries. Despite this, these articles tend to assimilate 'person' to 'human person.' The *Dizionario delle idee* goes so far as to list finiteness as one of the characteristic notes of the person: cf. L. Stefanini, "Persona," *Dizionario delle idee*, Centro di Studi Filosofici di Gallarate (Florence: G.C. Sansoni Editore, 1977) 859.
[29] De Smet, "Is the Concept of 'Person' Congenial to Śāṅkara Vedānta?" 111-112 below. Cf. also S. Grant, *Śaṅkarācārya's Concept of Relation*.
[30] De Smet, "The Loss of the Person" 61-67 below.
[31] De Smet, "Categories of Indian Philosophy and Communication of the Gospel," *Religion and Society* 10/3 (1963) 22.

[32] De Smet, "The Rediscovery of the Person" 75-76 below; "Towards an Indian View of the Person" 120-121 below; "*Vyakti* / Person" 156 below.
[33] De Smet, "Is the Concept of 'Person' Congenial to Śāṅkara Vedānta?" 112 below. "It is important... to notice that the term 'sagunatva', which is too commonly translated 'personality', can only designate empirical personality. This radical anthropomorphism prevents it from being a transcendental term and we should never accept 'saguna *Brahman*' as a correct rendering of our 'personal God'. The true God cannot be anything but nirguna since, strictly speaking, he 'has' nothing, but 'is' all perfections." De Smet, "Indian Contribution to General Metaphysics," [1961], Collected Papers B, 357 = Collected Papers D, 22 (italics as in text). See also De Smet, "Materials for an Indian Christology," *Religion and Society* **12** (1965) 9-10 = "Towards an Indian Christology," *The Clergy Monthly Supplement* 7/6 (1965) 257.
[34] De Smet points out that Śaṅkara actually used the method of *anvaya-vyatireki*; it was his disciple Sureśvara who systematized this in terms of *jahad-ajahal-lakṣaṇā*: cf. Guidelines in Indian Philosophy, cyclostyled notes for students (Poona: De Nobili College, 1968) 303; also, "Forward Steps in Śaṅkara Research," *Darshana International* **26** (1987) 41.
[35] De Smet, "Is the Concept of 'Person' Congenial to Śāṅkara Vedānta?" 112-113 below.
[36] De Smet, "Categories of Indian Philosophy and Communication of the Gospel," *Religion and Society* **10**/3 (1963) 22.
[37] De Smet, "Early Trends in the Indian Understanding of Man" 105 below.
[38] De Smet, "Early Trends in the Indian Understanding of Man" 105 below.
[39] De Smet, "Towards an Indian View of the Person" 135 below.
[40] Malkovsky, "Introduction" 12.
[41] De Smet, "Indiens Beitrag zur allgemeine Metaphysik," *Kairos* **3**/4 (1961) 180. I use here the English original, "Indian Contribution to General Metaphysics," [1961], Collected Papers B, 356-357 = Collected Papers D, 22 (Sanskrit words not italicized in the original). By 1972 De Smet seems to have changed his ideas about the integrality and integrative function of the Vedāntic *ātman*: cf. "Is the Concept of 'Person' Congenial to Śāṅkara Vedānta?" 114-115 below.
[42] De Smet, "Materials for an Indian Christology," *Religion and Society* **12** (1965) 9 = "Towards an Indian Christology," *The Clergy Monthly Supplement* 7/6 (1965) 256-257.
[43] Cf. the proposal in I. Coelho, "Applying Lonergan's Method: The Case of an Indian Theology," *Method: Journal of Lonergan Studies* **22**/1 (2004) 1-22.
[44] Chs. 1 and 2 below.
[45] Chs. 8 and 9 below.
[46] In the article of 1957, De Smet notes that there is a golden thread in the bewildering variety of meanings of *ātman*; this golden thread is the conviction, shared by the Platonists in the West, that the real and the true (*sat*, *satyam*) is the stable and the enduring. This explains why the dominant Indian tendency is towards analysis and discrimination (*viveka*) rather than synthesis and integration. Cf. "*Persona*, *Anima*, *Ātman*" 31 below.

[47] This is explained very well in "Concerning the Indian View of Man" 37-40 below, and in "Towards an Indian View of the Person" 124-6, 127-130 below.
[48] De Smet, "Towards an Indian View of the Person" 125 below. On creation in Śaṅkara at least, see De Smet, "Śaṅkara and Aquinas on Creation," *Indian Philosophical Annual* **6** (1970) 112-118; or "Origin: Creation and Emanation," *Indian Theological Studies* **15**/3 (1978) 266-279.
[49] De Smet, "Towards an Indian View of the Person" 129 below; "Concerning the Indian View of Man" 38 below.
[50] De Smet, "Concerning the Indian View of Man" 38-39 below.
[51] De Smet, "Towards an Indian View of the Person" 130 below.
[52] De Smet, "Towards an Indian View of the Person" 131-137 below. De Smet does, however, make the disclaimer that a more extensive examination would be required to establish the suitability in greater detail: cf. "Is the Concept of 'Person' Congenial to Śāṅkara Vedānta?" 117 below.
[53] De Smet, "Towards an Indian View of the Person" 136-137 below.
[54] De Smet, "Towards an Indian View of the Person" 137-138 below.
[55] De Smet, "The Rediscovery of the Person" 75 below.
[56] The contrast between the organic conception of the human person and the atomic concept of individuality is explained at length in chs. 5 and 6 below.
[57] De Smet, "Towards an Indian View of the Person" 121 below.
[58] De Smet, "Materials Toward an Indo-Western Understanding of the Dignity of the Human Person" 223 below.
[59] Cf. De Smet, "*Ātmā – Ihetara Jīvana* / Self – Afterlife" 147-148 below.
[60] The consequences of a lack of such familiarity became painfully obvious to us at a dialogue with a Swamiji (probably Swami Krishnananda) at the Rishikesh ashram in 1989: cf. I. Coelho, "Fr. Richard V. De Smet (1916-97): Reminiscences," *Divyadaan: Journal of Philosophy and Education* **8**/1 (1997) 9-11.
[61] *Encyclical Letter* Fides et Ratio *of the Supreme Pontiff John Paul II to the Bishops of the Catholic Church on the Relationship between Faith and Reason*, 14 September 1998, n. 36; cf. I. Coelho, "Inculturation in *Fides et ratio*," *Divyadaan: Journal of Philosophy and Education* **10**/2 (1999) 254-278.
[62] Cf., for example, "Early Trends in the Indian Understanding of Man" 107-108.

1

PERSONA, ANIMA, ĀTMAN[1]

1. *Persona*

The fortune of the word *persona* (*prosôpon* in Greek) was made when the Stoics borrowed it from the language of the stage where it belonged and meant 'mask.' They had been the first among Greek philosophers to conceive the Supreme Being and Cause of the universe clearly as a providential God. The world was a big stage, history a cosmic drama, Providence the wise and powerful director who devolved upon each being, especially upon each human being, the irreplaceable part which he had to enact in harmonious connection with his fellow actors. Hence they naturally applied a technical stage term which had already extended its meaning from mask to character and part, to signify human destiny as distributed by God and delineated in his fundamental gift to each one, namely, in the characteristic nature by which each individual is distinct from every other.

After this decisive passage from the realm of external objects to the realm of the subject, the term *persona* was ready to be used not only by the Roman jurists but also by the Latin Fathers of the Church. The latter were in search of a term by which the newly born 'science of the Christian faith' or 'supernatural theology' would be able to translate adequately the truths of Revelation, especially the mystery of the Holy Trinity and of the human incarnation of the eternal Word.

Christ, the God-Man, could not be said to be two; he was one, though in two distinct natures, the divine and the human. These, though intimately conjoined, were in no way mixed in him: his divine nature remained, absolutely transcendent, unchanged, untainted by any finiteness; his human nature was not absorbed in his divinity, which stood perfect and complete.

Still, this inner duality of natures did not detract at all from the absolute unity of his being.

If the meaning of *persona* could not be refined further than its Stoic usage allowed, it would be useless to them; for, then, it would simply remain a synonym of 'individual nature.' Fortunately, jurists were already accustomed to use it in order to designate those human beings to whom the law attributed not only duties but rights; (hence, a slave was not *persona*). Thus the term could now be predicated of a complete being, no longer of its nature only, provided of course this being enjoyed consciousness and freedom and, hence, could be the subject of attribution of duties and rights. Without therefore any violence to the accepted meaning of the term *persona*, the Christian divines could now with a slight precision generalize it and denote by it *any single and complete subsistent, endowed with intellect, and considered as an ultimate subject of attribution of knowledge, free activity and rights*.

Applying this elaborated notion to the revealed mysteries they defined Christ as one divine Person in two distinct natures, and God as a Trinity of Persons, subsisting equally in the perfect unity of the one divine nature, and distinct only by virtue of their mutual relationships.

Further every human being, including slaves, women and even infants, was to be considered and treated as a person. Angels also, i.e., bodiless but finite spirits, were rightly to be called persons.

The high watermark of this semantic evolution was reached by Boethius (470-525 AD) when, in his *De duabus naturis et una persona Christi*, ch. III (Migne, *Patrologia Latina*, LXIV:1343 D), he proposed the following definition, which, although slightly imperfect, was to remain classical during the whole Middle Ages: "*Persona proprie dicitur naturae rationalis individua substantia*" (The proper definition of 'person' is 'individual substance endowed with an intellectual nature').

After that, the Schoolmen had an easy task. Theirs was only to clarify even further the terms of this definition. I shall now propound briefly the results attained by them.

(1) A person should be a *subsistent being*. 'To subsist' means 'to exist in itself,' not in something else. This excludes not only genus, species and individual notions, which, as such,

exist only in minds and have no independent being, but also parts, which have no existence apart from the whole, and accidents, which depend entirely on the act of being of their substance. Further it excludes also all substances which happen to exist by the act of being of another, for instance, by the being of God according to some forms of pantheism. The Christian teachers reject pantheism in all its forms. This is the reason why they had to explicate the term *substantia in* Boethius' definition by limiting it to mean only self-subsistent substances.

(2) A person should be a *distinct* or *singular* subsistent being. This precision is made with the intention of excluding the narrowness of the term *individua* in Boethius' definition. Things are distinct when they cannot be predicated *in recto* or by identity of one another. Singularity is that kind of distinction which is proper to subsistent beings. In order to be singular, such a being may have to be distinct not only from all other beings in general, but also from all other species, and from all other individuals in its own species. God is distinct from all finite beings by the very transcendence of his nature. Since he does not belong to any genus or species, his singularity is absolutely perfect. In God the three divine Persons are distinct from one another only in virtue of their mutual relations. Angels, on the other hand, are conceived by the Schoolmen as so many spiritual species or degrees of being. Hence the principle of their singularity is their own essence or nature, which contains exhaustively the full perfection of a particular degree of being. Since such a degree is necessarily finite, it sets them apart from God, and since it is exhaustively realized in a single such being, the question does not arise of distinguishing an angel from fellow-angels of the same degree. The plurality of angels is therefore merely 'formal,' not predicamental or strictly numerical. But all other beings, on account of their materiality, are distributed in classes or species. The ontological perfection represented by such a material species, though truly verified in all its members, is yet never realized exhaustively by any of them, but only in an imperfect fashion. It is by such degrees of imperfect realization of the same nature that individuals of one species differ from one another. But, their nature being similar, they are much less distinct from one another than species among themselves or than God from the universe of his creatures.

Hence, individuality is but the last and most imperfect degree of singularity. And while personality always implies singularity, it does not necessarily require individuality. Indeed, among persons, only men are individuals.

(3) It follows immediately from what precedes that a person should be a *complete* being in itself. Indeed, for a reality to be distinct from all others, it should not be a part of something else. Hence, nothing that is by nature a part can be a person. For instance, the human soul, though it is subsistent, is not a person; only the complete man, soul and body, is strictly speaking a person. This necessity of being complete is called the incommunicability of the person. With regard to it, two restrictions must be made, the first concerning the human person, the second concerning every person as such. First, human personality, since it denotes the lowest and least perfect kind of person, admits secondary communicability together with fundamental and primary incommunicability: while existing in himself and by virtue of his own being, man is also sociable and a part of the human genus; however, this unity with his fellow-men is not substantial but consists wholly in a net of variegated relationships. (Similarly, there exists a necessary communication of the relational type not only among angels but between all members of the created universe, and, at a deeper ontological level, between all finite beings and God, since as creatures they depend entirely upon him for their preservation, their activity and their end as well as for their beginning.) Secondly, the incommunicability of the person does not exclude communication either through activity in general or through knowledge and love, since, on the contrary, this type of relation is, as we shall now see, characteristic of personality.

(4) All beings that verify the first three notes are called 'supposits,' but the exclusive mark of the personal supposit is that it should be *an ultimate subject of intellectual, free activity and rights*. In other words, its nature should be an intellectual one. Its mode of knowledge, freedom and rights will differ according to its degree in the hierarchy of persons, but all persons are by nature capable through their intellect and will of relating themselves consciously to all beings and especially to God. This spiritual union with God and, in him, with all finite existences constitutes their supreme end and bliss. And on

account of this inner ordination they are, and must be treated as, ends in themselves and never as pure means. To enthrall them and treat them as mere 'objects' is to offend against this fundamental right and dignity.

Such are the precisions brought forth by the Western Schoolmen to clarify the notion of person which formed the pole, rising from man to God, around which revolved their theocentric humanism and their civilization.

The scope of this paper being limited to ascertaining some definitions, I must resist the desire of further describing the history of *persona*. Let it suffice to say that in the hands of the well-intentioned but anarchic philosophers of later days it hardly succeeded in retaining its ontological status and was in the end almost monopolized by positivistic Psychologists who could but grant it a very extrinsic meaning. However, the modern trend towards 'Personalism' may succeed in recovering its authentic signification.

2. *Anima*

The meaning of *anima*, soul (*psychê* in Greek), has remained much more homogeneous through the centuries since it was first defined by Aristotle. It designates the *first inner principle of life and activity in all living bodies*. As such it pervades the whole body and is by nature distinct from the bare matter which it informs and determines by elevating it to a certain degree of life. This determination, however, can never be perfect because it is counteracted by bare matter, the other inner cause which we are bound to infer as a pure principle of indetermination and receptivity in order to explain metaphysically the individuation of bodies and their multiplicity within the same species.

The scale of degrees in corporeal life allows us to distinguish several kinds of souls: vegetative, animal and intellectual. The animal soul performs also the functions of a vegetative soul, and the intellectual soul those of a vegetative and of an animal soul.

The term 'spirit' (*pneuma* in Greek) applies properly to the intellectual or human soul, but not exclusively, for there exist spirits, such as angels and God, which are not to be called souls, since they are not the inner principle of life in any body. God, indeed, though he is more immanent to all creatures than their own substantial form or soul, is at the same time so absolutely transcendent that he may not be conceived as the animating principle of anything, not even of the whole universe. Unfortunately this difficult synthesis of divine immanence *and* transcendence has escaped the grasp of many philosophers, especially the strict pantheists.

The human soul, because it is a soul, cannot begin to exist except in a body which individualizes it and to which it communicates life, thus making it its own, and by the instrumentality of which it issues forth into action. On the other hand, because it is as truly a spirit, this dependence upon its body either to be or to act is merely extrinsic, as witness the very transcendence and self-reliance of its spiritual activity of knowing and willing; it can, therefore, even after its separation from its own body, continue to exist and to act spiritually.

The other kinds of souls, on the contrary, do not manifest this intrinsic independence in the midst of extrinsic dependence, and lacking this evidence we are not allowed to attribute to them any kind of spirituality or immortality.

3. *Ātman*

The first meaning of *ātman* is clearly that of the reflexive pronoun. And strictly speaking the reflexive pronoun refers to the whole subject, but not necessarily to the integrity of its aspects. Indeed, there are many ways of approaching and grasping a subject, the scale of which extends from the most extrinsic to the most intrinsic. A subject can be spoken of with regard to his material possessions (*artha*), his relations to other subjects (*svāmin*, *mitra*, *strī*, *putra*, *guru*), his substantial relation to his gross body (*deha* or *annamaya*, figuratively *kṣetra*), his accidental relation to the external form (*rūpa*) of this body, or to its name (*nāma*), his instrumental relation to its vital functions (*prāṇa*), its organs of action (*karmendriya*) or of sensuous perception (*jñānendriya*), the formal objects of the latter (*tanmātra*), the internal sense (*antaḥkaraṇa* or *manas*), the function of individuation (*ahaṃkāra*) and its self-conceit (*abhimāna*) (this function when disturbed can give rise to a double or plural *abhimāna* or multiple personality), the faculty of cognitive and volitional decisions (*buddhi* or *mahat*), its modifications (*vṛtti*), especially, discriminate knowledge (*vijñāna*), and its characteristic, consciousness (*caitanya*), finally, with regard to his ontological root (*mūla*), the supreme *Brahman*.

The term *ātman* has been used in all these cases and the list I have drawn is far from being exhaustive. Such a variety of applications, which may well bewilder the modern scholar in śāstric lore, was fortunately a spur rather than a puzzle to the *ācāryas* of old, and it is possible to recover from their speculations the golden thread which will guide our way out of that labyrinth.

Their reflexion always comes back to a fundamental conviction which they have in common with Plato, St Augustine and the Platonists, though doubtless independently of them. It is the conviction that in all cases that is most real and true (*satyam* or *sat*) which is most enduring, subtle and pervading.

It follows immediately that the wise man should endeavour to discriminate (*viveka*) true reality from what does not deserve to be called so in the first place and with full right. Hence Indian thinking is characterized by analysis, dissociation, purification, isolation (*kaivalya*), rather than by the effort to retain, in spite of analysis, the integrity and the variety of the experience from which philosophical enquiry is bound to start. This was also the direction which philosophy first took in the West, but it was soon counterbalanced by Aristotelianism and later by Christianity which is ineradicably catholic, i.e., totality-minded. We have seen an example of this in the development of the notion of person.

Sadviveka has permeated Indian research in all fields of knowledge. For instance:

> That is being (*sat*) which is the object of a knowledge which does not fail; that is non-being (*asat*) which is the object of a knowledge which fails. (Śaṅkara, *Bh. Gītā Bh.* 2, 16)

> There are two sounds (*śabda*) in the words that we speak: one, the essence of sound; the other, used for indicating an object… The sound (*sphoṭa*) in the *buddhi* is the cause of the various sounds heard (*nāda*). (Bhartṛhari, *Vākyapadīya* 1, 44-46)

All the words of *Veda* mean common *jātis*; for otherwise the whole fabric of *Mīmāṁsā* would fall to the ground, since all individual objects are ephemeral. (*Mīmāṁsāsūtra* 1, 3, 33 and 1, 4, 10)

The idea of difference (between syllables) is conditioned by accidents distinct from, and superimposed upon, the *ākṛtis*; ... recognition is caused by the intrinsic nature (*svarūpa*) (of the syllables). (Śaṅkara, *B.S.Bh.* 1, 3, 28)

The authority of the *Veda* depends upon its eternity (*nityatva*) and "this eternity of the self-dependent *Veda* has been established from (the fact that there is) no remembrance of any author (of it) and from other (arguments)" (Śaṅkara, *B.S.Bh.* 1, 3, 29).

Perfect *vidyā* is that knowledge only which endures uncontradicted forever (*abādhita*); "it is characterized by uniformity (*samyagjñānamekarūpam*), because it depends upon actually existing things (*vastutantratvāt*); for true reality is that which persists in one and the same form through all its states (*ekarūpeṇa hyavasthito yo 'rthaḥ sa paramārthaḥ*)" (Śaṅkara, *B.S.Bh.* 2, 1, 11).

Such quotations could be multiplied and find parallels in the West. Does not St Augustine write: "All creation I beheld and I saw that it neither is absolute being nor absolute non-being. Because it is from Thee, it is; still it is not what Thou art, and therefore it is not. That indeed truly is, which endures beyond the reach of change" (*Confessions* 7, 11)?

It was but natural that the *ācāryas* should pursue this search for the unchangeable as a search for inner causes, even unto the supreme and universal cause of everything.

Now hardly any philosopher would deny that actual causation implies a certain kind of presence of the cause in the effect. Still, there is room for a division of causes into *samavāyi* and *asamavāyi kāraṇa*, including under the latter head all these *hetus* such as *nimitta kāraṇa*, *karaṇa*, etc. which the effect does not need continuously in order to remain what it is. It is in the group of *samavāyi* or permanent and pervading causes that we shall find *ātman* in its philosophical sense. Let us listen again to Śaṅkara:

It is obvious that the effect, which is limited and gross, is pervaded by its cause, which is unlimited and subtle. Just as earth (is pervaded) by water, similarly each preceding (element) must be pervaded by the succeeding one. Thus the purpose of (Gārgī's) enquiry reaches up to the *ātman* that is within all. Here the five elements, combined in an ascending order, are arranged according to their degree of subtleness and their pervading causality. And, on this side of the supreme *ātman*, independently of it, there is no other reality, for the *śruti* says, '(It is) the Truth of truth,' and 'truth' is the five elements, and 'the Truth of truth' is the supreme *ātman*. (*Bṛh. Up. Bh.* 3, 6, 1)

Commenting upon the pre-Sāṁkhya text of *Kaṭhopaniṣad* 3, 10-11, he follows the well-known pedagogy of *Arundhatī-nyāya*, and points successively first to the objects of the senses, then to *manas*, *buddhi*, the *ātmā* of *buddhi* (i.e., *Hiraṇyagarbha*), further still to *avyakta*, and lastly to *Puruṣa*. Of each one of them in turn he says that it is superior, more subtle and greater than the preceding one, and that it is its inner *ātman*; but of the *puruṣa* he says that it is "the utter limit, the culmination, the climax of subtleness, greatness and inner-selfhood" (*sūkṣmatva-mahamattva-pratyagātmatvānāṃ sā kāṣṭhā niṣṭhā paryavasānam*).

In *Kaṭhopaniṣadbhāṣya* 6, 12, he explains that the elimination of effects terminates in existence: "Thus, indeed, this effect (the world), when followed along the ascending series of its more and more subtle (causes), leads ultimately to the pure awareness of 'being.' Even when, through the elimination of objects, the intellect itself is eliminated, it is full as it were of the embryo of *sat* when it is eliminated. For the intellect is our instrument in the perception of the truth of *sat* and *asat*. If the world had no cause, this effect, being associated with nothing but *asat*, would at every step be grasped as 'non-being only.' But it is not so. On the contrary, it is at every step grasped as 'being only,' just as the effect of clay, etc., namely jar, etc., is associated with clay, etc. Therefore the *Ātman* should be conceived as being the root of the universe, not otherwise."

On the other hand, "pure consciousness is *ātman*... for whereas the objects betray their own form, consciousness never fails" (*Praśnopaniṣadbhāṣya* 6, 2). Thus in analyzing our inner experience we can, no less than in our analysis of the external world, arrive at a supreme and immutable cause, the Ear of the ear, the Sight of sight, the Thought of thought, the illuminator in all cognition, and therefore the supreme *Ātman*. Only through *lakṣaṇā* or indirect indication can words signify Him somewhat. Thus, for instance, in the sentence, "*Satyaṃ jñānamanantaṃ Brahma*," "the term *jñānam* expresses the perfect actuality of the abstract idea which it conveys" (*bhāvasādhana jñānaśabdaḥ*, *Taitt. Up. Bh.* 2, l), for "knowledge is the proper form of the *ātman*; it is not separate from it, hence it is permanent indeed" (*ātmanaḥ svarūpam jñaptirna tato vyatiricyate ato nityaiva*," ibid.). On account of his supremacy, this illuminating *caitanya* must be conceived as the universal first cause of all cognition, and therefore as one for all (*sarvātman*). According to Aquinas also, "God Himself causes the natural light in us to be preserved; He Himself directs it that we may see; obviously, therefore, the perception of truth must in the first place be ascribed to Him" (*Comm. on Boethius'* De Trinitate, Proemium, 1, 1, 8).

The relation between all effects and their supreme *ātman* is called *tādātmya*, a term which in this context should not be rendered by 'identity,' since it rather means 'having that as one's own *ātman*.' This relation is not reciprocal for "inspite of the non-otherness of cause and effect, it is the effect which has its *ātman* in the cause, but not the cause in the effect" (*ananyatve 'pi kāryakāraṇyoḥ kāryasya kāraṇātmatvaṃ natu kāraṇasya kāryātmatvam*) (*B.S.Bh.* 2, 1, 9). "Nor can (the universe), being no *ātman*, be the *ātman* of anything" (*Na cānātma sansarvamātmaiva bhavati kasyacit*) (*Bṛh. Up. Bh.* 2, 4, 14). Because nothing can either be affirmed or be apart from the supreme *Brahman-Ātman*, things may be said to be non-different (*ananya*), not utterly separated (*nātyantabhinna*) from it, but this *Śāntātman* itself is completely transcendent and other than them.

We may now conclude to the philosophical meaning of the term *ātman*. According to its original meaning it designates either the whole subject or more often something intimately connected with the subject. On account of its constant equivalence in *śāstra* with other terms, such as *kāraṇa*, *svarūpa*, *adhikaraṇa*, *pradhāna*, *upādāna*, *svabhāva*, *pratyagātman*, it must be interpreted as a causal principle of the *samavāyi* or immanent type. Because it is considered as *gauṇa* (figurative) rather than *mukhya* (primary, prcper) unless it is somehow replaceable by such terms as *jña*, *antaryāmin*, *sākṣin*, *upadraṣṭṛ*, *dṛksvarūpa*, *caitanyajyoti*, *pramātṛ*, *cetayitṛ*, *jñāna*, *jñāpti*, it must be thought of as a conscious inner principle and even ultimately as pure undifferentiated consciousness. Finally, in its supreme sense (*paramārthataḥ*), it applies only to the universal Cause, immanent in everything and at the same time separated (*pṛthak*), transcendent, other than and superior to, everything.

In short, *ātman* can be defined as *inner conscious principle*. It is divided into finite *ātmans*, which verify the definition properly but not absolutely perfectly, and the infinite *Ātman*, which verifies it perfectly and has the property of being absolutely transcendent and, by nature, utterly free from any relation to anything else whereas everything else depends on It to be affirmed and therefore to be.

Among finite *ātmans* can be ranged what Western philosophers have called *soul*, while, on the other hand, their notion of *persona* applies perfectly to the supreme *Ātman*.

Note

[1][First published in *Proceedings of the All-India Philosophical Congress*, part II (1957). Reprinted under the same title in *The Philosophical Quarterly* (Amalner) **30**/4 (January 1958) 251-260. Subtitles have been added. Permission to reprint has been obtained from *The Philosophical Quarterly* and is gratefully acknowledged.]

2

CONCERNING THE INDIAN VIEW OF MAN[1]

Georg Landmann's article "Soul, Self and *Ātman*," published in *Kairos* 1966 (pp. 44-49),[2] catches the attention of the reader through its compactness, clarity and acuteness. He traces with great exactness the main lines of the development of an idea that is central to Indian thought: the idea of the inner principle of life, knowledge, consciousness, conceived by some as single and all-encompassing, by others as diverse and individual, but always as at least relatively transcendent. This transcendence is such that it never allows a 'substantial unification' of the transcendent *ātman* with the matter in which it dwells. The *ātman* is never a soul in the Aristotelian sense of the word. It is akin rather to the Platonic conception of a soul as an immaterial monad exiled in a body. If it might be called a self, it is never to be taken in that comprehensive sense in which the classical Christian thinkers understood the human person as bearer of spiritual and corporal potentialities and activities, but rather in the Cartesian sense of a thinking ego, without any natural connection with the body that it appears to ensoul. Only when it is identified with *Brahman* does it become an integral Self, although now a divine Self that is absolute Spirit (*cit*). We could well say that in Sanskrit the single concept *ātman* stands for all the three concepts in the title of the article mentioned above. And this confirms Landmann's comment, in his introduction, about the duality acknowledged in the human person by Indian thinkers of this trend of thought, as a combination of spirit and matter. The human person is for them a temporary appearance, a way leading towards an *ātman* that is neither human nor animal nor divine, but that can during its wandering take any of these forms or even remain without any form whatsoever. Their understanding of man ultimately does away with man himself!

Nevertheless, by stressing these trends of thought—admittedly the dominant ones—we run the danger of not keeping the whole picture in mind. It may therefore be useful to recall briefly other, opposing trends in Indian thought.

Let us begin with the Indians of the *Vedic age*. These do know about the presence of a principle in man that survives death, yet at the centre of their religious thought and rites stands the concrete, this-worldly man, who belongs to the family and the social order, acquires cattle and wealth, has very material desires and needs, and turns to gods that are corporeal but invisible, with whose cosmic functions he cooperates through sacrifice. Their hymns to the gods are the expression of the relationships of very concrete men to very individualized divinities. Even in their prayers and sacrifices, these men strive only after the three inner-worldly goals: *artha* (wealth), *kāma* (enjoyment of pleasure) and *dharma* (morality as correspondence with the traditional laws, on which one's reputation in the community is founded). The concept of *mokṣa* (liberation from the conditions of this world) is still unknown to these people. It will first emerge in the Upaniṣads—as will the other concepts that mark what we have been calling the dominant trend in the Indian tradition.

But the Upaniṣads were not able to bring this trend to dominance without opposition. The greatest dissident was the Buddha. With 'diamond hardness' he rejected the Eternalism of the doctrine of the *Ātman* (*ātmavāda*) in order instead to stress the changing nature of human beings and of all beings, even to the point of absurdity. One must note that he did not oppose a theory of the individual soul in the Aristotelian sense of animating principle of matter and the forms intimately connected with it, but rather a theory about the *Ātman*, understood as an eternal, unchanging and independent essence—either in atomic form or as all-pervading—of unhistorical reality and actionless consciousness. When only this kind of substantiality could be guaranteed, he preferred to reject such a substance. For he could not turn his attention away from the concrete man, the suffering man filled with desires and needs of all kinds, the anxious and restless animal in which he was unable to find any element of actionless calm and transcendent equanimity. If therefore he rejected the doctrines of the *Ātman* or *puruṣa* preferred by the

Upaniṣadic and early Sāṃkhya thinkers, and if on the other hand he knew no better theory of the soul or substantial form, he explained the stream-like unity of man as a purely dynamic aggregation of successive momentary effects that apparently solidifies under the directions of vital or other desires. Here we must perhaps add that such a theory could well have led to an adequate understanding of man, if only it had succeeded in including within its characteristic dynamism also the aspect of reality that we find exaggerated in *Ātmavāda*.

In this context it is worth mentioning the Buddhist Personalist school (*pudgalavāda*), which belongs to the Hinayāna tradition and represents an effort to make good the shortcomings of the no-*ātman* theory (just as the *Sarvāstivādins* or Realists were trying, at the same time, to overcome the limits of the theory of impermanence). The *pudgalavādins* thought that behind the aggregates or groups (*skandha*) of mental and physical conditions observed by introspection, there must be a substrate. Had not the Buddha, in a well-known passage, spoken of the 'bearer of the burden'—an expression seeming to indicate some sort of ego underlying the aggregates? At the same time the *pudgala* could by no means be identified with the *Ātman*, because it was merely an integrating function demanded by the aggregates and expressed by them. Nevertheless this school did not last long, because its teaching came too close to the dreaded heresy of Eternalism.

Turning now to Jainism, we can regard also their conception of man as an attempt to reconcile *Ātmavāda* with a sense of the unity of the human essence. While acknowledging life monads that are naturally eternal, all-knowing and at rest, Jainism regards these as really connected with bodies of non-living matter and burdened with them, so long as they are born and reborn. From these intimate connections with matter arise qualities that make them very similar to the Aristotelian souls: in accordance with the volume of the bodies clothing them, they extend or contract themselves, just like a source of light fills the entire room in which it finds itself. Further, the Jaina epistemology is realist and regards empirical knowledge as correct even though imperfect information about reality. All said and done, however, the Jaina doctrine is preponderantly on the side of *Ātmavāda*—although the prescription of non-violence towards life (*ahiṃsā*) seems to imply the consubstantiality of the life monads and their bodies, insofar as the use of violence against the latter also disturbs the life monads themselves.

The *Cārvākas* or materialists, on the other hand, brought forward innumerable arguments against any such eternal *Ātman*. Insofar as they explained everything in terms of the four elements, they regarded consciousness as a mere epiphenomenon. Just as the intoxicating qualities of alcohol arise from the particular mixture of its components, so consciousness arises from a particular combination of material elements, as is the case in certain organic bodies. Although it was never very influential and practically disappears as a teaching from the seventh century AD, this materialism in the Indian tradition stands as a witness to the fact that reflection can never lose sight of the substantive unity of man. It survives today in different forms inspired by the West, and the basic reason for this seems to be the unsatisfactoriness of an extreme idealism that does not take the whole of man into consideration. The early Vedic exegetes of the Pūrva-Mīmāṁsā school also held a completely materialist non-*ātman* doctrine, but this arose more from their Vedic conservatism (in the form of a rigid ritualism) rather than from a real effort to understand the human being. Later on the Mīmāṁsā school succumbed to the attraction of *Ātmavāda* and took over the concepts of *Ātman* and *Mokṣa*.

The philosophers of the Nyāya-Vaiśeṣika school had their own peculiar theory of man. On the one hand they taught that the psycho-physical organism was a substance composed of countless eternal atoms, while on the other hand they accepted that there was an *ātman* in this organism, eternal and all-pervading, but also really affected and characterized by knowing, acting, etc. Such an *ātman* is in itself completely unconscious, and its liberation from matter can only mean a condition of non-conscious peace. As a system the teaching of this school was hardly satisfactory, though from our present standpoint we must say that it represented an attempt to be faithful to the entire human phenomenon. From the epistemological point of view, it maintained the existence of an *ātman*, because without this the unified knowledge and understanding of the objects of sense experience would be impossible. From the moral standpoint it drew the same conclusion, because it would not have been wrong to harm others if they had no *ātman* capable of suffering physical violence and moral evil. This double argumentation makes it clear that the *ātman* is closely connected to the organism and is marked by knowing, willing, pleasure, pain and other psycho-physical changes. On the other hand these philosophers considered the proofs for rebirth as convincing, and this demanded an eternal and all-pervading *ātman*, even if not naturally all-knowing and blessed.

Philosophical systems do not necessarily have a strong influence on the popular imagination of men, but religions can lend them lasting power and life. Among the most important religions of India is to be numbered Śaivism. In its Pāśupata-stage Śaivism describes man as the *kārya* (effect) of organs of knowledge embedded in matter, of knowledge, and of the individual soul. This soul is called *paśu* (beast), so as to emphasize its total dependence on *pati* (the Lord, i.e. Śiva), and like a beast of burden it is attached to a bond (*pāśa*), i.e. matter. Through ascetic vows (*vrata*) and special means (*dvāra*) for the worship of Śiva—all ordering the body to the service of the soul—it can achieve the cessation of suffering (*duḥkhānta*) and eternal blessed union (*yoga*) with Śiva. This Pāśupata-teaching attributes to man a dependent but real personality that endures even in union with the divine. Matter is regarded as the bond of the soul, but its function is not merely negative, insofar as it serves the purposes of the soul in ascetical practices and devotions connected with the body. We must also note that the soul can free itself from its bonds without the help of divine grace.

The Śaivism of the *Āgamas* (28 canonical texts) deepens the idea of *paśu*, showing that the dependence on *pati* also implies the dependence on divine grace (*anugraha*) in the matter of liberation; but this interpretation seems to go too far, because it understands liberation not merely as union but practically as identification with Siva. Still, the blossoming of Āgama-Śaivism into the hymns of the Tamil saints (*nāyanār*) brought forth a religion of love (*patti* for the Sanskrit *bhakti*) and childlike trust in the saving grace (*arul*) of Śiva.

The Śaiva-Siddhānta is the theology of this monotheist and non-brahmanic religion. It offers not merely a pure concept of the divine *pati* and a differentiated concept of the *pāśa* as consisting of *ānava* (ignorance), *karman* (effects of actions) and *māyā* (not illusion but empirical reality), but also a developed conception of *paśu*. *Paśu*, the soul, is endowed with knowledge, will and action, but needs an impulse from outside in order to move from isolation (*kevala*) to wholeness (*sakala*) and ultimately to purity (*śuddha*). In the first state it is actionless and inert, bound with *pāśa* (cf. the embryonic human form). In the state of wholeness it appears differentiated and subjugated to both *pāśa* and Śiva: clothed with a body it traverses the *saṃsāra* of worldly existence in the sixteen stations from plant life to the discipline of Yoga, in order to reach the state of purity. The means of this progress are first the purification of knowledge, will and action, then the dedication of the soul to cosmic *śakti* (divine power), and lastly its surrender to the 'good teacher' (*sadguru*) Śiva. The attainment of the third state means liberation, consisting of perfect union (*yoga*) of *paśu* with *pati*—a state that is 'full of life,' not a dissolution but rather the highest self-realization of the soul in perfect dependence on Śiva: the liberated soul has given up all the activities that it could itself give up, and so it now enjoys no separate blessedness, but rather participates intimately in the pure blessedness of Śiva. True, such a doctrine is marred by the teaching about rebirth and matter as a bond; yet its anthropology is much less marked by all those alienations to which man as man is subject in the Brahmanic Ātmavāda doctrine. It is interesting to note that, as the Brahmins of Kashmir developed their own Śaivism, it became a new monism, similar to the strictest Vedāntic *Ātmavāda*.

Even within Vedānta itself the Transcendentalism and Acosmism of Ātmavāda had to make place for a more humanistic conception. In his Viśiṣṭādvaita (qualified non-dualism), Rāmānuja tried to draw the consequences of the idea that world and man are somehow included in the absolute *Brahman*, through the use of what Ninian Smart calls "an *analogia corporis* or perhaps better an *analogia personae*."[3] From his analysis of man Rāmānuja obtained the concept of body as an instrument linked to *ātman*, ruled in its movements by this *ātman* and serving its goal through the realization of the highest perfection. Between body and *ātman* (*deha* and *dehin*) there is a relationship of inseparability (*apṛthaksiddhi*). Every organic body has an *ātman*, and every *ātman* is in a body. The difference between the two consists in this, that the body does not itself have experience but rather conditions the experience, whose conscious and critical owner is the *ātman*. Thus Rāmānuja defines the body as "that substance that a conscious being can completely support and use for its purposes, and that in its essence is ultimately subordinated (*śeṣa*) to that being." (*Srībhāṣya* 2, 1, 9). The chief quality of the conscious *ātman* is *jñāna*, by which is commonly understood thinking, feeling and willing. The *ātman* transcends the body, but needs it as natural tool, addition, effect, way, field of action (*kṣetra*) and area of dominance (all descriptions used by Rāmānuja).

The microcosmic harmony of soul and body in the unity of the human person is used as a suitable analogy for the macrocosmic harmony of God and world in the unity of *Brahman*. The material reality (*prakṛti*) is the great body of the divine Lord, the *ātmans* wandering through *saṃsāra* are his subtle body, the liberated *ātmans* are his blessed body. He freely brings them forth through modification (*pariṇāma*) of himself, directs them from within as their inner guide (*antaryāmin*) and so allows them to serve his own goal: the perfect worship of his glory. What he changes, in order to bring them forth, is his own purely transcendent body. This body is eternally in his perfect light, beauty, sweetness, youth and strength. It is pure *sattva* (the element of glorification that is next only to spirituality). Since the difference between the Lord, who is Spirit, and his many bodies cannot lie outside the one *Brahman*, which is therefore differentiated from within, there emerges a whole range of interpersonal relationships between the Lord and the embodied souls, whether migrating or liberated. In this way this genuinely pantheistic form of Advaita becomes at the same time a religion of love and of grace. It is, further, also a very comprehensive humanism, one that possesses possibilities of adaptation even for the modern world.

Another *bhakti* theologian, Madhva, breaks so radically with pantheism as to present a radical dualism between world and God. The two are ontologically fully independent of each other. But in their dynamic activities nature and living souls (*jīvāḥ*) are really ruled and guided by the divine Lord. Each soul is essentially spiritual consciousness (*cidrūpaiva hi sarve jīvāḥ*), but its knowledge, activity and blessedness—necessary aspects of its spirituality—can be darkened during the period of its embodiment. In its essence however it is similar to the Lord, whose image (*abhāsa*), reflection (*pratibimba*), 'separated part' (*bhinna aṃśa*) it is—though surely a self-subsisting image (*nirupādhi*). Although like an instrument it responds to the guidance of the Lord, it still has its own nature (*svabhāva*) that it did not receive from him and that he cannot change. This explains why some do not succeed in reaching liberation, and either fall into hell or wander forever through *saṃsāra*. Anthropologically, Madhva's dualism is a radical humanism that is embedded in a deeply religious worldview. The power to create other beings is taken away from God, but only in order to protect the self-subsistence and the inalienable properties of all worldly beings and especially of human beings.

Landmann's article has, generally speaking, and especially in the light of his introductory statements, stressed the Upaniṣadic and Vedāntic streams of Indian thought, even though he has not neglected the so-called theistic and other trends. Through a somewhat impressionistic treatment I wanted to make his presentation more complete, especially with regard to the Indian conception of man. Landmann rightly remarks: "around their [the Indian] conception of God turns also their understanding of man and of the world" (p. 49). But it cannot be denied that the idea of God also in its turn changes according to the different conceptions of man—arising from the investigation of the self, but often unexpressed—or at least according to the never fully satisfied need for a correct understanding of man. Already in the nineteenth century, many influential Indians were drawn to the different varieties of atheistic humanism in Europe, while others, not less influential, filled the old wineskins of Hinduism with large doses of gospel-influenced social humanism.[4] The picture of the Indian tradition which can be put together from the contributions of Landmann and myself, wishes to explain why the mixtures that have arisen from it have revealed themselves to be not very satisfactory. The contemporary thought and life of India tend to different types of world humanism, for which the preoccupation with religion is either obsolete or meaningless or simply irrelevant. This is doubtless a consequence of the fact that none of the religious philosophies of India offered an explicit philosophy of man comprehensive enough to do justice to man in all the dimensions of his being. Nevertheless, what they have said about him is anything but meaningless, and it surely contains important building blocks for a renewed religious humanism of the future.

Notes

[1] [First published in German under the title "Zum indischen Menschenbild," *Kairos: Zeitschrift für Religionswissenschaft und Theologie* (Salzburg) **8**/3-4 (1966) 179-202. Translated by Ivo Coelho. Permission to publish has been obtained from De Nobili College, Pune, and is gratefully acknowledged.]

[2] [Georg Landmann, "Soul, Ṣelf and *Ātman*," *Kairos: Zeitschrift für Religionswissenschaft und Theologie* (Salzburg) **8**/1 (1966) 44-49.]

[3] N. Smart, *Doctrine and Argument in Indian Philosophy* (London: George Allen & Unwin, 1964) 109.

[4] Cf. G.K. Mookerjee, "Neuer indischer Humanismus—Vinoba Bhave," and also S. Dhar, "Asien, Christentum, Menschheit," in *Kairos: Zeitschrift für Religionswissenschaft und Theologie* (Salzburg) **5** (1963) 250-260, and **7** (1965) 7-33 respectively.

3

THE DISCOVERY OF THE PERSON[1]

When the invitation came to me from the Registrar of the University of Madras to deliver this year the Sri L.D. Swamikannu Pillai Endowment Lectures, I felt humbly grateful for the undeserved privilege of addressing the worthy company which would assemble here and, beyond the trustees of this endowment my gratitude turned towards the great scholarly gentleman whose love for truth it perpetuates for our common benefit.

The subject of my lectures is the concept of the Person, its emergence and discovery, its obscuration and loss, and its rediscovery in our times. Upon the person are focused the studies and concerns of the philosophers and the priests, the psychologists and the sociologists, as well as of those responsible for maintaining the rights enshrined in our Constitution and fulfilling the promises born from our adoption of democracy. But the concept of the person is a highly complex and perfectible one. It is loaded with consequents derivable from it which affect the very direction of our life for our weal or woe. It will, therefore, be no idle enquiry to study the course of its ascertainment from ancient times to our own century.

1. Emergence of the Term 'Person' in Greek and Latin Antiquity

Long before the adoption of the term 'person' men had ways of designating those subjects which they held to be intelligent and responsible agents. For this they used proper nouns and pronouns or other indicative expressions. But the Greeks and Romans had the particular habit of referring to the whole agent by mentioning his most prominent aspect or the part of his individuality which appeared most directly engaged in a given manifestation or behaviour. Thus Homer sings of 'the abominable wrath of Achilleus' (rather than of the irate Achilleus), of 'the will of Zeus,' of 'the destiny' or 'the honour' or 'the shame' of his heroes and he speaks of their 'liver' or their 'thorax' or their 'arms' as responsible for their prowess in battle. Hesiodes and Lycurgos use the term 'body' (*sôma*) to signify an individual, as we still do in English. Pythagoras and Plato play on the similarity between *sôma* and *sêma*, body and tomb, and hook up on this pun philosophies which exalt the universal and disparage the particular. Against Plato, Aristotle vindicates the individual existent as the paragon of reality and calls it 'primary or first substance' (*prôtê ousia*) in opposition to the 'secondary substance' which is merely conceptual. For him, the 'first substance' is *hypostasis*, i.e., subject, but this term is not yet specialized and he uses it to mean all possible sorts of subjects, substrates, supports, supposits or subject-matter. Thus Greek thinkers have met early with the problem whether individuality is something superficial or deep, a negligible or an important value, a property of parts or of the whole subject.

The next development concerns the term *prosôpon* which Polybios (200-120 BC) seems to have been the first to use in the sense of person. Its first meaning is 'face' since a face consists of that which is found 'near and around the eyes' (*pros* + accus. of *ops*) and it was quickly used to designate the made up faces or masks of the Greek theatre. Its Latin cognate *persona*, which is perhaps of Etruscan origin, was popularly understood to indicate the utility of those masks as loudspeakers. But the first function of such masks was to present in an immediately recognizable form the various roles or *dramatis personae* of the tragedy or comedy. Here again, a part, the mask, stood for a whole personage and impersonation. The *prosôpon Basileôs* or *persona Regis* began really to signify, almost in our own sense, the person of the king, the king as king. But this implied a differentiation between the personage and the actor who sustains him, between the social figure and the empirical man. The Stoics tried to suppress this subtle difference with their theory that the world is a stage set by God and each man has been entrusted with a part to play on that stage. As given by God each such part constitutes the very nature, temperament and destiny which make a man what he is. Thus for the Stoics the *prosôpon* or *persona* is not an impersonation taken up by a man but rather his very individual essence; it is this very man as constituted by God. Of course, such a personality is mysterious and reveals surprises to its owner himself as it unwinds and develops under the omniscient guidance of the divine Producer. The Stoic conception is religious, interiorizing, holistic and dynamic but it depends on a too simple notion of divine Providence and, hence, fails to secure for man the full measure of his dignity.

In the law-courts, on the other hand, *persona* has entered the juridical vocabulary precisely to express the kind of dignity which the law recognises. From the end of the second century AD the *persona* is the subject of legal rights, i.e., concretely, the Roman citizen. The slave, on the contrary, is a *non-persona*, being deprived of any right. However, a new religious influence, that of Christianity, is already at work, though still in the underground, to vindicate the rights which every man, be he even a slave, owns by nature and, hence, inalienably.

About the same period, Plotinus is reviving Platonism and his concept of the human being is not at all holistic. According to his analysis, man is made of body, soul and spirit, causality being the link which unites these three. But "it is in the spirit (*nous*) that we are mostly ourselves; that which comes before is ours (not we). We are up there, directing the animal from that top" (*Enneades* 1, 1, 7). Plotinus goes back to the primitive meaning of *prosôpon* and compares men under the influence of the discursive reason to "a number of faces (or masks) which are turned outwards though inwardly they are attached to one head. But if one of us, like one of these faces, could turn round either by his own effort or by the aid of Athene, he would behold at once God, himself and the whole" (quoted by Caird, II, 296).[2]

Thus what Plotinus contributes to this evolution is a dimension of religious depth which links man more radically to a less anthropomorphic God than the one of the Stoics. But he tends to reduce personality to its spiritual centre whereas the Stoics' view tends towards a larger integrality.

2. The Individual in Indian Antiquity

Before taking up this Western development to its next stage, it will be enriching to enquire about the views which paralleled it in ancient India.

Here also the individual is usually referred to by proper nouns and pronouns, among which the reflective pronoun *ātman* is destined to a great philosophical career. What is more interesting is that the Indian mind manifests early a bent towards reflective analysis and discrimination (*viveka*) which, applied to this term *ātman*, transfers it from the outer to the inner man. While *ātman* does not cease completely to designate the gross body or its main part, the trunk, it progressively comes to designate in turn the complex of life made of breaths (*prāṇa*), the complex of the senses (*indriya*), each one of the great intellectualising functions (*manas*, *ahaṃkāra*, *buddhi*) or their whole complex (*antaḥkaraṇa* or *manas*), up to the innermost reaches of knowledge (*vijñāna*) and bliss (*ānanda*). This kind of analysis is pursued by various thinkers whose formulations differ but it is systematized in the doctrine of the five sheaths (*pañca-kośa*) of which man is comprised, as found in *Taitt. Up.* 2, 1-5. The first sheath, the gross body (*annarasamaya*), is said to be filled with the second (*prāṇamaya*), the second with the third (*manomaya*), and so forth. Each inner sheath is said to be other than, interior to, and the *ātman* of its containing sheath. Śaṅkara will add that it is also higher than it. Man is thus conceived as a hierarchy of *ātmans* whose inner imbrication resembles that of the Chinese balls. We may remember here that that Indian conception of human society is also essentially hierarchical as opposed to equalitarian.

The same *Taittirīya* text designates man as the *puruṣa*. Like the Latin *persona*, *puruṣa* is probably of non-aryan origin and its etymology is uncertain but its basic meaning seems to be 'male being.' Popular etymologies connect it with the ideas of whole and all-inclusiveness. The mythical *Puruṣa* of *Ṛgveda* 10, 90 is the cosmic male Giant from whose sacrificial dismemberment the whole world has originated. We learn from the *Brāhmaṇas* that the brahmanic sacrifice is meant to reintegrate symbolically this *Prajāpati* who is the Whole (*Sarva*) and thus to secure the integrity and wholesomeness of the world and of man who by it becomes also all (*sarva*).

This idea of plenitude or integrality should not be neglected. In the *Brāhmaṇas*, it directs the search for affinities (*bandhu* or *bandhutā*) between the three realms of the sacrifice, of the cosmos or macrocosm, and of man the microcosm. The powers at work in the sacrifice are set in correspondence and even identified with the *devas* who preserve the order (*ṛta*) of the cosmos and with the inner functions discoverable in man. The sages of the *Upaniṣads* continue this search for such connections and do not hesitate to call man's senses and higher inner functions *devas* or *devatās* or *puruṣas* as well as *ātmans*. Here again they introduce the idea of hierarchy and the resulting picture of man is that of a city (*pura*) rather than that of a monad.

Yet, the sense of man's unity asserts itself too. Reflection upon the three states of waking, dreaming and dreamless sleep suggests to those thinkers that the lower functions which first appeared to be separately active though ruled by the higher ones in the waking state do in the other states return to their ruling functions and merge within them, and these in the heart or in pure consciousness or in bliss. The practice of yoga further suggests that these functions which we first grasp as psychological are also cosmogonical. *Yogo hi prabhavāpyayau* (*Kaṭha Up.* 6, 11): "Yoga, indeed, is emanation into existence (*prabhava*) as well as resorption (*āpyaya*)." Hence, the unity of man results from causality, and this causality is that which characterises the inner causes, variously called *pradhāna*, *upādāna*, or *ātman*. Śaṅkara will later explain that in their ascending ladder each such cause is "higher, more subtle, greater, and more 'inner ātman' than its emanation" (*para sūkṣmatara mahattara pratyagātmabhūta*: *Kaṭha Up.* 3, 10-11).

Thus man appears as a field of cosmogonic forces and these forces are no longer the *puruṣas*, *devas* and *devatās* who, in earlier texts, appear to act as efficient causes, but rather the emanating and resorbing inner causes which *yoga* suggests.

However, man is aware of himself as agent (*kartṛ*), patient (*bhoktṛ*) and knower (*jñātṛ*). This gives rise to other pictures of man. As knower and witness he is the 'knower of the field' (*kṣetra-jña*). As conscious enjoyer and responsible agent, he is the rider of the body-chariot, led by the *buddhi*-charioteer towards a goal which is the supreme *Puruṣa* or *Ātman* (*Kaṭha Up*. 3, 3-11). The relation of man as knower and rider with this supreme *Puruṣa* towards whom he journeys but who also somehow inhabits, pervades, impels and illumines him, exercises the minds of the upaniṣadic thinkers.

The analogy of the wheel indicates the progress of their reflection. In *Bṛh. Up*. 1, 5, 15, the hub of the psychic wheel is the finite *ātman*. In *Bṛh. Up*. 2, 5, 15, the wheel is psychic-cosmic and its hub is the infinite *Ātman*. Similarly, it is the highest *Prāṇa* in *Chānd. Up*. 7, 15, 1 and the greatest *Puruṣa* in *Praśna Up*. 6, 6. Finally, in *Śvet. Up*. 1, 6, the finite *ātman* is the wild goose (*haṁsa*) fluttering about in the universal wheel whose Impeller is the One God favoured by Whom the *haṁsa* passes to immortality. In the parable of the two birds, which *Śvet. Up*. 4, 6, adapts from *Ṛgveda* 1, 164, 20, the witnessing is totally attributed to the divine *Ātman* and the fruit-eating to the finite *ātman*. Thus, in the later Upaniṣads, the two *ātmans* are neatly distinguished.

But their relation is very intimate "Of the measure of a thumb, the *Puruṣa* abides within the *ātman*" (*Kaṭha Up*. 4, 12). The two are unborn, minute and great; however, the inmost *Ātman* (*Antar-ātman* of 6, 17) is "more minute than the minute (*ātman*) and greater than this great (*ātman*)" (ibid. 2, 20). Just as the active functions emanated from *prāṇa* and were periodically resorbed into it, so also the finite *ātman* is originated from the supreme *Ātman* and is to return to Him. How? Through knowledge favoured by His grace. This is but an application of the conception of the inner cause which underlies many Upaniṣadic statements. Any inner cause transcends its effects but is also immanent to them; they originate from it, abide and subsist in it, and are resorbed into it (cf. *Taitt. Up*. 3, 1). The inner cause is the innermost reality of its effects, though it transcends them and is not resoluble into them.

To sum up, man is not an entity closed upon itself but rather the play-field of a hierarchy of psychic-cosmic functions at the top of which stands the divine Energy-Consciousness which is Fulness, Existence and Bliss imperishable. His individuality radiates from his self-awareness which posits him as an 'I' (*aham*) encountering a world of objects and responsibly active in their midst. But he can discover that his very individuality is, as it were, open upwards and shot through with the transcendence of a universal *Ātman-Brahman* apart from which it has no consistency and towards which it is directed to find there its blissful fulfilment.

However, its consistency is hardly holistic since it resides in the unity of layers or sheaths linked by inner causality. Yet, in the Upaniṣadic conception of this causality, these layers are resorbable into their inner cause and, therefore, not altogether perishable. But in Buddhism the analysability of the individual is much more radical and the unity of the *dharmas* or elements which constitute him is due to the special causality of *karman*, to the exclusion of any *ātman*. The resulting doctrine hardly gives place to any positive conception of personality.

3. The Christian Adoption of the Term 'Person'

Coming back to the Mediterranean world, we have now to consider the development of the concept of person in the hands of Christian thinkers.

At the centre of the Christian experience was a man, Jesus of Nazareth, who had exhibited extraordinary knowledge and powers. He had presented himself as the Son of God as well as the Son of Man. He had appeared to synthesise in himself both the divine and the human attributes in a most intimate way and without flaws. What was he? A mere man in whom the inner presence of the Creator in all his creatures had attained special transparency? Or a holy man raised by divine grace to adoptive sonship? Or, as he claimed, the original and eternal Son of God, made man to partake[3] with all men his unique Sonship?

The answer of most of the Christian believers was the latter assertion which they called the 'Good News' or Gospel. It is in their effort to spread it that they got hold of the term 'person' and some other terms and endeavoured to give them a higher precision.

The Greek and Latin culture contained pairs of terms, the notion of which was still floating and ambiguous. These pairs were *prosôpon – persona*; *hypostasis – substantia / subsistentia / subjectum / suppositum*; *ousia – essentia/substantia*; *physis – natura*.

In Greek, the term *prosôpon* was currently retaining its ancient denotation of face / mask / role / character / aspect, whereas in Latin its cognate *persona* was fast becoming used in the sense of *subjectum juris* (subject of rights, citizen), first by the law-courts, then by the ordinary people. Among the Greeks, it was the term *hypostasis* which was acquiring this meaning of *persona*, whereas its Latin cognate *substantia* only meant for the Latins essence (Gk. *ousia*) or substance or nature (Gk. *physis*) for which they also used *natura*. Hence, for a long time there was a lot of haggling about the correct terms between Greek and Latin Christian theologians.

Finally, during the fourth century AD, they agreed to say that Christ was, in Latin, one *persona* in two distinct *naturae* or *substantiae*, in Greek, one *hypostasis* in two *physeis* or *ousiae*, i.e., one person uniting in himself two complete but distinct and unmixed natures, the divine and the human. Similarly, they declared that God the Unique is one incomplex Essence or Substance (*Ousia / Substantia*) in three Persons (*Hypostaseis / Personae*), Father, Son and Spirit, each identical with the divine Essence but distinct through their mutual relations.

This precise application of the term *persona* or *hypostasis* to Christ and to God clarified indirectly its application to man and opened up the field to Christian humanism. Indeed, man was created in the image of God and, therefore, every man must be said to be a person in the proper sense of the term. Personality would no longer depend on the rights granted to some by positive law but was something ontological and inherent to human nature. It was the birthright of everyone, whether citizen or slave. The proclamation of this dignity was to have great consequences for the emancipation of man from all kinds of oppressions and for the whole development of Western culture and even for the destiny of all mankind.

Around 500 AD, Boethius formulated an imperfect but, nevertheless, highly successful definition of 'person.' Properly speaking, he said, the term 'person' designates "any individual substance possessed of a rational nature." We shall see later on the corrections which this definition demanded but, imperfect as it was, it sufficed to provide a solid conceptual root to the new humanism.

To conclude this first lecture, we may enunciate a few main features of this personalistic humanism:

(1) In opposition to classical Greek thought, which is dominated by the ideas of universality and of the ordered *cosmos* in which man plays but a lowly part, it puts the central emphasis on the unicity and dignity of every human being and of his relation to God.

(2) The individual human being is no longer a crossroads where several participations in general realities meet (matter, ideas, etc.) but an indissoluble whole, of which the unity is prior to the multiplicity because it is rooted in the Absolute.

(3) It is not the abstract tyranny of a Destiny, or of a heaven of Ideas, nor is it an impersonal Thought indifferent to men's individual destinies that reigns over them, nor even a Stoic Producer of the world drama. It is a God who is himself personal, albeit in an eminent degree. It is a God who through love brings men into existence; a God who offers to each person a relation of unique intimacy, of participation in his divinity; a God who affirms himself not at all by what he takes away from man but by granting man a freedom analogous to his own.

(4) The profound purpose of human existence is not to assimilate itself to the abstract generality of Nature or of the Ideas, but to accept to become exalted and divinised.

(5) To this transformation each man is freely called. Liberty is constitutive of his existence as a created person.

(6) This absoluteness of the person neither cuts him off from the world nor from other men. The unity of the human race is for the first time fully affirmed and doubly confirmed; every person is created in the image of God; every person is called to full citizenship in the Kingdom of God, which is the Kingdom of divine Love.

In the next lecture, we shall see, first, how the medieval schoolmen improved Boethius' definition of the person, and then, how it became obscured and lost to the detriment of mankind. In the third lecture, however, we shall assist at the rediscovery and enrichment of the conception of the person in our own times.

Notes

[1] [This was the first of three lectures delivered at the University of Madras under the Sri L.D. Swamikannu Pillai Endowment, 1969-70 (delivered on February 25-27, 1970, according to the indication given by De Smet himself in "Early Trends in the Indian Understanding of Man," cf. n. 2 in chapter 7 below). It was subsequently published in the *Indian Philosophical Quarterly* 4/1 (1976) 1-9. The three lectures, together with "The Aristotelian-Thomist Conception of Man" (cf. below, chapter 11), were reprinted by the same *Quarterly* as an abstract under the title *A Short History of the Person*. Permission to publish has been obtained from the *Indian Philosophical Quarterly* and is gratefully acknowledged.]

[2] [Edward Caird, *The Evolution of Theology in the Greek Philosophers: The Gifford Lectures Delivered at the University of Glasgow in Sessions 1900-1 and 1901-2*, vol. II (Glasgow: James MacLehose, 1904) 296.]

[3] [By 'partake' here De Smet probably means 'share.']

4

THE LOSS OF THE PERSON[1]

The philosophical search for the adequate definition of a concept may appear an idle occupation of intellectuals but we should be aware that in all scientific disciplines concepts are the basic media of thought whose value for life may depend very much on their adequacy. For instance, to define such a term as 'person' adequately is to gain a proper view and evaluation of those beings that are persons and it enables one to adopt the proper attitudes and relations towards them. If, on the other hand, the meaning of 'person' becomes falsified, those relations are disturbed to the detriment of persons themselves.

1. The Refinement by the Schoolmen of the Notion of Person

For Boethius, 'person' meant an individual substance possessed of a rational nature. The terseness of this definition made its success but I have already indicated the dissatisfaction which it was to arouse in the best of the medieval schoolmen.

First of all, they objected to the term 'substance' on account of its ambiguity. 'Substance' could mean either that part of a finite essence which is the basic support of accidents and which is also called 'nature' or it could, according to the prevalent usage of Aristotle, mean the whole existent subject, the complete *hypostasis*. Richard of St Victor and St Thomas Aquinas insisted that this second meaning alone could suit a definition of 'person.' Aquinas explained further that what is proper to the subject thus understood existentially and holistically is that it subsists, i.e., exists in its own right. As such, it exists by its own act of being, its own inner energy (*energeia*) of existing, whether it is identical with this energy as in the case of God, the Absolute, or whether it receives it in a limiting essence as in the case of creatures which are existentially dependent on this Absolute as on their total Cause. The term 'subsistence' must, therefore, be substituted for 'substance' and we must say that the first condition to be a person is to be subsistent. 'Subsistence' had already been introduced into Latin by Rufinus at the end of the fourth century AD to render the Greek *hypostasis* in the sense of 'person' and had been used as such by Pope John II in 534 and by the Church Council of Lateran in 649.

A further refinement introduced by St Thomas is that the subsistent to be personal must be understood in its totality. The meaning of 'person' is holistic. "It must," he says, "comprehend the whole reality of the subject, i.e., not only its essential elements, (such as its nature or substance in the restricted sense of the term and its intellectual and other faculties) but also its individuating qualities and other accidents. Thus only will it retain the denotation of totality which the notion of 'person' requires." (*In III Sententiarum* 5, 3, 2, 3.)

St Thomas, therefore, opposes the Platonism of many philosophies which reduces the person in man to man's soul or conscious 'self.' This, he thinks, is neither proper linguistic analysis, for it fails to give a right account of linguistic usage, whether of the Church or of the secular culture, nor does it tally with the desire rooted in man's very nature for the salvation and fulfilment of his whole self. "By nature," he says, "man desires, that his whole self be saved; his soul, on the other hand, is not the whole man but only a part of the corporeal man: my soul is not myself; hence, though it be saved in the other life, this does not yet mean that I am saved or that any man whatsoever is saved" (*In I Cor.* 15, 2.) But the Christian promise of the resurrection assures that the whole person of man, body and soul, will be granted full redintegration by God.

Many other assertions of St Thomas become clear in the light of his teaching of the holistic character of the person. Man's soul, he says, is immortal but man himself is mortal. Death is not the freeing of the spirit from the jail of the body but a physical evil, a disaster which breaks asunder the natural unity of the human person. To impose it unjustly upon any man is a moral evil, a sin against the inviolability of the person. Christ died the victim of such a sin and, between his death and his resurrection, he was no longer absolutely speaking a man, since his soul was deprived of his body. Further, we should never consider the living Christ as a human person or as a conjunction of two persons, one human and the other divine, but only as one divine Person in two natures. Indeed, the human nature he took up does not exist by a created 'act of being' of its own level but by the existential energy of the divine Person who assumed it; hence, it lacks the subsistence which personality requires. Finally, in the case of God, the two conditions for personality so far demanded are obviously fulfilled. For God being the Absolute is the very subsistent *Esse*, the perfect existential Energy whose fulness implies in identity all the illimitable ontological perfections. He is without qualities, *nirguṇa*, not because He lacks them but because they are not present in Him as accidents of a substance. Rather than having them, He is them: He is their Fulness, incomplex. undiversified, simple. This is the Christian conception of God, Subsistence of Being and Fulness of all perfections, as sanctioned by the first Councils of the Church and faithfully adhered to by St Thomas Aquinas.

In his definition Boethius had indicated that a person must be an individual. Now, this term also required further refinement. In Latin, '*individuum*' originally meant 'undivided' and designated the 'monadic' character of unparticipable units which could usually retain their wholeness and particularity and oppose themselves to others as original centres of existence, resistance and activity. The above explanation of the holistic character of 'person' has already taken care of this meaning. However, a natural consequence of the undividedness of individuals is that they are by the very fact 'divided from others' or, at least, ontologically distinguishable from them. Individuals are generally observed as single units, distinguishable by their individuating characters; but they are also generally groupable into classes according to their more universal characters. Such are the individuals presented to us by common experience and we are not directly acquainted with any 'concrete universal,' i.e., with an individual which would at the same time be a universal. However, this would not be in itself absurd since the subsistent forms of Plato and the angels of Christianity are defined as subsistent species. Besides, for all those who hold the unicity and transcendence of the divine Fullness, God is singular and other than all the rest and, in that sense, He is the perfect 'concrete universal' or the supremely 'universal individual.' To include such considerations while avoiding the ambiguities to which they might give rise, St Thomas opts for the term 'singular' or 'distinct' in preference to 'individual.' Thus the twofold term 'individual substance' of Boethius' definition is so far replaced by the threefold term 'singular (or distinct) integral subsistent.'

Boethius had said finally that a person is 'possessed of a rational nature.' This is important since it marks the difference between personal and non-personal subjects. But the term 'rational' must be understood as Boethius probably meant it, namely, as equivalent to the Greek *logikos*, 'of the nature of the *logos*,' i.e., intellectual. And 'intellectual' must be understood in reference to the intellect proper, which is characterised by the total reflection of self-consciousness and the transcendence which permits to evaluate any object in terms of being. Neither animal intelligence nor the so-called intelligence of machines gives any evidence of reaching that level although they are capable of quasi-judgments and quasi-reasonings. On the other hand, reasoning activity as a matter of combinatory calculus would not be intellectual if it were not permeated by the power of the intuitive intellect. Rationality, therefore, stands on the lowest rung of the scale of intellect and the discursivity it generally denotes is not a property of intellect as such but only of the human intellect. Hence, it is better to say that a person must be 'possessed of an intellectual nature.' The term 'possessed of' translates here a mere Latin genitive and does not imply that there should be a distinction between a person and his nature or his intellect. Indeed, we know that in the case of God any such distinction would be absurd. Because He is subsistent *Esse*, God is Consciousness, is Knowledge, is Intellect, just as He is Power, Freedom, Bliss, etc.

The role of a definition is to provide the primary elucidation of a notion but the properties which are derivable from it may extend considerably our understanding of it. In the case of the person, these properties are furthermore of vital importance.

First of all, since a person is a subsistent, he is either the pure act of being (God) or in possession of an act of being received from God (created persons). Hence, every finite person is as such grounded in God and the self-awareness of which he is capable extends virtually to an apprehension of his ontological dependence upon the Absolute and he may recognise the hyperpersonality of this Absolute God who verifies eminently all the constitutive notes of the definition of 'person.' Thus the religious dimension is introduced into the world of persons by the bias of the *esse* or energy of being which is intrinsic to personality.

Secondly, since a person is possessed of an intellectual nature, he is endowed with the will which follows the intellect. This means that, consequent upon his acknowledgement of realities and his intellectual evaluation of their goodness, he can choose to bypass them or adhere to them in the measure of their goodness. The proper object of the will is the good as such. Whatever is good attracts the will insofar as it is good, i.e., if relative relatively, if absolute absolutely. The absolute desire for the supreme Good constitutes the human will as a dynamic tendency innately oriented towards a fulfilment which can only consist in a blissful possession of the Godhead. Short of the latter, a man's will is characterised by liberty of choice. It can either adhere to finite goods insofar as their deficient similarity with the divine Good suits this man or neglect them because their goodness is ever deficient. God himself, so long as a man's intellect is still unable to present Him to the will through a perfect intuition, stands within the scope of this liberty of choice. But once revealed through a perfect intuition, He immediately obtains the complete self-surrender of that man whose will has attained its perfect object. In this ecstasy of love, man is still free though not of the freedom of choice but of the freedom of self-determination.

Thirdly, being possessed of an intellectual nature which makes him the free author of his activity, a person is either the pure Energy of the perfect Activity of absolute Bliss (God) or endowed with the dynamism of a constantly self-integrating and spiritually progressing being. The human person tends innately towards this spiritual self-integration. His personality is meant to grow on every level, physical, psychological, social, intellectual, moral and affective. St Thomas, in his Treatise on Man in the *Summa Theologica*, constantly recalls this dynamism of growth and refuses any static conception of the human person.

Fourthly, besides God who is the noblest of all beings, created persons are the noblest of all creatures. Because of the perfection of their nature and the greatness of their end, they have the dignity of ends-in-themselves as opposed to the inferiority of means or instruments. In reference to this, St Thomas quotes Book of *Wisdom* 12, 18: "You have dealt with us, O God, with great reverence." Human persons, though the lowest in the scale of persons, are capable of spiritual activities, even ultimately of knowing God by intuition and loving Him in blissful self-surrender, which in the realm of activity are ends, pursuable for their own sake, and not only steps towards a final attainment. In such highest activities, they accomplish the purpose of the whole creation which non-personal creatures can only subserve but not attain. This is why men are ends-in-themselves, are inviolable, have rights, and are lovable for their own sake. This is why the least of men is to be respected and not abused of, and I may sacrifice my own life for his sake. This is why also the good even of the whole human society must not be sought by trampling on the essential rights of any individual. In brief, the whole of ethics and morality derives from this acknowledgement that each man is an end in himself.

Fifthly, because of his freedom and his spiritual powers, the human person is capable of initiating interpersonal relations of dialogue, free exchange, free contracts, friendship, love, service of love, etc. with other persons. Through these relations he extends and fulfils himself and helps others to fulfil themselves. What has been called the 'I–Thou' relationship is an exigency of his very nature. It must constitute the fabric of human society. As a member of that society, each man is bound to contribute his part of the common work in view of the common good of the whole of his species. But, as a person, he transcends this society, and must above all pursue his own personal vocation. This consists in uniting himself by the love of friendship with his human brethren and with God. Since each man has such a personal vocation the common good is subordinate to each individual's personal good. Hence, the temporal order and welfare is an end (because it is the common good of persons) but only an intermediary end. Not being ultimate, it is to be pursued during the whole course of human history in a way which is autonomous but subordinate to the ultimate end of each human person.

2. The Twilight of the Person

The views of St Thomas concerning persons become a living part of medieval culture and have never ceased to inspire what we may call the silent majority of Christian orthodoxy. But many of the philosophers who came after him followed contrary winds of thought and, often unwittingly, jeopardized his comprehensive doctrine.

The first rent was made by Duns Scotus. He was a voluntarist and a formalist. His fundamental theory asserted that the universe consisted of absolute individuals depending exclusively on the absolute Free-Will of God. Whereas St Thomas, the intellectualist, had explained that the Will of God, though absolutely free, should never be considered apart from His Intellect and Wisdom, Scotus considered it absolutely, as a purely arbitrary power. For him the laws of nature and morality do not express ontological exigencies of being at its various levels but are pure impositions of the divine Will. God could have willed their opposites. He could have willed that evil acts be acts of virtue, that lies, hatred, murders be good deeds, etc. Similarly in man the will is given primacy over the intellect and the blissful end of man is to be obtained in a supreme act of the will rather than in a supreme intellectual intuition. This will is no longer Aquinas' 'rational appetite' but an absolute power free of any necessary relation to reason. It is no longer derivable from the possession of an intellectual nature but an isolated datum. Thus Scotus initiated a voluntaristic trend which afterwards reappeared again and again and gave rise to such nefarious political doctrines as Fascism and Nazism.

He also endangered the Thomistic understanding of the integrality of the human person. Better gifted for analysis than for synthesis, he multiplied the distinctions and conceived man as a bundle of 'formalities,' i.e., of intelligible elements set side by side but not linked by any intrinsic relation. Scotus' conception of personality remained apparently holistic but in reality it was emptied of the necessity of inner unity without which it is liable to all forms of disintegration.

Ockham, whose thought was to dominate the fourteenth and fifteenth centuries, opposed this Scotistic riot of ontological formalities through his theory of terminism but this theory closed the door to any deep metaphysics of man. Further, he retained and even exaggerated Scotus' voluntarism.

The fourteenth century saw an important revival of Thomism but which, in Suarez at least, remained too eclectic. Suarez failed to see the constitutive role of the act of being, the *esse* of St Thomas, in the ontological making of personality. Therefore, he invented the astonishing theory that personality is only a mode which is superadded to the subsistent essence. Thus it becomes merely accidental and perhaps alienable.

Modern philosophy at least up to Kant is dominated by the influence of Descartes. The problem of personality is at the centre of his philosophy. His *Cogito* reveals immediately the intellectual nature of the human person. Unfortunately the *Cogito* is already an abstraction: it brackets out not only the *cogitata* but also the sensible as such. This is serious because sensing is intrinsic to the act of concrete knowledge, the direct judgment, which is synthetically sensitive and intellectual and which alone should be our adequate point of departure. On the basis of his narrowed starting-point Descartes could only discover that the I who thinks is a thinking reality. According to his definitions of substance and attribute, this thinking reality is a substance, characterised by the fundamental attribute of thinking; hence, it is distinct, complete, absolutely simple and, consequently, spiritual and immortal. If this were correctly derived, I would indeed be a person since the defining notes of 'person' are verified here (subsistence, distinction, completeness, intellectuality) but I would be only a mind. Yet, Descartes has to face the fact that to all evidence he is also a body. But he cannot prove it to himself indubitably except through a queer roundabout way. He first proves—by arguments which, I think, are invalid—that God exists as the infinitely perfect Being, supremely personal and the all powerful and free Cause of the universe. Now those of our ideas which are clear and distinct can only be innate and, hence, received from God. But God would not be God if He were not truthful. Hence, those ideas cannot be erroneous. But among them is the idea of matter or extension, and since it is warranted by God, I am right in thinking that a material universe exists and that I am not only mind but body.

The question, however, comes up, what is the relation between mind and body. The first answer of Descartes is that each of the two is a complete and independent substance. But it seems monstrous to say that man consists of two independent substances. Their union, answers Descartes, is stricter than the merely accidental union of the pilot and his ship but it cannot be the substantial union affirmed by St Thomas because two substances can never merge into one. Neither can it be a necessary union because each of the two can be conceived apart from the other. Hence it is contingent and consists in a certain interaction of which Descartes avows the mystery. To clarify this somehow, he has recourse to the voluntarism which he has inherited from the late medieval thinkers. God, he says, has willed these two substances to co-exist and interact, and God's will is absolute and independent of rationality though assuredly good.

To sum up, Descartes bequeaths to his successors the so-called body-mind problem. It is already the problem of the mind in the machine, since for him an animal and, hence, a human body too is only a highly complex machine, and it will after Hume become the problem of the ghost in the machine. Thus, for Descartes, the human person is no longer a unitary and integral subsistent, it is no longer the centre and source of a whole network of relations, and the will of man like the will of God has been isolated from his intellect. The kind of radical individualism which dissolves society into a mere aggregate of isolated units and was to triumph at the French Revolution has its source in Cartesianism.

Spinoza abolishes the body-mind problem but at the high cost of his monism of the substance. For him, the correspondence between psychic events and physical events results from the fact that these two forms of existence express the same eternal reality, which is divine. Since, for him, there is only one substance, Descartes' difficulty over the interaction of substances is avoided. The supposed interaction of body and mind is for him an illusion. To believe that it occurs would be to make the mistake of someone who, seeing the same action in a number of mirrors, believed that what he saw in one mirror was caused by what he saw in another. Plurality is due to the variety of the modes of the one substance which is simply expressed in various ways as a thought can be expressed in diverse languages. Man is neither a substance nor an original source of activity and relations, but only a peculiar mode of God. He has only an appearance of freedom, for determinism, both physical and rational, reigns supreme and admits of no contingency.

Leibniz refuses the monism of Spinoza and flatters himself that he has overcome the Cartesian dualism through his doctrine of the monads. His reduction of space to an infinity of points leads him, first, to an atomic conception of matter. And matter is not merely extension, as for Descartes, but it resists pressure, it exerts a certain force, which is not the case with mere extension. The source of the force thus exerted cannot be merely a geometric point; it must be a point endowed with force. This is the final indivisible element of material reality, the monad. On the other hand, Leibniz tells us, minds as thinking substances are indivisible in space like monads and, like them, have force. Could not each thinking substance be regarded as a monad, and each monad as a thinking substance? The virtue of this idea would be to conceive the whole universe as made up of substances of the same nature and thus avoid the dualism of Descartes. This idea would constitute a sort of monism, not the monism of Spinoza but a unitary view of reality which reduces all forms of being to substances of one and the same kind. Leibniz' monism is a spiritual monism; each monad is conceived as a kind of mind, either actually or virtually conscious. Each monad mirrors the whole universe from its particular angle and position. Leibniz calls this its perception. Conscious monads are aware of this *perception*. This awareness is their *apperception*. The internal force of a monad is called *appetition*. In this view of the universe each monad is 'windowless'; it remains shut up in its own universe and its own internal structure determines the entirety of its changes and development. Solipsism is avoided by recourse to the hypothesis of a pre-established harmony among monads. In brief, reality is conceived by Leibniz as a complete series of monads which differ imperceptibly from each other and which constitute a harmonic scale extending up to God. God is the perfect Monad whose apperception is equal to his perception and whose appetition is unrestricted Free Will. His decrees, however, are governed by the principle of the best which imposes moral necessity upon his Freedom.

Leibniz' monads retain some essential traits of the 'person' but his extreme rationalism perverts his understanding of personal freedom, and hence, of interpersonal relationships, of society, of the transcendence of God, of the sovereign freedom of His creative causality, etc.

After considering the reduction of the person in the hands of rationalists, we may look at the other end of the philosophical spectrum and see what happened to it in the hands of empiricists.

Hobbes eliminates the Cartesian dualism by subjecting man's reason totally to his senses and describing him in a mechanistic language in which the genuine notion of freedom is reduced to mere absence of external constraint. But Hobbes inaugurates a new kind of dualism between the natural and the social states of man. In this he is probably inspired by the modern theory of Natural Law. This theory is itself a novelty as compared with the ancient or classical theory of Natural Law of St Thomas Aquinas and other medieval thinkers. For the latter, man is a social being by essence and metaphysical reflection upon this essence can descry the necessary principles which form the basis of private and social morality. All positive law must develop in conformity with this order of nature. For the moderns, on the contrary, man is first of all an individual and autonomous being independent of any social attachment. It is from the inherent properties of this isolated individual that these jurists extract or deduce the first principles of social order. This is what they call the state of nature, which is logically prior to social and political life. The passage from the natural to the social and political state is a matter of contracts or covenants. In Hobbes we find a similar passage from man to the commonwealth, from the state of nature where man is "solitary, poor, nasty, brutish and short" to the artificial state of commonwealth where he accedes to pure rationality but by entering into political subjection. For Hobbes the social is restricted to the political. Indeed, if man is not social by nature, one can pass from the individual to the group only in terms of 'covenant,' i.e., in terms of conscious transaction or artificial design. And what can the individual bring into the bargain except 'force'? It is by pooling their forces, more or less contractually, that isolated individuals can constitute the political Leviathan which subjects them to itself despotically. This despotism is mitigated only by Hobbes' assertion of the natural convergency of the social good with the individual good.

For Locke as for Hobbes the origin of society is contractual but he evades the consequence of despotism by distinguishing two contracts. The 'social' contract introduces the idea of fellowship in equality; the 'political' contract introduces subjection to a ruling agency but only in terms of Trust. Citizens retain their rights, especially to property, except the right of coercion which they entrust to a limited monarchy. The triple power of such a monarchy originates in the people who retain the faculty of claiming it back even through violence and revolution. The political doctrine of Locke is thus liberal and more favourable to persons but his conception of the origin of society and, we must add, of morality and religion, views them as rational constructs rather than postulates of man's nature. For him also the human person rather than being social by essence is radically an isolated atom.

Berkeley, though he belongs to the empiricist current, is to a large extent a reactionary. He dematerializes the ego but asserts its permanent subsistence as spirit. Rejecting the static conception of substance of the Rationalists, he comes nearer to St Thomas' dynamic conception when he affirms that this spirit is not an inert substratum of accidents but an active principle endowed with intellect and free-will. He also retains the essentials of the classical conception of God as the Personal Absolute though he weakens God's transcendence by his perceptionism. However, Berkeley's influence does not seem to have been determinant in the development of social philosophy.

Hume's radical phenomenism is much more influential in this evolution. He does away with the Berkeleyan active self and sees the ego only as the pure possibility of a series of felt phenomena. As to the foundation of morality and social life he cannot see it in God, whose existence we cannot know, or in reason, which cannot prescribe anything, but he sees it only in the natural instinct for general utility and in the natural feeling of 'humanity.' The universality of moral ideas results from the strength of social habit. Regarding the birth of political society, he rejects the theory of the divine right of kings as well as the theory of the social contract and attributes the birth of nations solely to force or ambition. The legitimacy of a government remains constantly dependent on its actual efficiency in pursuing the common good.

To end this survey, let us turn to J.J. Rousseau. Like Hobbes, Rousseau posits a discontinuity between the man of nature and political man whose 'social contract' marks the actual birth of humanity proper. He also starts from premises which are extremely individualistic to proceed to anti-individualistic conclusions. And he too endeavours to legitimize social order and the transcendence of the Sovereign, though in his case the Sovereign is not Hobbes' Ruler but the General Will and is thus in a sense identified with the subjects. Rousseau's position of the problem is purely utopian: "Some form of association," he writes, "must be found as a result of which the whole strength of the community will be enlisted for the protection of the person and property of each constituent member, in such a way that each, when united to his fellows, renders obedience to his own will and remains as free as he was before."

And this is the startling solution which he immediately proposes: "The complete alienation by each associate member to the community of all his rights".[2]

Another quotation may bring forth even more forcefully the paradoxical nature of Rousseau's theory: "To institute a People (means) to change, as it were, the very stuff of human nature; to transform each individual who, in isolation, is a complete and solitary whole, into a part of something greater than himself, from which, in a sense, he derives his life and his being".[3] Truly we are here not far from the divinised State of Hegel.

Such are the vicissitudes of the person from the fourteenth century to the eve of the French Revolution. It has been atomized, formalised, and disintegrated into a bundle of formalities by Duns Scotus; modalised by Suarez; dualised by Descartes; pantheised by Spinoza; monadised and mentalised by Leibniz; desocialised and despotised by Hobbes and even by Rousseau; and fictionalised by Hume.

Towards the end of the eighteenth century the theories of these philosophers begin to yield their fruits, good and bad, in the Declarations of the Human Rights and in social and political revolutions, especially the French Revolution. I intend to study what happened to the person during the tumultuous period inaugurated by this revolution and to pass on finally to our own in which, I believe, a recovery of the person is increasingly taking place.

Notes

[1] [The second of three lectures delivered at the University of Madras under the Sri L.D. Swamikannu Pillai Endowment, 1969-70. It was subsequently published in the *Indian Philosophical Quarterly* 4/1 (1976) 10-23. The three lectures, together with "The Aristotelian-Thomist Conception of Man" (cf. below, chapter 11), were reprinted as an abstract under the title *A Short History of the Person*. Permission to publish has been obtained from the *Indian Philosophical Quarterly* and is gratefully acknowledged.]

[2] J.J. Rousseau, *The Social Contract*, Book I, chapter vi.

[3] Rousseau, Book II, chapter vii.

5

THE REDISCOVERY OF THE PERSON[1]

Philosophers may appear to deal in abstractions and to live in ivory towers but their ideas seldom remain uninfluential on the course of human history. In the event of the French Revolution we see in an exemplary way the mutation of intellectual views into principles of social transformation and directives for revolutionary action. Other factors contributed to its explosion but what gave them structure and thrust is the conjunction of ideas regarding man and society disseminated by the unorthodox thinkers of the seventeenth and eighteenth centuries.

1. From the Hierarchical to the Equalitarian Society

What the French Revolution meant to accomplish was not a mere political change but a radical transmutation of the social system. Ancient society was hierarchical and aristocratic; the new society would be equalitarian and democratic; it would be a triumph of the atomic individual, of the particular citizen, in the liberty, equality and fraternity of a self-ruling People.

In order to bring into focus the difference between the hierarchical and the equalitarian society, I shall summarize two paragraphs of Alexis de Tocqueville in Chapter 2 of his *Democracy in America*. He speaks there of the social system of the aristocratic nations of old Europe but we may listen to his description with the model of the Hindu society of castes in our mind.

> Among aristocratic nations, as families remain for centuries in the same condition, often on the same spot, all generations become as it were contemporaneous. A man almost always knows his forefathers, and respects them; he thinks he already sees his remote descendants, and he

> loves them. He willingly imposes duties on himself towards the former and the latter [...]. Aristocratic institutions have moreover, the effect of closely binding every man to several of his fellow-citizens [...]. As all the citizens occupy fixed positions, one above the other, the result is that each of them always sees a man above himself, whose patronage is necessary to him, and below himself another man, whose co-operation he may claim. Men [...] are, therefore, closely attached to something placed out of their own sphere, and they are often disposed to forget themselves. It is true that [...] the notion of human fellowship is faint, and that men seldom think of sacrificing themselves for mankind; but they often sacrifice themselves for other men. In democratic ages, on the contrary, when the duties of each individual to the race are much more clear, devoted service to any one man becomes more rare; the bond of human affection is extended, but it is relaxed.
>
> Amongst democratic nations new families are constantly springing up, others are constantly falling away, and all that remain change their condition; the woof of time is every instant broken, and the track of generations effaced [...]. The interest of man is confined to those in close propinquity to himself [...]. Aristocracy had made a chain of all the members of the community, from the peasant to the king; democracy breaks that chain, and severs every link of it. As social conditions become more equal, [...] men owe nothing to any man, they expect nothing from any man; they acquire the habit of always considering themselves as standing alone, and they are apt to imagine that their whole destiny is in their own hands. Thus not only does democracy make every man forget his ancestors, but it hides his descendants, and separates his contemporaries from him; it throws him back for ever upon himself alone, and threatens in the end to confine him entirely within the solitude of his own heart.[2]

Tocqueville's description thus shows the profound gap that separates the ancient societies from the societies of the modern Western type. The first were based on the natural order of things and had evolved their structures after the manifested data of life. In them the persons were, as soon as born, caught in a network of relations which immediately gave substance and reality to their natural sociality. They were distinct, singular, as Aquinas emphasised, but as essentially related. They pertained to the group before discovering their autonomy and through the group this very autonomy was shaped and their personality moulded on a pattern of participation and co-adjuvancy. The groups themselves were hierarchised into an overall structure of mutual dependence and collaboration sanctioned more or less strictly by religion. The social held primacy over the political. The state was an important but secondary formation which found its rationality in its conformity with the exigencies of the naturally hierarchical society. Through this society it was connected with something universal and religious, the conception of a cosmic order antecedent to any ordering of man's fabrication. In short, hierarchy integrated the ancient societies of men by reference to their universal values. Such societies could, of course, become rigid and their organisations oppressive but at their best they offered individuals the proper scope for exchange, co-operation and mutuality which are demands of the essential relatedness of human persons.

As against those societies which based themselves on the given sociality of human nature, the equalitarian societies were born from a desire to be 'rational' by breaking away from nature in order to set up an autonomous human order. Drawing their inspiration from Hobbes, Locke, Rousseau and other philosophers of the so-called Enlightenment, their creators started with the postulate that men are by nature isolated individuals and that the problem of making them live together lies exclusively within the competence of reason. Nature provides only the basic equality of those individuals and its absolute demand is the equalitarian principle which directly negates the old hierarchies.

This equalitarian principle is not simply equivalent to the moral principle of equality so strongly inculcated by Christianity. The latter affirms that all men, even the least, are equal in nature, dignity, inviolability and natural rights; it does not deny their concrete inequalities, their complex relatedness, their mutual complementarity; it does not affirm their basic identity. The equalitarian principle, on the contrary, posits this basic identity of all men whom it conceives as pre-social atoms to be socialised by the Social Contract which is the work not of nature but of reason.

The chief consequence of the equalitarian principle is to deny the legitimacy of the intermediary group-structures which ramified society and to set up the democratic state directly over against the multitude of individuals. The state is supposed to result from the compact of their many wills. It can begin anew by means of a constitution approved by a popular referendum or by elected representatives of the people. Once set up, it organises society through structures which too are, ideally at least, determined and controlled by the will of individuals manifested by vote. The power of such a state tends to become ubiquitous since it is no longer mediated and possibly counterchecked by hierarchical intermediaries independent of itself. The political threatens to devour the social.

The creation of democratic societies secured many positive results. It did away with the worst excesses of inequality. It proclaimed solemnly the Fundamental Rights of Man which became the norm of the codes of law elaborated for their furtherance. And its offspring, the modern state, has been an apt instrument of modernisation made possible by the progress of industry and technology.

However, the unmediated polarity of the isolated individuals and the Leviathan state has remained to a large extent unreconciled. Hegel's attempt in his *Philosophy of Right* to reconcile freedom and authority ended in his glorification of the Prussian state. He conceived that law is rational as the deepest expression of man's freedom but also that it is prescribed in opposition to the individual's freedom. He belonged to the voluntaristic tradition begun from Duns Scotus and Ockham and his paradox is that law is 'Liberty' because it is 'Will,' command, but it is only the positive will of the State. In line with the philosophers of the Enlightenment, he persisted at looking at society in exclusively political terms. He disregarded with contempt the unwritten customs and mores of peoples. For him as for Hobbes or Rousseau the conscious individual is abruptly called to recognize in the State his higher self, and in the State's command the expression of his own will and freedom.

Hegel's posterity branched off into a 'right' and a 'left,' which respectively accepted only either the positivistic or the rationalistic ('critical') aspect of his doctrine. Marx believed in the natural perfection of the individual so much that he dreamed of ultimately abolishing all class-distinctions and even the state. But his economic interpretation of history persuaded him that his dream could only be realised by violent revolution, abolition of private property, economic collectivisation and political dictatorship of the proletariat. The rightist current produced another kind of dictatorship, that of the fascist totalitarian state.

Against this background of the modern age in the West, we may consider briefly the parallel evolution in India. We shall have to distinguish here the speculations of the philosophers and the concrete reality of man and society. The ideal man of the philosophers is not the empirical member of society but the renouncer (*saṁnyāsin*) who prepares for liberation (*mokṣa*) and has already isolated himself from the secular bonds and concerns of society. In this renouncer they value essentially the radically free spirit (*puruṣa* or *ātman*) or even, if they are Buddhists, the pure freedom which substitutes for *ātman*. The empirical man is only a name-form (*nāma-rūpa*), fictitious and evanescent, and for most of them society deserves no abiding interest.

This society, however, continues its course and bears within itself a certain conception of man. It is a hierarchical society, a society of castes and sub-castes. Castes are permanent groups which are at once specialized, hierarchised and separated (in matters of marriage, food and physical contact) in relation to each other. The common basis of these three features is the opposition of pure and impure which is part of the religious outlook. This opposition is of its nature hierarchical and implies separation in customs and life and specialisation in occupations. Thus the foundation of the caste system is not power, economic or political, which may be important in practice but is distinct from, and subordinate to, the hierarchy. According to L. Dumont, the relation between hierarchy and power is as follows. Hierarchy culminates in the Brāhman; it is the Brāhman who consecrates the power of the Kṣatriya, which otherwise depends entirely on force. While the Brāhman is spiritually supreme, he is materially dependent; the gifts made to Brāhmans transform material goods into spiritual values. Whilst the Kṣatriya is materially the master, he is spiritually subordinate. A similar relation distinguishes the two superior ends of man in society, *dharma* (action conforming to) universal order, and *artha* (action conforming to) utilitarian interest. These two are hierarchised in such a way that *artha* is legitimate only within the limits set by *dharma*. Thus hierarchy is the integrating concept of the whole society. It never attaches itself to power as such, but always to religious functions and dignities from which power may then derive or by which it may be sanctioned. Hierarchy integrates the Hindu society to its universal values which are religious because religion is the form that the universally true assumes in this society.

Within this caste society, persons are being focussed on the three values or constellations of values, *artha*, *kāma* (bonds of sexual and family affection) and *dharma*. These form the realm of activity (*pravṛtti*), of actions and results (*karman* and *phala*), which is governed by the law of *karman*. The maintenance of *dharma* tends to make this society extremely conservative, the ideal being to preserve the hierarchy of the castes and the distinction of each caste and sub-caste duties. The unity of this complex society arises from the fixed complementarity of its constituent groups which is expressed in the *jajmāni* system of dominant and dominated castes. The caste system is essentially social, not political, so that the Hindu society has been able to preserve itself almost untouched by political upheavals till recent times.

Such a society does not itself favour the singularity and the autonomy of human persons but rather their relatedness and their religious rootedness in universal values. The call of freedom comes from outside the society, from the renouncers who propose spiritual emancipation (*mokṣa*) through *nivṛtti* (abstention from activity) but it reaches all the groups and polarises them on an end which is beyond and apparently opposed to the aims of society. It is the great merit of the *Bhagavad Gītā* to have discovered a reconciliation of the demands of the hierarchical society with the call of the renouncers. Its rule of *niṣkāma karma* (disinterested action) introduces renunciation within activity itself and thus redeems activity dedicated to the welfare and maintenance of the caste society.

Traditional India encounters the modern ideas almost as soon as they become active in the West but its confrontation with them is much less immediately radical and metamorphosing. For almost the whole of the nineteenth century the changes advocated are mainly partial reforms, corrections of excesses, whereas the structure itself of the society of castes is seldom if ever put into question. Liberal individualism, democratic nationalism, positivism, socialism are catching the minds of intellectuals but they hardly become aims of systematic pursuit and points of political programs before the turn of the century. And when they begin to dominate and finally triumph they do so only on the political level, and this level has not succeeded in swallowing the social level. The Constitution of Independent India may abolish the legality of the caste system but the latter remains the organisation of society as such; the Constitution may be secular but religion continues to permeate the lives of families and most individuals. The way that has been found to take in the new while retaining the old passes through the federalism of the state, a secularism not opposed to but benevolent towards religions, the recognition of linguistic boundaries, a communalism and a casteism officially denied but often upheld in practice, a planned and partly socialized economy respectful of petty mercantilism and private capitalism, and in general a healthy sense of pluralism. More than compromise or synthesis, there is duplication and conjunction and the overall change is evolutionary rather than revolutionary.

Without denying the validity of many possible complaints, I venture to say that contemporary India accepts a conception of man which is congenial to the development of persons. This conception is made of various elements: the old hierarchical casteic conception of society, which provides the roots and ligaments that prevent Indian citizens from ever being isolated individuals; the modern conception, which sanctions the basic rights and freedoms of each man and abolishes excessive privileges or disabilities; the philosophy of Neo-Hinduism, which mingles the lofty transcendentalism of the Upaniṣads with the humanism of the Sermon on the Mount and the self-sufficiency of Hinduism with the universal openness of religious and cultural pluralism. The conjunction of these three has opened India to all the chief dimensions of the human person.

On the contrary, with regard to divine personality we suffer in India at least from a linguistic embarrassment. We here speak of 'personal' and 'impersonal' as if they were synonyms with '*saguṇa*' and '*nirguṇa*.' Thus we fail to recognize the personality of the *nirguṇa Brahman* and the parallel *nirguṇatva* (simplicity befitting the Absolute) of the personal God of Christianity and of most Western conceptions. In this we follow the guidance offered by the great translators of Sanskrit works during the late nineteenth century. But we can trace their understanding of the term 'person' to the trend of rationalistic individualism studied earlier and, more precisely, to F.H. Jacobi, the philosopher of faith as the sense of reality. Jacobi appears to be the first in the whole Western tradition to have considered that 'person' necessarily implied limitation and relational dependence so that it could not be applied to God except anthropomorphically. A small number of Protestant thinkers, chiefly Germans, accepted his ruling and we have inherited their usage. But we must be aware at least that it is contrary to the larger tradition of European and Christian thought and idiom within which the term 'person' received its original denotation.

2. The Redintegration of the Person

Passing now to our own century, we may on a broad estimation say that it is marked with a renovated sense of the person and a will to promote its welfare.

This redintegration of the person is, first of all, observable in the sciences of life or of man. In biology, for instance, J.S. Haldane holds that physiological events should no longer be interpreted in terms of lower levels of physico-chemical laws but from the higher standpoint of consciousness. At the same time, we should cease to consider consciousness or personality as a mere parallel of the organism and to suppose that man as a person is anything different from his organism perceived and understood more fully. The advance in the social sciences has revealed anew the social dimension of human personality. It has shown it as a datum both of nature and of nurture or culture. The new-born infant is received and cradled by a network of social relationships, thanks to which he can emerge as a self and unfold his particular potentialities into realisations which in turn affect society. In psychology, we have attained to the notion of personality as a dynamic unity of traits or as a body-mind complex of dispositions. Even extreme behaviourists would not deny this position taken by James, Dewey, Haldane, Mead, etc. Psychology further acknowledges the inequalities between persons and, in view of measuring them, resorts to various types of data obtainable from life-situations (L), objective tests (T), questionnaires (Q), population sampling (P-technique), etc. The structure which is thus being measured is a complex typical pattern of traits, dispositions, needs, interests and values which are in dynamic relationship to each other and to the environment in a given situation. The psycho-analytical approach has destroyed the Cartesian domination of consciousness and mapped out the various levels, conscious and subconscious, of the mind. The perceptual-motivational research has demonstrated that the configuration of personality does not result from mere conditioning by stimuli but from the need-system which motivates the organism. As to the origin of the religious sentiment, it is less and less attributed to the sex instinct or to the so-called religious instinct but it is found, by Selbie for instance, in the fact that many primitive motives work in such a way that they attract a person closer to the religious interpretation of the Universe. Thus religion is seen as a product of persons' rational reflection as much as the sciences. Psychology, in order to isolate and measure the various traits and factors of personality, had initially to take man to pieces but, beyond that analytic procedure, there has now emerged a dynamic concept of the self, a new holistic picture of personality.

In philosophy, there is a similar convergence towards a holistic, anti-Cartesian understanding of personality. Husserl opens up the *Cogito* by placing intentionality at the centre of his doctrine. Bergson dynamises completely the conception of man and relates him more satisfactorily both to matter and to the living and personal God of open religion and mysticism. Blondel centres on the question of man's destiny his great book on *Action* and his later trilogy on *Thought*, *Being and Beings*, and *Action*, together form the most comprehensive and, perhaps, most impressive system of this century. Lavelle develops his dialectics of participation by which man discovers himself as sustained by the personal Absolute and constantly dependent on this Source but as a free being entrusted with the choice of his own destiny. The Neo-Thomists restore the personalism of St Thomas and find in it valuable directions to guide them in their encounter with science and technology, social development, international relations, violence, dictatorship, etc. Existentialists, without denying the experience of the *Cogito*, explore, often with rewarding results, the complementary experiences either of anxiety (Heidegger) or of hope and commitment (Marcel) or of pure contingency and absurdity (Sartre). More recently, the structuralists have drawn our attention to the *a priori* but external systems of relations which pertain to language, symbols and culture, thus anteceding each man and conditioning his social personalization.

In order to illustrate more vividly the trend which I have just outlined, I shall now report briefly on three thinkers, Max Scheler, Emmanuel Mounier, and P.F. Strawson.

Scheler, the most illustrious of Husserl's disciples, is the phenomenologist of sympathy and of the polar sentiments of love and hatred. His central view may be expressed as follows: Love can explain all things (i.e., God and the universe) because it is directed to the person which is the supreme and synthetic value. Love is manifested as the aspiration towards values. But values are realised by the person, which synthesises them and transcends each of them as well as their sum. We love a person not simply as a totality of values but as something more and unique, an 'unaccountable Plus' (*unbegründliche Plus*), says Scheler. He calls it "the concrete (or vital) unity of our being in all its activities" (*die konkrete Seinseinheit von Acten*). The whole person is committed in each act and varies in each act without exhausting its being in any one of them. The person is necessarily individual and thus unique in the sense of unrepeatable. To talk of a general person or, in Kant's way, of 'consciousness in general' is nonsense. The person is doubly autonomous, firstly, through personal insight into good and evil and, secondly, through personal volition concerning the good or the evil as concretely given. Due to this autonomy and transcendence, the person is never part of a world but always its correlate. However, the essence of the human person is found in the fact that his whole spiritual being and activity is rooted both in individual reality and in membership in a community. Man enjoys an elemental and irreducible religious experience: the divine element belongs to the primitive givenness of his consciousness. God is subsistent Being, Consciousness, Power, Holiness, Infinity. Thus He is personal, the person of persons. The reproach of anthropomorphism against attribution of personality to the Absolute is misdirected because it is not true that God is conceived according to man's image but rather that the only notion of man which makes sense is 'theomorphic.'

Mounier (1905-1950) was not only a professor of philosophy but the founder of the Paris review *Esprit*, a leading periodical which has remained in the van of progressive thought as the organ of a movement also called *Esprit*. This movement tries to achieve a peaceful revolution which will be personalistic and communitarian. Mounier's *A Personalist Manifesto* delineates the features of such a revolution in the various spheres of private life and education, economy and politics, international and intercultural relationships. These features are commanded by his conception of the human person which he sets forth in contrast with the Cartesian and sub-Cartesian conceptions.

Against dualism, he proclaims that "*I exist subjectively, I exist bodily* are one and the same experience." "Man is a body in the same degree that he is a spirit, wholly body and wholly spirit." But against materialism, he asserts that although man is a natural being, he transcends nature. "The singularity of man is his dual capacity for breaking with nature. He alone knows the universe that enfolds him, and he alone transforms it." Against liberal individualism, he upholds communication as a primordial requirement of personality. "Individualism is a system of morals, feelings, ideas and institutions in which individuals are organized by their mutual isolation and defence." "Man in the abstract, unattached to any natural community, the sovereign lord of a liberty unlimited, and undirected; turning towards others with a primary mistrust, calculation and self-vindication; institutions restricted to the assurance that these egoisms should not encroach upon one another, or to their betterment as a purely profit-making association—such is the rule of civilization now breaking up before our eyes. It is the very antithesis of personalism." "In its inner experience the person is a presence directed towards the world and other persons. It is thus communicable by its nature." "One might almost say that I have no existence, save in so far as I exist for others, and that to be is in the final analysis to love." Self-recollection is the complementary opposite of communication. Persons must be assured privacy for self-withdrawal and concentration. "Discretion and reserve are the homage that the person renders to the sense of an infinite life within." And this leads to a "surpassing of the self", a self surrenders to the transcendent divine. "Personalists, however, cannot willingly surrender the person to anything impersonal. (On the contrary they finally) deduce all values from the unique appeal of the one supreme Person."[3]

P.F. Strawson published in 1959 *Individuals: An Essay in Descriptive Metaphysics.*[4] "Descriptive metaphysics," he explained, "is content to describe the actual structure of our thought about the world, revisionary metaphysics is concerned to produce a better structure. Broadly (speaking), Descartes, Leibniz, Berkeley are revisionary, Aristotle and Kant descriptive." The first part of this *Essay* aims at establishing the central position which material bodies and persons occupy in our conceptual scheme as it is. At the outset, he puts two questions: (1) why are states of consciousness ascribed to anything at all? and (2) why are they ascribed to the very same thing as certain corporeal characteristics, a certain physical situation, etc.? His answer, on p. 98, is that states of consciousness could not be ascribed at all, unless they were ascribed to the same things as certain corporeal characteristics, etc. And what he means by the concept of a person is precisely the concept of a type of entity such that both of those distinct predicates are equally applicable to a single individual of that single type. He maintains that the concept of a person is primitive, i.e., it is the ultimate subject of this twofold attribution and is not analyzable into more ultimate subjects, such as body and soul, or reducible to the Humean fiction. Thus Strawson restores in his own way the holistic character of 'person' and bars the way to any dualism or scepticism in this matter. This vindication of the primitiveness of the concept of person permits me to speak of a rediscovery of the person even in the uncongenial atmosphere of contemporary British philosophy.

3. Conclusion

Our survey of the troubled history of the notion of person may have revealed several things: the centrality and the primitiveness of this notion; the difficulty of defining it correctly, i.e., of providing for it a well-conducted piece of descriptive rather than revisionary metaphysics; the need for considering not only the pronouncements of philosophers in this matter but also the views implicit in the ways of life and the institutions of the different peoples and cultural areas; the active role played by the several competing conceptions of the person in the transformation and revolutions of mankind, including

India, especially during the last two hundred years; the difference between individualism and personalism and the lag between many of our conceptions, institutions and ways of behaviour and what appears to be the richest and most adequate conception of person and personalism.

Surely in this matter more than in any other one the wish is true that we should not only *explain* but *transform* and that theory should usher in *praxis*.

* * *

Selected Bibliography

Berdyaev, N. *The Destiny of Man*. London: Bles, 1937.

Bertocci, P.A. and Millard, R.M. *Personality and the Good*. New York: David C. Cook, 1963.

Buber, M. *I and Thou*. Edinburgh: T. & T. Clark, 1937; 2nd ed., New York: Scribner's Sons, 1958.

Copleston, F. *Contemporary Philosophy*. London: Burns and Oates, 1956, esp. pp. 103-124.

Chatterjee, M. *Our Knowledge of Other Minds*. London: Asia Publishing House, 1963.

De Raeymaeker, L. *The Philosophy of Being*. London: Herder, 1954, esp. pp. 240-247.

De Smet, R.V. "*Persona*, *Anima*, *Ātman*." *The Philosophical Quarterly* (Amalner) **30**/4 (January 1958) 251-260.

Drennen, D.A. *A Modern Introduction to Metaphysics*. New York: Free Press of Glencoe, 1962 (esp. pp. 561-600).

Flewelling, R.T. *The Person*. Los Angeles: The Ward Ritchie Press, 1954.

Frings, M.S. *Max Scheler: A Concise Introduction*. Pittsburgh: Duquesne University Press, 1965.

Kelly, W.L. and Tallon, A. *Readings in the Philosophy of Man*, 2nd ed. New York: McGraw-Hill, 1972.

Kale, S.V. "Personality in Philosophy and Psychology." 33rd Indian Philosophical Congress (Psychology Section), 1958.

Kardiner, A. *The Individual and His Society*. New York: Columbia University Press, 1939.

MacMurray, J. *Persons in Relation*. London: Faber and Faber, 1961.

Maritain, J. *The Person and the Common Good*. London: Bles, 1937.

Merleau-Ponty, M. *L'union de l'âme et du corps chez Malebranche, Biran et Bergson*. Paris: Vrin, 1968.

Mouroux, J. *The Meaning of Man*. London: Sheed and Ward, 1948.

Müller, M. "*Persona*." *Collected Works of F. Max Müller*, vol. 10. London: Longmans, Green, 1912.

Strawson, P.F. *Individuals: An Essay in Descriptive Metaphysics*. London: Methuen, 1959.

Trendelenberg, A. "A Contribution to the History of the Word Person." *The Monist* **20** (1910) 336-363.
Van Peursen, C.A. *Body, Soul, Spirit: A Survey of the Body-Mind Problem.* London: Oxford University Press, 1966.
Wahl, J. *The Philosopher's Way.* New York: Oxford University Press, 1948 (esp. pp. 226-232).
Wisdom, J. *Other Minds.* Oxford: Blackwell, 1952.
Zacharias, H.C.E. *Human Personality.* London: B. Herder, 1950.

Notes

[1] [This is the third of three lectures delivered at the University of Madras under the Sri L.D. Swamikannu Pillai Endowment, 1969-70. It was subsequently published in the *Indian Philosophical Quarterly* 4/3 (1976) 413-426. The three lectures, together with "The Aristotelian-Thomist Conception of Man" (cf. below, chapter 11), were reprinted as an abstract under the title *A Short History of the Person.* Permission to publish has been obtained from the *Indian Philosophical Quarterly* and is gratefully acknowledged.]
[2] Alexis de Tocqueville, *Democracy in America*, chapter 2. [The French original was published in 1835; several English translations are available, among which the Penguin Classics edition of 2003.]
[3] All Mounier quotations are taken from his *Personalism*, tr. P. Mairet (London: Routledge and Kegan Paul, 1952).
[4] [P.F. Strawson, *Individuals: An Essay in Descriptive Metaphysics* (London: Methuen, 1959).]

6

THE OPEN PERSON vs THE CLOSED INDIVIDUAL[1]

The subject of this study is the ambiguity that confounds the two terms 'person' and 'individual.' It is hoped to show from the data of history that 'person' implies an openness which deserves greater consideration by philosophers as against the atomic closedness implied by 'individual.' This becomes important after P.F. Strawson has demonstrated anew that 'person' is a primitive concept which no further analysis can resolve. Indeed, if this is true, the ascertaining of the proper intention and dimension of 'person' is part of the fundamental tasks of philosophy.

We may approach this task by considering first that the tension and rivalry between 'person' and 'individual' belongs to the modern period from Descartes to our own days, i.e. to a time which witnessed, on the one hand, the wonderful growth of Classical Physics but also its more astonishing substitution by Modern Physics, and, on the other hand, the sudden blossoming of rationalism and the philosophies of the understanding but also their reversal by philosophies of intuition. Thus the last four centuries present us with the succession of two formulations of reality which correspond to two ways of viewing the world. Let us clarify these two approaches.

Classical Physics and the philosophies of understanding, whether rationalistic or empirical, operate on the assumption that we should primarily search for individual, unique, atomic entities, such as 'things,' and 'events,' 'ego' or 'substances,' and only secondarily link, relate and unify them by a unity of our own imposition which may solidify their sheer contingency. The primacy of 'reality' within this approach is given to the atomic individual unit, separated in its recognition from the rest of reality. This is perhaps the commonsense approach to reality or, at least, it is the approach of elementary science for we see it in the various atomisms and the lists of elements, categories, *tattvas* and *padārthas* which mark the beginnings of science in Greece and India.

Modern Physics and the philosophies of intellective intuition operate on the opposite assumption that we should primarily search for the totality and only secondarily for individual entities, the most 'real' aspect of any entity being its participation in the larger pattern. In other words, to perceive anything is to perceive it as a sub-system, as a pattern in a field of stresses. Thus, whereas the classical physicist would tell us, "here, on this instrument, now, there is this signal which manifests the presence of a particle, say an electron," the modern physicist only says, "here is an area where the field is strong." Similarly, Bergson advises us to recover our power of intuition and view reality as duration crossed by creative lines of *élan vital*; Husserl views it as a bi-polar totality of experience axed on transcendental ego and objective reality and traversed by lines of intentionality; existentialists give prominence to all-underlying moods or unparticularized feelings which seem to reveal either the absurdity or the meaningfulness of existence and invite us to cut as it were holes of freedom which will negate the opacity of the given; neo-Augustinian spiritualists, like Lavelle or Sciacca, speak of 'total presence' and participation, interiority and communication or, like Nédoncelle of the 'reciprocity of consciousnesses'; neo-Thomists, like Maréchal or Rahner, dynamise the whole realm of analogical being and break down all arbitrary limits by the transcendental thrust of intentionality; Blondel develops his dialectic of implication and integration, and Teilhard de Chardin writes that "as soon as science outgrows the analytic investigations which constitute its lower and preliminary stages and passes on to synthesis, it is at once led to foresee and place its stakes on the future and on the *all*."

Let us now see in what precisely the concept of 'person' pertains to this second way of viewing reality whereas 'individual' pertains to the first.

The history of 'person' goes back to late Antiquity but its place in Philosophy was assured by the Christian teachers of the fourth century AD who decided to adopt it for their own purpose and by Boethius who, around 500 AD, formulated a rough but terse and highly successful definition of it. "Person," he said, means "individual substance possessed of a rational nature." This definition clearly belongs to the first atomistic approach to reality and it is interesting to observe what happens to it in the hands of a man of deep metaphysical insight, such as St Thomas Aquinas.

First of all, every term of it is replaced by a more satisfactory one: substance by subsistent; individual by singular or distinct, and rational by intellectual.

Now, for Aquinas, 'subsistent' means 'that which exists by its own *esse*, i.e., by its own act or energy (Aristotle's *energeia)* of being.' Such a being exists in its own right, whether it is created or uncreated. It matters little whether it has qualities and other accidents and is in that respect a substance, or whether, as in the case of God the Absolute, it is so integral and perfect that it stands beyond the scope or the verb 'to have' and simply *is* in the utmost positive sense or the term. What matters is that this subsistent, if it is to be acknowledged as a person, must exhibit ontological wholeness. "It must," Aquinas writes, "comprehend the whole reality of the subject, i.e., not only its essential elements but also its individuating qualities and other accidents. Thus only will it retain the denotation of totality which the notion of 'person' requires" (*In III Sententiarum* 5, 3, 2, 3). In the case of man, this requirement means that the person is his whole self, not simply his soul or spirit: "the soul," says Aquinas, "is not the whole man but only a part of the corporeal man: my soul is not myself" (*In I Cor.* 15, 2). In the case of God, wholeness does not result from an integration of parts but from the very plenitude of the subsistent *Esse.* Aquinas' emphasis on wholeness is consonant with Strawson's rediscovery of the primitiveness of the concept of 'person.' Both mean that in the ontological line the person is the ultimate subject of attribution to which both states or consciousness *and* physical characteristics are ascribable in such a way that it is simply absurd to look for further subjects of ascription such as the soul and body of Cartesian philosophies. Indeed, for Aquinas, the first and functional idea we have of the person is that of "the ultimate subject of attribution of a certain set of activity and passivity." And what is remarkable is that, when passing from this functional to the above ontological definition, he finds that in order to be that ultimate subject of attribution the person must be, not a nucleus, but the total subject.

Passing now to the substitution or 'individual' by 'distinct' or 'singular,' let me recall that in Latin *individuum* originally meant 'undivided' and designated those unparticipable units which could stand as original centres of existence activity and resistance. The Thomistic notion of 'integral subsistent' has already taken care of this meaning. However, the kind of individuals presented by ordinary experience, namely, the members of the various species of living beings, appear to be such due to the poverty rather than to the richness of their being. Indeed, it is the distance between the full, ideal, perfection of their species and their own defective realization of it which marks off the individuality of each one. In other terms, none of them is a maximum.

The term 'person,' on the contrary, directly indicates a perfection which opens upwards towards the greatest maximum. It is not restricted to human persons which realize defectively the perfection of their species. It applies also to concrete universals and surely to God who, as Absolute, is the most concrete universal, and is as such distinct from all the rest by the very transcendence of his fullness. This explains why St Thomas adopts 'distinct' or 'singular' in preference to 'individual.'

The substitution of 'intellectual' for 'rational' is commanded by a similar consideration. For St Thomas, only the lowest grade of intellect is rational in the sense of 'bound to reasoning and discursiveness.' The higher grades are intuitive; and even man tends through his discursive activity to an intuitive knowledge short of which he cannot find his final happiness. Aquinas is fond of recalling the Isidorian etymology of *intelligere* as *intus legere*, to read within, to 'intuit,' and of repeating that our knowledge begins with sense intuition and tends through the reasoning discourse to intellectual intuition. Hence, again because 'person' is designative of perfection it must be said to imply not simply rationality but intellectuality. This, of course is its most characteristic note, that which distinguishes persons from non-personal subsistents.

Intellectuality is also that which radically prevents the person from being a mere atomic individual and gives it that holistic character and universal dimension which we found suggested by our analogy with the particles of wave-mechanics. Philosophers have repeated since Aristotle that "the intellect is in some way everything." Our intellect is all things virtually and intentionally. The divine intellect is all things in self-awareness because God is eminently every possible reality. Hence, the person, from man to God lives actually or virtually its identity with the whole. Not like Leibniz's windowless monads which mirror the whole universe through their 'obscure perceptions,' somehow as magnetic tapes contain in their silent tracks a whole universe of music. No, human persons are not subjects which pre-contain all their possible predicates. Their becoming is real, not illusory. Their dynamic development is not a simple passing from obscure to clear perceptions, a mere analysis. It is a growing synthesis with the whole and the All, through comprehension resulting from the intellect, and selective appropriation resulting from the free-will which necessarily accompanies the intellect. It is therefore through knowledge in all its intellectual forms and through the exercise of the will in all its options but particularly those of love that the human person is incessantly concerned with the whole, i.e. not with an abstraction but with all beings from the lowest creature to God himself. Omitting many important other considerations, such is the core or the Thomistic view of the person.

What happened to this view and how the person was denatured into the modern 'individual' is to a large extent the history of post-Thomistic philosophy.

The first adulteration was initiated by Duns Scotus. A voluntarist, he asserted that the universe consists of absolute individuals depending exclusively on the absolute free will of God. Free will is an arbitrary power, independent of the intellect and therefore alien to the ontological relations and connections of the universe. For Scotus, indeed, the laws of nature and morality do not express ontological exigencies of being at its various levels but are pure impositions of the divine will. God could have willed their opposites. Further, Scotus also jeopardised the integrality of the human person, this time as a formalist. Multiplying the distinctions in an Avicennian way, he presented man as a bundle of 'formalities,' i.e. intelligible elements set side by side but unlinked by any intrinsic relationship.

As regards Descartes, his *Cogito* reveals immediately the intellectual nature of man. Unfortunately, this *Cogito* is already an abstraction: it brackets out not only the *cogitata* but also the sensation-element of our initially concrete knowledge. Hence it is in a very roundabout way that Descartes can assure himself that he is not only a *res cogitans,* a thinking thing, which he understand be a distinct substance, but also a body, i.e., an extended substance different from the mental one. But how one man can be two substances is, Descartes avows, a disturbing mystery. The *commercium mentis et corporis,* i.e., the interaction and intercourse between soul and the body, being merely contingent, cannot point out to Thomistic substantial union of the two but only to a voluntaristic explanation, such as a free decision of God that they should coexist and interact. Thus, on the one hand, Descartes bequeaths to successors the so-called body-soul problem conceived as the problem of the mind in the machine, and on the other hand, he reduces the person, the intellectual subsistent, to a mental unit, deprived of connatural relationship with the world of matter and sensations, with the society of other men, and even with its own body. This is why Descartes is the genuine father of modern individualism.

Leibniz tried to overcome those two shortcomings of Cartesianism by supposing that all the centres of force and resistance in the material universe are virtual minds, of the same kind as the actually thinking monads, and by postulating further that each monad precontains the whole range of all its possible predicates and relationships, in such a way that it can adequate the universe and yet be windowless and that its changes and development are merely analytical. Solipsism is avoided through the voluntaristic appeal to pre-established harmony.

In England, Thomas Hobbes proposed to eliminate the Cartesian dualism by subjecting man's reason completely to his senses and reducing freedom to mere absence of external constraint. But he inaugurated a new kind of dualism, this time between the natural and the social states of man. For him, man's life in the state of nature is free from external constraint but "solitary, poor, nasty, brutish and short." He can accede to the social state and its benefits but only on the condition that he renounces his freedom and subjects himself to a political authority. This accession is conceived by Hobbes in terms of 'covenant' or 'compact,' i.e., of a bargaining transaction. And what can the individuals bargain with except their brutal 'forces'? The contractual pooling of such forces constitutes the state as the despotic Leviathan which coerces individuals in the pursuit of the social good.

John Locke evaded the consequence of despotism by distinguishing two contracts: the 'social' contract which ushers in fellowship in equality, and the 'political' contract which introduces subjection to the state but only in terms of Trust and Limited Monarchy. Though liberal and, as such, favourable to persons, his conception continues to view man as naturally isolated and society, morality and religion as rational constructs rather than exigencies of man's nature.

In reaction against the arbitrary postulates of Hobbes and Locke, David Hume attributes the birth of nations only to force or ambition, the origins of social life to the natural instinct for general utility, and the universality of moral principles to the strength of social habit. As to the existential subsistent that we affirm our self to be, it is but a fictitious construct of a series of felt phenomena.

Such are the most outstanding phases of the denaturation of the person into the modern individual from the fourteenth century to the eve of the French Revolution. The person has been atomised and disintegrated into a bundle of formalities by Duns Scotus, dualised by Descartes, mentalised and monadised by Leibniz, desocialised and despotised by Hobbes and hardly rescued from that by Locke, and, finally, fictionalised by Hume.

Towards the end of the eighteenth century, their theories begin to yield their fruits, good and bad, in the various Declarations of the Human Rights and in social and political upheavals, especially the French Revolution. In this tumultuous event, we see in most exemplary fashion the mutation of theoretical views of unorthodox thinkers into principles of social transformation and directives for revolutionary action.

What the French Revolution meant to, and did, indeed, accomplish was not a mere political change but a radical mutation of the social system. Ancient society was hierarchical and aristocratic; the new society would be equalitarian and democratic; it would be a triumph of the atomic individual, of the particular citizen, in the liberty, equality and fraternity of a self-ruling People. Let us consider a little more attentively the differences between those two types of society.

The ancient, hierarchical societies were based on the naturally occurring order of things and had evolved their structures after the manifested data of life. In them, the persons were, as soon as born, caught in a network of relations which immediately gave substance and reality to their natural sociality. They were distinct, singular, but as essentially related. They pertained to the group before discovering their autonomy and through the group this very autonomy was shaped and their personality moulded on a pattern of participation and mutual adjuvancy. The groups themselves were hierarchised into an overall structure of mutual dependence and collaboration sanctioned more or less strictly by religion. The social held primacy over the political. The state was an important but secondary formation which found its rationality in its conformity with the exigencies of the naturally hierarchical society. Through this society it was connected with something universal and religious, the conception of a cosmic order antecedent to any ordering of man's fabrication. In short, hierarchy integrated the ancient societies of men by reference to their universal values. Such societies could, of course, and did become rigid and their organisations oppressive; but at their best, they offered the proper scope for exchange, cooperation and mutuality which are demands of the essential relatedness of human persons.

As against these societies based on the given sociality of the human nature, our modern equalitarian societies were born from a desire to be 'rational' by breaking away from nature in order to set up an autonomous human order. Their creators, drawing their main inspiration from Hobbes, Locke, Rousseau, started with the postulate that men are by nature isolated individuals, and that the problem of making them live together lies exclusively within the competence of Reason. Nature did provide only the basic equality of those individuals and its absolute demand was the equalitarian principle which directly negated the old hierarchies.

This equalitarian principle is not simply equivalent to the moral principle of equality as inculcated by Christianity. The latter affirms that all men, even the lowest, are equal in essential nature, dignity, inviolability and natural rights. It does not deny their concrete inequalities, their complex relatedness, their mutual complementarity, it does not affirm their basic identity. The equalitarian principle, on the contrary, posits this identity of all men whom it conceives as pre-social atoms to be socialised through the Social Contract which is the work not of nature but of reason.

The chief consequence of the equalitarian principle is to deny the legitimacy of the intermediary group-structures which used to ramify society. It sets up the democratic state directly over against the multitude of single individuals. This state is supposed to result from the compact of their many wills. It can begin anew by means of a constitution approved by popular referendum or by elected representatives of the people. Once set up, it organises society through structures which too are, ideally at least, determined and controlled by the will of individuals manifested by vote. The power of such a state tends to become ubiquitous since it is no longer mediated by hierarchical intermediaries independent of itself. The political threatens to devour the social.

The creation of democratic societies secured many positive results. It did away with the worst excesses or inequality and privilege. It proclaimed solemnly the Fundamental Rights of Man which became the norm of the codes of law elaborated for their furtherance. Further, the modern state has been an apt instrument of modernisation once this was made possible by the progress of industry and technology.

However, the unmediated polarity between the isolated individuals and the Leviathan state has remained to a large extent unreconciled. Hegel's attempt in his *Philosophy of Right* to reconcile freedom and authority ended in his glorification of the Prussian state. He conceded that law is rational as the deepest expression of man's freedom but also that it is prescribed in opposition to the individual's freedom. His paradox is that law is 'Liberty' because it is 'Will,' command, but this command is only the positive will of the state. This is unredeemed voluntarism. He also persisted in viewing society in exclusively political terms. And for him, as for Hobbes or Rousseau, the conscious individual is abruptly called to recognize in the state his higher self, and in the state's command the best expression of his own will and freedom.

Hegel's posterity branched off into a 'right' and a 'left,' which respectively accepted only either the positivistic or the rationalistic ('critical') aspect of his doctrine. Marx believed in the natural perfection of the individual so much that he dreamed of ultimately abolishing all class distinctions and even the State. But his economic interpretation of history persuaded him that this dream could only be realised by violent revolution, abolition of private property, economic collectivization and the political dictatorship of the proletariat. The rightist current, on the other hand, produced another kind of dictatorship, that of the Fascist totalitarian state.

During the last hundred years a number of philosophers have slowly rediscovered the holistic conception of the person and eschewed both kinds of dualism, the Cartesian and the Hobbesian. But the modern state and society remains essentially faithful to the ideologies of individualism and contractualism which presided over its birth at the French Revolution. The new philosophical awareness has not yet won the day but it may be of interest to record briefly the main manifestations of its appearance.

This redintegration of the person is, first of all, observable in the sciences of life. Physiological events have ceased to be interpreted exclusively in terms of physico-chemical laws and consciousness has consequently ceased to be considered as a mere parallel of the organism. One no longer supposes that man, the person, is anything different from his organism perceived and understood more fully. The advance in the social sciences has revealed anew the social dimension of human personality as a datum not only of culture but of nature. In psychology we have attained to the notion of personality as a dynamic unity of traits or as a body-mind complex of dispositions. The structure which the psychologist tests and measures is a complex pattern of needs, interests, values, traits and dispositions which are in dynamic relationship to each other and to the environment in a given situation. The psycho-analytical approach has destroyed the Cartesian domination of clear consciousness and mapped out the various levels, conscious and unconscious, of the mind. The perceptual-motivational research has demonstrated that the configuration of personality does not result from mere conditioning by stimuli but from the need-system which motivates the organism. Psychology had initially to take man to pieces but beyond that analytic procedure there has now emerged a dynamic concept of the self, a new holistic picture of personality. Personality is said to be the whole organisation of an individual's instincts, emotions, habits and intellectual life. In the words of A.C. Danto: "A person *is* the body, *is* the appearance, *is* the self-conscious and rational individual, *is* the source and object of rights and obligations, *is* that which takes roles and discharges functions." Its characteristic notes are said to be totality, independence, intelligence, unity, singularity. Mounier calls personality "an active life of self-creation, communication and adhesion, capable of grasping and knowing itself in its acts." All this would have gladdened the heart of the medieval Alain of Lille who explained that *persona* meant *per-se-una*, "by itself one."

In philosophy proper, we find a similar convergence towards a holistic, anti-Cartesian understanding of personality. Husserl breaks open the *Cogito* by placing intentionality at the centre of his doctrine. Bergson dynamises completely the conception of man and relates him more satisfactorily both to matter and to the living, personal God of open religion and mysticism. Blondel centres on the question of man's destiny his great first book *Action*, and his later trilogy on *Thought*, *Being and Beings*, and *Action*, which together form the most comprehensive and, perhaps, most impressive system of this century. Lavelle develops his dialectics of participation by which man discovers himself as sustained by the personal Absolute and constantly dependent on this Source but as a free being entrusted with the choice of his own destiny. The New Thomists restore the personalism of Aquinas and find in it valuable directions to guide them in their encounter with science and technology, social development, international relations, violence, dictatorship, racialism, etc. Existentialists, without denying the experience of the *Cogito,* explore, often with rewarding results, the complementary experiences of anxiety (Heidegger) or of hope and commitment (Marcel) or of pure contingency and absurdity (Sartre). In Merleau-Ponty's course of 1947-48 on *The Union of Soul and Body in Malebranche, Biran and Bergson*, this most influential French philosopher confides that this problem has haunted the whole of his thought and that he has pursued its solution in the direction of a holistic, anti-individualistic conception of the person. Max Scheler, whose phenomenology of values is centred on a definitely holistic conception of the person, says that we love a person not simply as a totality of values but as something. more and unique, an 'unaccountable Plus' (*unbegründliche Plus*). And he defines the person as "the concrete (or vital) unity of our being in all its activities" (*die konkrete Seinseinheit von Acten*). Due to its autonomy and transcendence, the person is never mere part of the world but always its correlate. However, the essence of the human person is found in the fact that its whole spiritual being and activity is rooted both in individual reality and in membership in a community. In France, the personalism which Mounier initiated in opposition to the totalitarianisms of right and left, was based on a holistic and open conception of the person. Liberal individualism is "the very antithesis of personalism." "In its inner experience the person is a presence directed towards the world and other persons. It is thus communicable by nature." "One might almost say that I have no existence, save in so far as I exist for others, and that to be is in the final analysis to love." I have already alluded to P.F. Strawson's *Individuals*. At the outset he puts two questions: (1) why are states of consciousness ascribed to anything at all? and (2) why are they ascribed to the very same thing as certain corporeal characteristics, a certain physical situation, etc.? His answer, on p. 98, is that states of consciousness could not be ascribed at all unless they were ascribed to the same thing as corporeal characteristics, etc. And 'person' means precisely a type of entity such that *both* of those distinct predicates are equally applicable to a single individual of that single type. This is why the concept of a person is primitive as the ultimate subject of this twofold attribution and as not analyzable into more ultimate subjects, such as body and soul, or reducible to the Humean fiction. Thus Strawson restores in his own way the holistic character of the person and bars the way to any dualism or scepticism in this matter. His vindication of the primitiveness of the holistic concept of person heralds the rediscovery of the person from the very uncongenial area of contemporary British philosophy.

In conclusion, we may say that the philosopher is privileged to live as a person more consciously and responsibly than most other men because he can coincide through reflection with the very openness of the person to the divine, to the cosmic and to fellowship with all men. He may also feel more vividly the importance of his calling after being reminded that philosophical theories have engendered such radical revolutions as the French and the Russian ones and may perhaps give rise to a more satisfactory transformation of our human society.

* * *

Bibliography[2]

De Raeymaeker, L. *The Philosophy of Being*. London: Herder, 1954, esp. pp. 240-247.

Wahl, J. *The Philosopher's Way*. New York: Oxford University Press, 1948, esp. pp. 226-232.

Copleston, F. *Contemporary Philosophy*. London: Burns and Oates, 1956, esp. pp. 103-124.

Drennen, D.A. *A Modern Introduction to Metaphysics*. New York: The Free Press of Glencoe, 1962, esp. pp. 561-600.

Le Trocquer, R. *What is Man?* London: Burns and Oates, 1961.

Mouroux, J. *The Meaning of Man*. London: Sheed and Ward, 1948.

Wisdom, J. *Other Minds*. Oxford: Blackwell, 1952.

Strawson, P.F. *Individuals: An Essay in Descriptive Metaphysics*. New York: Doubleday Anchor Books, 1963.

Chatterjee, M. *Our Knowledge of Other Minds*. London: Asia Publishing House, 1963.

MacMurray, J. *Persons in Relation*. London: Faber and Faber, 1961.

Maritain, J. *The Person and the Common Good*. London: Bles 1937.

Kale, S.V. "Personality in Philosophy and Psychology." Psychology Section, 33rd Indian Philosophical Congress, 1958.

De Smet, R.V. "*Persona, Anima, Ātman*." *The Philosophical Quarterly* (Amalner) **30**/4 (January 1958) 251-260.

Zacharias, H.C.E. *Human Personality*. London: B. Herder, 1950.

Merleau-Ponty, M. *L'union de l'âme e du corps chez Malebranche, Biran et Bergson*, ed. Jean Deprun. Paris: J. Vrin, 1968.

Dumont, L. "The Modern Conception of the Individual. Notes on its Genesis." *Contributions to Indian Sociology* [The Hague: Mouton] **8** (Oct. 1965) 13-61.

Notes

[1] [This piece was delivered as the Presidential Address of the Goa session (May 23-26, 1970) of the Indian Philosophical Association, as indicated in "Early Trends in the Indian Understanding of Man," ch. 7, note 2 below. It was published in *Indian Ecclesiastical Studies* **9**/3 (1970) 161-171, and only later in the *Journal of the Philosophical Association* **15**/47 (1974). Permission to publish has been obtained from *Indian Theological Studies* (earlier *Indian Ecclesiastical Studies*) and is gratefully acknowledged.]

[2] [De Smet had not arranged this bibliography alphabetically.]

7

EARLY TRENDS IN THE INDIAN UNDERSTANDING OF MAN[1]

He knows to-morrow, he knows the world and what is not the world.
By the mortal he desires the immortal, being thus endowed....
Man is the sea, he is above all the world.
Whatever he reaches he desires to go beyond it.

—*Aitareya Āraṇyaka* 2, 1, 3

The growing importance of the humanistic outlook in modern India and its diffusion into outlets of revolutionary ardour call our attention to its sources and to its significance and validity. In its more overt manifestations, it seems to be inspired mainly from Marxism. But, as a deeper current, it continues the movement of the Indian Renaissance in its thrust towards greater fraternity, equality, liberty and the assured dignity of every human being. This movement, it is well known, resulted from the Indian discovery of Western values as emphasised in the philosophies of the eighteenth and nineteenth centuries with their special interest in the individual and the state and as justified by a recourse to certain layers of the Indian tradition. Today, after the large success of this adaptive development, it is no injury to remark on the limitations of several of those philosophies as well as of that Indian rethinking of its own sources. On other occasions this year I have concerned myself with reassessing the Western conceptions of man either as a person or as an individual.[2] This time I intend to research our Indian heritage—briefly for significant materials concerning the Indian understanding of man.

1. The Contribution of the Sacrificers

Each Vedic sacrifice is performed for an individual, the *yajamāna*, who assumes its costs. But this individual is very different from the individual of modern society whose aim is self-sufficiency to do and live as he pleases and whose values are social equality, unhampered mobility and the right to follow his own choice in everything. The aim of the Vedic individual is maintenance, maintenance of the cosmic order (*rta*), maintenance of the mutual support that binds gods and men, maintenance of the sacrificial ritual which is the instrument of that support, maintenance of his own social rank and status. His view of the world is basically optimistic because beyond the sight of accidents, failures, illness and death, it adheres to the vision of some great archetypes which assures him that the universe has been well made and made for the good of all creatures. His deepest conviction, therefore, is that this situation has to be preserved and that the only change admissible is from the relaxation of order brought about by the wear and tear of ordinary life to the ritual recovery of its archetypal integrity. The very archetype of man is the *Mahāpuruṣa* of *Ṛgveda* 10, 90 from whose sacrificial dismemberment the whole (*Sarva*) universe has originated, and we learn from the *Brāhmaṇas* that sacrifice is meant to reintegrate this *Prajāpati* and thus to secure the wholesomeness of world and man. By it man himself becomes all (*Sarva*).

This holistic idea of man is important as it is opposed to his conception as a mere part. The Vedic man is not insulated by his empirical limits. He is prolonged not only by his wife, children, cattle and pasture lands, but by his very complementarity with the other *Varṇas* and with the gods themselves. These are his allies and friends. He feeds and praises them and they in turn provide him with the bounty of well-regulated nature. He does not hanker after independence and isolation but rather seeks association and integration with his natural auxiliaries. He does not fear any blind necessity but is, on the contrary, confident that he can with their help fulfil intelligently the role for which his birth and station have prepared him. His religion is not something otherworldly but rather the sacralisation of the precise network of all his links with the beings of the three worlds.

A new turn is given to this self-idea of the Vedic man by the *bandhutā* theory of the *Brāhmaṇas*. S.K. Belvalkar had rightly marked the importance of this theory for the beginnings of philosophical speculation in India.[3] L. Renou and several other important Indologists have confirmed his judgment. In the Brahmanic pantheon each *deva* has a definite function and also specified associates and paraphernalia. These are his *Bandhus*. Indra, for instance, has Indrani for his wife, Agni, Soma, Varuṇa, Pūṣan, Bṛhaspati, Brahmaṇaspati, Parvata, Kutsa, Viṣṇu and Vāyu as his companions, and is associated with the number eleven, the metre *Triṣṭubh*, the season *Grīṣma* (summer), the mid-day oblation, and so forth. Between a *deva* and his *bandhus*, there is a subtle connection (*bandhutā*), a mysterious bond, which leads to their identification. For the word *bandhu* the texts use more or less synonymously the words *rūpa*, *tanu*, *nāma* and, more rarely *pratimā*, *ātman*, *manas*, *nidāna*, etc. They all indicate a close degree of identification and throw light upon the subsequent identity-statements of the *Upaniṣads*. Now the *bandhutā* theory contains another presupposition, namely, the distinction of the universe into three parallel but equivalent realms: the realm of the sacrifice, the macrocosm and the microcosm. When we pass from the *Brāhmaṇas* to the *Āraṇyakas* and the *Upaniṣads*, the conviction increases that the powers and functions at work in the first realm are identically those at work in the other two or, at least, have their authentic *bandhus*. The search for these correlated *bandhus* leads insensibly to the quest for the most sacred power, the *Brahman* which sustains their hierarchy, and to its identification with the deepest *Ātman* of man the microcosm.

If, therefore, there exists this extensive affinity between sacrifice, cosmos and man, the latter must now be considered as a field of forces, and verily of the same forces that are active in the sacrifice and in the cosmos. Indeed, the *Prāṇas* and *Indriyas* which energize man are unhesitatingly called *devas*, *devatās*, *puruṣas* and *ātmans*. They constitute the same hierarchical society as the cosmological *devas*. Their disputes about which of them is the highest recall the rivalries between *devas* and *asuras*. Inversely, the progressive discovery in man of deeper and deeper layers or functions, such as *manas*, *hṛdaya*, *vijñāna*, *ātmā mahān*, *ānanda*, *antarātman*, *prājñātman*, *śāntātman*, which are ultimately subsumed under that biggest *Ātman* which is *Brahman*, is paralleled by the gods' discovery that they owe their victories to a Power higher than their own (*Keṇa Up*. 3-4) and by Prajāpati's instruction to Indra and Virocana concerning the supreme *Ātman* (*Chānd. Up*. 8, 7-12). The forces of which man is the field are thus conceived as personal, cosmological, hierarchical and ultimately as polytheomorphic manifestations—let us recall the synonyms of *bandhu*—of a supreme and Absolute Godhead.

The resulting picture of man is that of a city (*pura*) rather than of a single organism. He is the meeting-place of a whole scale of powers apart from which he seems to be nothing. He is not their host or even their lodging-place but he is rather the very form of their encounter, the *rūpa* and *nāma* of their manifestation. Through this development of ideas the Vedic man has gained in wholeness but seems to have lost in solidity. Yet his social and functional solidarity with the members of the *varṇas* and with the *devas* has been expanded into a cosmic dimensionality and raised from the level of commonplace realism to that of metaphysical transcendentalism.

2. The Contribution of the Renouncers

In the Vedic society, the ideal man is clearly the householder solidly integrated within the hierarchical system of his pastoral-agricultural society. But at the end of the Ṛgvedic period we find clear allusions to the houseless condition of some who practise asceticism (*tapas*) in diverse forms. In *Maṇḍalas* 7, 9 and 10 of *Ṛgveda*, mention is made of the *muni*, rag-clad, ecstatic and driven by the gods, of the *Yati*, who makes the worlds swell, and of the *Ṛṣi*, powerful over gods and elements because of his *tapas*. The long hymn of *Atharva-veda* 11, 5 (7) describes the *Brahmacāri* not as a student but as a specialist of *tapas* by which he gains the *Brahman*-power. It is by his *brahmacārya* that the king protects his kingdom, girls obtain husbands, horses fodder, the gods immortality, and that Indra becomes the king of the gods. The whole 15th book of *Atharva-veda* is consecrated to the *Vrātya* whose claim of mastery over the cosmic powers is marked by a rather excessive freedom from all conventional rules. The attraction of ascetic life must have been strong since we see the Brahmanic society endeavouring to accommodate it to its own ways by gradually developing the scheme of the four *Āśramas*. Outside this society there is the vast proliferation of Śramanism which includes the *Ājīvikas* and other *Lokāyatas*, the pre-Jaina *Nirgranthas*, and soon the *Jainas* and the *Bauddhas*.

What are the consequences of this development for the Indian conception of man? I see mainly two, namely, first, the apparition of the individual in a quasi-modern sense of the term, and, second, a secularisation and an extenuation of the integrative ontology of man.

First of all, then, the apparition of the individual in a quasi-modern sense of the term. The Renouncer, the *Saṁnyāsi*, is deliberately the opposite of the Vedic householder. Whereas the latter was a centre of manifold relations and communications, i.e., a person with all the openness which this term implies, the renouncer, on the contrary, is a detached atom, a self-isolating individual. He has subtracted himself from the ties of family and the bonds of society, freed himself from the rights and duties of his *Varṇa* and status, and set himself in the margin of, or even completely outside, the very structure and hierarchical framework of secular society. He generally turns away with a shrug of contempt from the honoured triad of human goals, *artha*, *kāma* and *dharma*, to pursue a new and supreme value, *mokṣa*, understood as a complete liberation from the very forms of existence which the secular man cherishes and endeavours to prolong. He may, if he is a materialist, reject this ideal but even then he pretends to absolute freedom from the *dharma* which is so essential to his society and he both professes and practises antinomianism as the only reasonable way of life.

In later times, the renouncer dramatizes his death to the world. Distributing his possessions and ceasing to feed his sacrificial fires, he performs his own funerals with "sixteen *śrāddhas* of himself and *sapindīkaraṇa*".[4] But from this death he rises as an individual, isolated, monadic. Henceforth he is to rely only on himself. He may for a time follow a teacher, he may even enter a monastical *sangha*, but this does not mean that he reenters something like the society he has left. A *sangha* is no hierarchical structure of separate status and vertical complementarity. In the pursuit of *mokṣa*, the renouncer is strictly alone, as witness the words of the dying Buddha: "So,

Ānanda, you must be your own lamps, be your own refuges; take refuge in nothing outside yourselves" (*Dīgha Nikāya* 2, 100). He will, of course, endeavour to transcend or to extinguish this uncomfortable individuality but as compared to the householder in the world he will ever remain the man of his own choice.

I have said that the renouncer is an individual in a quasi-modern sense of the term. This point has been stressed, perhaps for the first time, by the French sociologist L. Dumont in several of his papers published in *Contributions to Indian Sociology*.[5] Both the renouncer and the modern individual conceived by Hobbes, Locke, Hume and Rousseau, and born from the French Revolution, exist with regard to their society in a state of denaturalisation. The modern individual is supposed to be by nature free of all social bonds and to accede to the social state only by choice through a social contract. The renouncer, though very much social by birth, overcomes the ties of his social nature through a contrary choice of self-emancipation. The modern individual while choosing society does not choose re-immersion into the natural type of society but opts for a society of artificial construct, dominated by the equalitarian principle and geared to be a political organisation rather than a participation in sociability. The renouncer if he ever turns again towards society does it as a preacher to introduce a new morality of universal compassion and equanimity towards all, a new polarity of *mokṣa* on which society has to readjust its secular aims, and some great spiritual movement in which people of all castes find a new fraternity. In the history of India, the renouncer is the provider of new ideas, the radical questioner and the initiator of new values. There is a tension between him and the householder who mainly preserves and maintains. But he is the strongpoint of this tension and it is the householder who yields, adapting himself, assimilating the new teaching and, at least grudgingly, finding a way of reconciling the ancient with the new.

A second point remains to be considered, namely, the new ontology of man introduced by the renouncers. We may notice, first, a process of secularisation. The divine cosmogonic forces of which the sacrificers' man was but a field are now increasingly replaced by mere physiological and psychological functions. These are either the categories of early Sāṁkhya or the seven *tattvas* of Jainism or the seven *kāyas* of Pakudha

Kaccāyana or the five *skandhas* of Gautama Buddha. Categories of this kind can be considered without awe. They have no more sacrality than the chemical elements or the particles of modern science. It is therefore possible to establish between them an order of value or even to devalorise all of them and to consider their conjunction as merely accidental. The renouncers are induced to adopt such attitudes by their attention to the three states of consciousness and by their practice of *yoga*. The natural withdrawal from the agitation of the waking state and the emotions of dream into the peace of deep sleep is emulated by the voluntary withdrawal of *yoga* which, bypassing the two forms of sleep, leads to the fourth state of super-peace mentioned in *Bṛhadāraṇyaka, Māṇḍukya* and *Maitri Upaniṣads*. This *turīya* is experienced in two possible ways, either as void (*śūnya*) by the Buddhists, or as fullness (*pūrṇa*) by the *Upaniṣads*.[6] In both cases, it implies a devaluation of man as an aggregate.

Indeed, the very experience of *yoga* leads the *yogī* to believe that the human elements and functions which appear distinct in their synchronic coexistence are resorbable so as to leave no residue of diversity. And this may incline him towards non-dualism (*advaitavāda*) with its strong emphasis on the unicity of the Absolute in us and its consequent relativisation of all finite forms. On the other hand, the detached witnessing by the yogic consciousness of the flux of *vṛttis* or mental forms in their diachronic succession suggests something like the Buddhist Law of Consecutive Origination (*pratītya-samutpāda*). This law reduces man's continuity to a mere appearance born from the close consecution of related but discontinuous instants of existence which can be viewed according to the sequence of act and fruit (*karma-phala*) Thus, whether the renouncer's analysis of human existence is synchronic or diachronic, it extenuates its cohesiveness and integrality.

Yet the renouncer introduces by his life even more than by his teaching another element which makes for consistency, namely, the dynamism of the intellect and the will. No doubt, he tends to suppress desire in the form of greed, lust, envy and other forms of *tṛṣnā* and *kāma*, but he is constantly sustained by a spiritual desire which burns like a flame until it is fulfilled by the perfect realisation of truth. This is a desire which makes man transcend himself so that "by the mortal he desires the immortal and whatever he reaches he desires to go beyond it" (*Aitareya Āraṇyaka* 2, 1, 3). It is "hope, greater than memory," which gives "unlimited freedom as far as it reaches" (*Chānd. Up*. 7, 14). It is "the love of the *Ātman* for the sake of which husband, wife, sons, wealth, *brahman*, *kṣatra*, worlds, gods or beings are dear" (*Bṛh. Up*. 2, 4, 5). It is the desire for knowledge from which are born all enquiries (*jijñāsa*). It is the desire for liberation (*mumukṣā*) and beatitude. As a dynamism of nature it appears first as the motive force of all active undertakings (*pravṛtti*). But when assumed as a spiritual drive it urges man to desist from all worldly pursuits (*nivṛtti*) and to opt exclusively for transcendence. In the Indian conception of man, this dynamism towards transcendence which is common to both the orthodox and unorthodox *sādhanās* is perhaps the most important piece though often unnoticed or taken for granted.

Dynamism redeems mechanicism as in the similes of the chariot, of the bow and arrow, or of the fire-drill. In such similes a man is compared to instruments made of separate parts and it would be easy to explain in Buddhist fashion that he is indeed nothing but a momentary aggregate of such parts. But in the *Upaniṣads* these instruments are considered at the height of their goal-seeking activity, the human chariot as driven skilfully by the charioteer *vijñāna* and "reaching the journey's end, Viṣṇu's highest abode" (*Kaṭha Up*. 3, 9); the human arrow as the self (*ātman*) sharpened by devotion and directed unerringly by the bow, *Om*, on to the target, *Brahman*, so that it becomes one with it (*tanmaya*) (*Muṇḍaka Up*. 2, 2, 34); the human fire-drill as revealing God like hidden fire by the twirling of the fire-stick, *Om* (*Śvet. Up*. 1, 14). The *yoga* context of these dynamic similes assures us that we owe to the same renouncers who have disintegrated the static image of the social man this dynamic picture of the individual ascetic redintegrated by will and spiritual purpose.

3. The Contribution of the Devotees

Spiritual dynamism introduces to the idea of polarity. It is the polarity between the two *ātmans* of *Kaṭha Up*. 3, 1 "lodged in the cave of the heart, in the seat supreme; the knowers of *Brahman* speak of them as shade and light." Their distinction is a characteristic of the more recent *Upaniṣads*. The successive forms of the wheel-analogy mark steps in that direction. In *Bṛh. Up*. 1, 5, 15, the wheel is psychic and its hub is the finite *ātman*, but ibid. 2, 5, 15 the wheel is psycho-cosmic and its hub is the infinite *Ātman*. Similarly it is the highest *Prāṇa* in *Chānd. Up*. 7, 15, 1 and the greatest *Puruṣa* in *Praśna Up*. 6, 6. Finally, in *Śvet. Up*. 1, 6, the finite *ātman* is the wild goose (*haṃsa*) that flutters restlessly in the universal Wheel whereas the one God is the Wheel-Impeller favoured by whom that bird-*Ātman* passes to immortality.

This idea that the human spirit attains immortality as a consequence of its being favoured and blessed (*juṣṭa*) by its divine Lord marks the transformation of at least some of the renouncers into devotees. It also marks a change in the conception of man. Instead of being a dynamic conqueror who by sheer will-power and concentrated attention can win the Godhead, he is now a receiver of divine grace, the beneficiary of a divine election (*Kaṭha Up*. 2, 23) which awakens in him the highest devotion, the *parā bhakti* of *Śvet. Up*. 6, 23. Whereas Yājñavalkya had long ago made clear that man must love and desire the absolute *Ātman* in all his loves and above all objects, the idea that this love could be reciprocated is a discovery of these late Upaniṣadic and probably post-Buddhistic times.

In the *Bhagavad Gītā*, it is entrusted by Srī Kṛṣṇa to Arjuna as his "highest word, of all the most mysterious." "I love thee well," He says, "thou art dear to Me" (*iṣṭo 'si me... priyo 'si me*: 18, 64-65). This is a revelation of an I-Thou relationship between God and man. And it reveals in both of them a dimension of personal intimacy and of elective communicability which had hardly been suspected before. That this is a dimension of the Absolute itself is, indeed, most mysterious and many have taken care to explain away the manifest meaning of the *Gītā* formulations. But the most recent commentator, R.C. Zaehner, urges us to read again with a free mind such a passage as 14, 27, where Kṛṣṇa declares, "*Brahmaṇo hi pratiṣṭhā 'ham*: For I am the base supporting *Brahman*." After examining carefully all the contextual relations of this passage, Zaehner writes: "Krishna's present statement, then, coming where it does, can only mean that He, as personal God, transcends even the absolutely transcendent. He 'is what IS and what is not and what surpasses both' (11, 37) as Arjuna, more percipient than most of the commentators on this magnificently subtle poem, intuitively saw."[7]

But, however important the *Gītā* formulations may be to reconcile in Indian terms divine absoluteness and personality, let us consider further their implications for the nature of man. Verse 18, 54 shows clearly what the *Gītā* adds to the view of the renouncers. "*Brahman* become, with self serene, he grieves not nor desires; the same to all contingent beings, he gains the highest love-and-loyalty to Me." "*Brahman* become," *brahmabhūta*, is not found as such in the classical *Upaniṣads* but is a stock-phrase in the Pali Canon to designate the man who, in the Buddhist view, has attained the highest state of excellence. The author of the *Gītā* adopts it to designate the *yoga* of sameness-and-indifference which is the highest aim of the *yogī* (cf. 5, 24, *sa yogī brahma-nirvāṇam brahmabhūto 'dhigacchati*). But it is only to cancel its ultimacy by revealing beyond it the divine gift of highest love, *parā bhakti*, which crowns as it were the human conquest of *Brahman*: *brahma-bhūtaḥ... mad-bhaktim labhate parām*. "To those men who are ever integrated and commune with Me in love, I give that integration of the intellect by which they may draw nigh to Me" (10, 10). "This I think, that of all yogis the most integrated (*yuktatama*) is the man of faith who loves and honours (*bhajate*) Me, his inmost self absorbed in Me" (6, 47). Love, therefore, a love of God communicated to man by God Himself, is the supreme integration of man. The self-emptying of renunciation or the absorption of the *jñāni* into the fullness of the *nirguṇa Brahman* are here subsumed into a higher absorption, the self-surrender of love through which man dies to all the perishable but gains the very immortality of the Imperishable.

4. Conclusion

It is time to gather the results of this limited survey. In early times the Indian man is essentially social. But his society is a hierarchy which beyond the visible *varṇas* of men includes the invisible gods. And he stands in his appointed station as a hub of horizontal and vertical relationships of complementarity and reciprocity through which he finds his wholesomeness and integration. The *bandhutā* theory accentuates this view to the point where man appears to be a mere field of divino-cosmic forces and, as it were, a name-and-form of their encounter and display.

In opposition to this paragon of social participation, the renouncer stands in the curiously quasi-modern stance of the pure individual who rejects all social impositions and dedicates himself to the exclusive pursuit of absolute freedom. He secularises the constituents of his own being, whether *tattvas* or past *karmas*, and in various ways devalorises and extenuates them in order by some kind of Yogic withdrawal to attain to an isolation (*kaivalya*) which he views either as void or as fullness. But what his stripping uncovers is the live wire of pure dynamism towards truth.

The discovery of divine love and grace and the beginnings of *bhakti* come as an answer from above to this assurging dynamism. The latter is more than a flame condemned to burn itself into extinction. It is the total aspiration of a being made to achieve itself in the self-surrender of love answering divine love. Thus the Indian mind discovers that the I-Thou relationship can endure beyond even the highest transcendence. The fullest integration of man, his integration with the Personal Absolute, is possible without loss.

Each one of these successive views of man stresses some important aspect of his complex being. Let me enumerate his relatedness and openness in the three directions: social, cosmic and divine; his complementarity with others; his dynamism towards integration on all possible levels; his radical freedom which enables him to refuse and reject whatever he deems worthless and to accept and embrace what he finds excellent; finally, his intrinsic worth as an end in himself proved by the fact that he is a desirable object of love (*iṣṭa*) for God Himself.

Neither these aspects nor the three contributions I have outlined do exhaust the Indian share in man's understanding of himself. But they have been chosen because they seem to complement and enrich what is usually said or published on this subject. In the past they have usually been thought about as alternatives rather than as aspects of a possibly unitary view of man. Yet, in the actual life of many, they appear to have been reconciled in diverse combinations of complementarity. This, to my mind, is especially true of the leaders of the Indian Renaissance. Once again, therefore, life opens up avenues for our reflection while from the past, history proffers experiences and views which can enrich and guide our troubled and uncertain present.

Notes

[1] [Six versions of this article are available: (1) "The Indian Understanding of Man," Presidential Address, History of Philosophy Section, 44th Session of the Indian Philosophical Congress, under the auspices of the University of Poona, 5-8 November 1970 (De Smet is listed as belonging to the Institute of Indian Culture, Bandra, Bombay, and De Nobili College, Poona); (2) "The Indian Understanding of Man," *The Call Divine* **19**/5 (1971) 211-223; (3) "The Indian Understanding of Man," *Indian Ecclesiastical Studies* **10**/3 (1971) 169-178; (4) "Early Trends in the Indian Understanding of Man," *The Divine Life* **33**/2 (1971) 60-67; (5) "Early Trends in the Indian Understanding of Man," n.d., paginated 1-8 and printed at Y.V.F.A. Press, P.O. Sivanandanagar (probably an offprint of version 4, given that *The Divine Life* is published from Sivanandanagar); and (6) "Early Trends in the Indian Understanding of Man," *Philosophy East and West* **22** (1972) 259-268. I have chosen to keep the title of the later versions, as it reflects more accurately the contents of the paper. The introductions of versions 2-6 are identical. The introduction of the first version is different; I reproduce it here:

> The privilege of having been elected President of the History of Philosophy section for this 44th session of the Indian Philosophical Congress affords me an opportunity of expressing my gratitude to all of you. I am, indeed, thankful not only to the Executive Committee for this undeserved honour but to all the members of this Congress for graciously and fraternally including me in their midst ever since our memorable Kandy session in 1954. While listening to your papers, sharing in your discussion and, at times, proposing my own modest contributions, I have gained access to your friendship as well as to your thinking and I have felt more than intellectually enriched.
>
> The time at my disposal does not allow for an assessment of the whole field reserved for this section. I can only reflect a particular facet but it should be of general interest. Now the growing importance of the humanistic outlook in modern India….

Permission to publish has been obtained from *Indian Theological Studies* (earlier *Indian Ecclesiastical Studies*), and is gratefully acknowledged.]

[2] Srī L.D. Swamikannu Pillai Endowment Lectures, University of Madras, February 25-27, 1970: "The Discovery of the Person;" "The Loss of the Person;" "The Rediscovery of the Person." Presidential Address of the Goa

session (May 23-26, 1970) of the Indian Philosophical Association: "The Open Person vs the Closed Individual." [Cf. above, chapters 3-6.]
[3] S.K. Belvalkar and R.D. Ranade, *History of Indian Philosophy*, Vol. II: *The Creative Period* (Poona: Bilvakuñja, 1927) 61-66.
[4] [Pandurang V. Kane, *History of Dharmaśāstra: Ancient and Mediaeval Religious and Civil Law in India*, 4 vols. (Poona: Bhandarkar Oriental Research Institute, 1941) **2**, II:958. The quotation and reference is missing in versions 4 and 5.]
[5] [Cf. L. Dumont, "The Modern Conception of the Individual. Notes on its Genesis," *Contributions to Indian Sociology* **8** (October 1965) 13-61.]
[6] ['Upanishadists' in versions 1 and 6.]
[7] R.C. Zaehner, *The Bhagavad-Gītā with a Commentary Based on the Original Sources* (Oxford: Clarendon Press, 1969) 358.

8

IS THE CONCEPT OF 'PERSON' CONGENIAL TO ŚĀṄKARA VEDĀNTA?[1]

1. The Traditional Christian Understanding of Person

Since the time of the great translators of Sanskrit works in the Max Müller era the custom has been established to render the terms *saguṇa* and *nirguṇa* by 'personal' and 'impersonal' although, strictly speaking, they denote either the presence or the absence of an endowment of *guṇas* whether the latter are understood as accidents of a substance in Vaiśeṣika fashion or as internal tensors which complexify a *prakṛti* as in Sāṁkhya. My contention is that such renderings are very unfortunate because they pervert the original and traditional understanding of 'person' and impede the task of comparative religion or philosophy especially when the traditions compared are Vedānta and Christianity. As a philosophico-religious term, 'person' has been coined and elaborated by the Christian thinkers so as to fit both man and the divine absolute and it is only in recent times (not more than 200 years ago) that some philosophers began to restrict it to man alone. I may therefore be allowed to recall briefly this traditional understanding of 'person.'

The term 'person' belongs to the realm of activity broadly understood as including such immanent activities as knowing, being conscious, etc. It designates the ultimate subject of attribution of all activities implying intellectual, namely suprasensuous knowledge and consciousness. Being ultimate, such a subject is not, like a function, subordinated to the purpose of another but acts for its own sake and exists autonomously. Hence, it is an end in itself and is characterised by ontological freedom and moral responsibility. It is signified by such pronouns as I, thou, he, which are indeed called personal pronouns. Since it assumes total responsibility it is not simply the conscious principle or element in the agent but the whole agent itself, not simply the spirit or the soul though it has to be spiritual. Thus 'person' is a holistic concept, it refers to the whole, to the integrality of the agent, whether the latter is pure spirit like God or rational animal like man. It is, however, immaterial whether the personal agent is in itself simple, partless, absolute spiritual substance without accidents and thus pure Consciousness, or whether it is a complex subsistent comprising parts and functions, spiritual and also corporeal. What matters is that its integrality be predominantly spiritual, i.e., intellectually conscious. This, indeed, is required to make it a subject of attribution ultimate, freely responsible and an end in itself.

Besides these, a remarkable property of the person is that it can initiate the kind of bi-polar relationships which we call interpersonal. These exist between persons as persons. They transcend utility for they imply an absolute valuation of the other as an end in itself. In order to be truly what they pretend to be, they demand in their subject a fair degree of selflessness without which there could be no opening up to the other as personal other.

Regarding relations, a question may arise: how can God, understood as the incomplex Absolute, be related to finite persons? Would not such relations accrue to him as accidents to a substance and thus complexify him?

The theory of relation of the Christian schoolmen, especially of St Thomas Aquinas, permits them to eliminate this difficulty. According to them, a relation need not be an ontological entity in order to be true. Its truth depends on its foundation or ground. If this ground is intrinsic to the subject of the relation, the latter is not only true but real. If, on the contrary, this ground is extrinsic to the subject and intrinsic to the term of the relation, the latter is true but only logical, not a real entity, in the subject though its correlation is real in the term. On the basis of this theory, the problem of the relations between the personal but immutable and absolute God and the perfectible finite persons finds the following solution. Since God's love for us, for instance, does obviously not change or perfect God but does perfect us, it is this change in us which is the foundation of the relation that arises from it. This foundation being extrinsic to God, the relation of God to us as our Lover is only logical though true (since it has a ground). As to our relation to him as the terms of his love, it is a perfecting actuation of our potentiality and thus an ontological complement of our being, that is to say, a real accident. Parallelly, our love for God perfects only ourselves and not God, hence gives rise to a similar unequal pair of relations, real in us but only logical in God. Since this solution derives from a general theory of relation, it is not merely an ad hoc solution of the case of interpersonal relations but is valid for all the relations between the Absolute and the relative beings. Thus creatorship, lordship etc., are logical whereas creatureship, dependence, etc. are real relations.

The conclusion of this is that none of the conditions for being a person, not even the property of initiating interpersonal relationships, prevent the absolute Deity from being considered as personal in the proper sense of the term. The concept of person transcends the opposition between *nirguṇa* and *saguṇa*, unqualified and qualified or rather incomplex and complex. Indeed, 'person' like 'being,' 'spirit,' 'bliss' (*sat, cit, ānanda*), etc. is not a predicamental but transcendental term whose highest range reaches the Absolute not only metaphorically but properly.

It must however, be recalled that no human term or concept, not even the transcendental ones, can apply in univocal fashion to God and creatures. To apply to God they must be de-finitised and elevated, i.e., analogised or, to coin a new term, 'lakṣaṇised.' And to apply to God in their proper sense, which is only possible for transcendental terms, their *lakṣaṇā* must be *jahadajahat*, that is, such that the *apavāda* moment of purification does not destroy their proper meaning or *svārtha* but only allows it to be elevated to its most eminent signification or *paramārtha.* As Śaṅkara explains clearly in *Taitt. Up*. 2, 1, even so the *Brahman* is not expressed but only indicated properly, i.e., defined, by such 'lakṣaṇised' terms: *tal-lakṣyate na tūcyate.*[2] He has also given there the rule that not only '*satyam jñānam anantam*' but all Upaniṣadic definitions of the *Brahman-Ātman* must be understood similarly through *jahad-ajahal-lakṣaṇā.*

The term 'person' as philosophically elaborated by the Christian tradition is obviously not Upaniṣadic. It has not even any adequate equivalent in Sanskrit. But when the question is put, is the *Brahman* personal, our answer should, it seems to me, take into account and even be based upon the original usage and understanding of 'person' as found in Christianity.

If this is done, there will be no doubt that we may and must say that the *Brahman*, even considered in the strict *Advaita* perspective of Śaṅkara's Vedānta, is most properly and eminently personal, indeed the Super-person. How could the supreme *Ātman* whose integrality is pure Consciousness and whose freedom is absolute not be supremely personal? Its very *nirguṇatva* and *akhandatva* are the marks of its perfection and fullness as person. The term 'person' is therefore perfectly suitable as an appellation of the absolute *Brahman* of Advaita Vedānta. Unlike '*saguṇa*' it is introduced not as a pedagogical device or a first but deficient approach but rather as an enrichment of the proper and correct (though ever inadequate) understanding of the Absolute according to the Upaniṣads.[3]

2. Person and the Vedānta Conception of Man

The second point to be treated in reference to my initial question is, how far is the term 'person' suitable to the Vedānta conception of man. Limiting myself to Śaṅkara's *advaitavāda* I shall refer chiefly to his *bhāṣya* on *Bṛh. Up*. 4, 3, 7 and to ch. 2 and 18 of his *Upadeśasāhasri* while not ignoring his other writings.

Śaṅkara agrees with the Mimāṁsā that "the self is the object of the notion 'I' (*ātmā aham-pratyaya-viṣayaḥ*)." But in his search for the uppermost *Ātman* he ascends with *Kaṭha Up*. 3, 10-12 through the ladder of more and more interior *ātmans* from the senses to the *Puruṣa*. The latter is really ultimate, it the inner source and ground of man and the absolute, self-luminous light (*svayaṁ-jyotiṣ*: *Bṛh. Up*. 4, 3, 9) which integrates him but it is not the ultimate subject of attribution of his actions and experiences. The *Puruṣa* or *Paramātman* is, indeed, neither an agent (*kartṛ*) nor a patient (*bhoktṛ*). It is, therefore, short of it that we must look for the ultimate subject of attribution of man's actions, etc. What we find immediately short of it is the *jīva* or *jīvātman* or ego (*aham, ahaṃkartṛ*). This is properly the 'I.' The innermost *Ātman* stands within the sphere (*gocara*) of the term '*aham*' but it is only indicated by it, not directly expressed. What is then this ego?

First of all, it is a reflection (*ābhāsa*), an image of the absolute *Ātman*, in the mirror-like inner sense (whether referred to as *buddhi, ahaṃkāra, manas* or *antaḥkaraṇa*). Its existence is contingent on the illumination of the inner sense by the *Ātman*. The latter is the prototype, the ego its image. The ego is, however, unequal to its prototype. Though similar to it in imitated consciousness, freedom, centrality, etc., it irremediably shares in the finiteness, mobility, passibility and other attending deficiencies of its reflector. Its being an image does not relegate it to the rank of illusions but it makes it ontologically relative and dependent, however wonderful an image of the *Ātman* it may be. It cannot find its truth in itself but only in its prototype. There is its true *vastu*. In this sense it is not *svārtha*, finding its meaning in itself, but *parārtha*. This does not mean that it exists and acts for the profit of the *Ātman* for the latter is self-sufficient and seeks no profit.[4] It only means that the ego finds its own sense, meaning and goal in another, namely, the *Ātman*. But in its life of action, enjoyment and suffering, it is autonomous insofar as it sets its own purposes and takes its own decisions as befits a *kartṛ*.

For a Christian there is nothing repugnant in this conception of the conscious ego as an image and reflection of the Absolute for Christianity has always cherished the teaching of *Genesis* that man is made at the image and similitude of God and its theologians have taught unanimously that this character of being an image of God resides essentially in man's intellectual soul.

The second thing to be noted in the Śaṅkarian ego is its integrative role with regard to the various functions and the body of man. This role it performs in intimate dependence upon its supreme *Ātman* and Prototype which shines in its midst like a luminous gem.[5]

> As an emerald or any other gem, dropped for testing into milk or a similar liquid, imparts its lustre to them, so does this luminous *Ātman*, being finer than even the heart or intellect, unify (*ekī-kṛ*) and impart its lustre to the body and organs, including the intellect, etc., although it is within the intellect; for these have varying degrees of fineness or grossness in a certain order, and the *Ātman* is the innermost of them all." (*Bṛh. Up. Bh.* 4, 3, 7)[6]

The reflection of the light of the *Ātman* is produced within the *buddhi,* which is its direct reflector. This reflection is the *jīvātman* which says 'I' and 'mine' and which acts and experiences. It is so similar to the *Ātman* that even wise men (*vivekinaḥ*) as a rule identify both and are unable to distinguish them. From it and through the mediation of the *buddhi*, the light of the *Ātman* passes on to the *manas*, and thence pervades the senses, the organs and the gross body. Thus there is established the existential unity of man signified by the verb *ekīkṛ*, the integration of his existence and essence, first radically by the luminous *Ātman*, then through an instrumental diffusion by the *jīvātman.*

In such a conception the Sāṁkhya dualism is really overcome. Man is no longer the heterodit assemblage of a blind and a lame. The due distinction of his different constituents is still made but he recovers the existential wholeness which the notion of person requires and guarantees. As in the parable of the chariot of *Kaṭha Up*. 3, 3-9, the *bhoktṛ* is "*ātman*, senses and mind conjoined."

A third point must now be considered. What about the self-subsistence and responsible autonomy which the conception of person also demands? Speaking again from a Christian standpoint, let me first remark that these are not understood in Christian metaphysics as closed and absolute. As a creature, the human person is totally dependent and dependent at every moment on its Creator, the absolute *Esse*. This is the innermost Ground of its subsisting and the uppermost Ruler even of its moral freedom. The spiritual soul of man is not a windowless monad, it is open to the world of persons and like the cosmic tree of *Kaṭha Up*. 6, it is rooted above in the Pure, the *Brahman*.

Yet if such a soul is only a reflection of pure Consciousness can it still be said to be spiritual? Yes, because a spirit need only be a centre of self-consciousness, it need not be pure and independent consciousness, it need not be *anādi*, without beginning, and even though it may be without temporal beginning, it cannot, unless it be the Absolute itself, ever exist apart and independently from this Absolute.

But should not a spiritual soul be *ananta*, unable ever to cease to exist? Absolutely speaking, i.e., considering only its ontological dependence upon God's power, the soul might cease to be if the divine radiation that produces it came to be withdrawn. But God is not a senseless or whimsical illuminator, he is Wisdom which has regard for the nature of its effects.[7] Now the nature of the spiritual soul is to be the immediate reflection of pure Consciousness. As such it has such a dignity that it must be said to be an end-in-itself and God, being wise, cannot annihilate an end-in-itself. Nevertheless, could not the soul as reflection come to an end through the dissolution of its reflector? Yes, if the simile of the mirror were to be taken literally as the absolute explanation of the soul. But the all-powerful and self-sufficient *Ātman* requires no reflector to sustain in existence the subsistent images of itself which the souls are.

A final difficulty may be raised insofar as *mokṣa* as the direct experience of the *Ātman* seems to imply a complete effacement and vanishing of the *jīvātman*. Regarding this, the Christian thinker might prefer the formulations of the *Gītā* to those of strict Advaita. But he stands all the same very close to these. For him also salvation consists in the return of the image to its Prototype, hence to its own supreme truth and reality. This return, however, is not physical in the manner of a jar turning back into clay; it is epistemic, a matter of knowledge and cessation of ignorance. This ignorance is that of the soul unaware of its nature as image and through the effect of its diffusing function towards the senses and the body, imagining itself as the absolute centre of the light it diffuses. This self-centredness, featured as *ahaṁkāra-mamakāra*, has to come to an end and, in that sense, the *aham*, the ego, is called to disappear. This happens when the *jīvātman* discovers its own truth in its own centre, the *Paramātman*. Such a discovery is so fulfilling, so blissful that there is no need in claiming a place in it for a separate self-affirmation which could only mar the ecstatic recognition of the one that is fullness. Many a Christian might hesitate to accept this formulation of the 'beatific vision' but the themes of the soul as image of God, of God as Light, of divine illumination have given rise in Christian theologians and especially in mystics to formulations either close to the Vedānta or which appear to be corollaries of it.

My conclusion is that the anthropology of those texts of Śaṅkara, without being itself formulated in terms of person, is at least consonant with the Christian understanding of the human person. This congeniality makes up a strong case for declaring that the term 'person' is not unsuitable to the Śāṅkara Vedānta conception of man. How close this suitability really is deserves attention and a more extensive examination.

Notes

[1] [First published under the title, "Is the Concept of 'Person' Congenial to Śāṅkara Vedānta?" *Indian Philosophical Annual* **8** (1972) 199-205. Reprinted under the same title in *Reflection* (Rajpur, Dehradun) **2** (1973) 3-9, and under the title, "Is the Concept of Person Suitable in Vedānta?" in *Indian Ecclesiastical Studies* **12**/3 (1973) 155-162. Subtitles have been added. Reprinted here with kind permission from *Indian Theological Studies* (earlier *Indian Ecclesiastical Studies*) and is gratefully acknowledged.]

[2] [The reference should be to Śaṅkara's *Taitt. Up. Bhāṣya*.]

[3] [I follow here the text of the 1972 version; that of the *IES* (1973) version is seriously defective.]

[4] [The *IES* (1973) text is defective in this and the previous sentence.]

[5] [The *IES* (1973) text is defective.]

[6] [The *IES* (1973) text is defective. In both versions, however, De Smet refers to the *Bṛh.Up.*, when he should be referring to Śaṅkara's *bhāṣya* on the *Bṛh.Up.*]

[7] [The *IES* (1973) text is defective.]

9

TOWARDS AN INDIAN VIEW OF THE PERSON[1]

It was rather unexpected to hear Dr T.M.P. Mahadevan declare on 5 March 1973, while inaugurating the seminar he had convened at the University of Madras on the concept of the 'person,' that "if the *Brahman* of Śaṅkara is anything it is surely not impersonal." Dr Mahadevan is a strict adherent of Śaṅkara's non-dualism (*Advaitavāda*) and it had become usual since the Max Müller era to hear such non-dualists assert contrarily that the *Brahman* of Advaita is impersonal. We were then witnessing an important linguistic change. The reason for it seems to be a better understanding in the Indian philosophical circles of the idea of 'person' as originally developed by Christianity for its own philosophico-religious uses and further elaborated along the centuries by Western thinkers. This better understanding may owe something to the increased participation by Catholic scholars in the many seminars, conferences and congresses of the diverse philosophical associations of India, especially during the last twenty years. More recently, interest in the person has been enhanced by the writings of Strawson whose M and P predicates are now haunting the minds of a large number of Indian philosophers.

The uncertain status of the notion of 'person' in India is conditioned by the fact that it is foreign to the Sanskrit tradition and has no adequate rendering in any of the Sanskritic languages. When dealing with man or the Deity Indian philosophy always worked with other concepts which rarely imported the holistic signification of 'person.' It will be useful to attend to the chief ones among them.

The term *ātman* whose original meaning is that of the reflective pronoun is used philosophically to designate the various results of the analysis of a being: the gross body, the vital energies called *prāṇas,* the outer senses, the inner sense which is threefold, viz. *manas* (mind), *ahaṃkāra* (ego-sense) and *buddhi* (intellect-will), the unmanifested matter (*avyakta*) which emanates all these, the individual monad (*jīva* or *jīvātman*) embodied (*dehin*) in them, and the divine Absolute which is the ultimate basis and sustainer of their whole hierarchy and, hence, is called supreme *Ātman* (*paramātman*). Each inner *ātman* acts as an internal cause (*upādāna*) giving reality to the element which precedes it in our enumeration but it does this without synthesising with it, i.e. only as a support. Hence, it is never equal to the whole being and misses the integrality of 'person.' Even to call it a self and to speak of a hierarchy of lower and higher selves is open to much ambiguity. This Upaniṣadic analysis remains an elementary presupposition of Indian thought and had to be recalled.

A closer equivalent of 'person' is *puruṣa* which means male, man. Philosophically, it was assumed to designate a sentient and usually an intellectual monad such as man's 'soul' (*jīvātman*), a god or a godly power, or 'the God within,' but also, as in some verses of the *Gītā,* to designate a cosmic entity, such as primordial matter. Monadic also is *jīva*, the living one, which denotes the sentient principle within living beings.

As to *vyakti* which is in current use today in the sense of 'individual,' it denotes strictly the individual within a genus so that when said of God, for instance of the three Persons of the Christian Trinity, it is a source of ambiguity and of difficulties in comparative religion.

When the term 'person' came to the notice of Indian intellectuals, it had already a long history of its own. Originally a designation of the stage-mask of Greek and Roman actors, it had quickly taken the meaning of stage-part or dramatic hero. Hence, the Stoics found it convenient to refer to man as endowed by God with a part to play on the world stage. This interpretation allowed the Roman law courts to call person a subject of legal rights and duties, i.e. a citizen as opposed to a slave. The dignity thus conferred upon the term 'person' induced the Christians to adopt it (not without some ambiguity at first) to designate the Three (Father, Son or Word, Spirit) in the one divine Essence and the One in two distinct natures (divine and human) otherwise known as Jesus Christ, the Word made flesh. Since Christians believed in the brotherhood of all men, they also began to consider them all as persons, whether free or slaves, citizens or foreigners. This development was summed up in the basic, though imperfect definition coined by Boethius: a person is an individual subject whose nature is rational.

The medieval Schoolmen realised that 'person' belonged to the realm of responsible action, intellectual and morally free, as the ultimate subject of single attribution of all predicates implying intellectual agency. Consequently, Aquinas refined Boethius' definition finally to declare that 'person' means an integral and unitary self-subsistent subject characterised by intellectual consciousness, moral freedom and all properties ensuing from these defining notes. Prominent among these properties were privacy, inalienability of end-in-itself, ownership of natural rights, moral responsibility, being a source of values in its own right, and capacity of initiating interpersonal relationships. It is to be noted with a regard to the Indian valuation of self-denial that such relationships demand a fair degree of selflessness and that this elaborate definition did not favour ethical individualism. It was also such that it could with due precision apply analogically to the divine as well as to human persons.

Such is the concept of the person which remained dominant up to Kant himself, but it is during the latter's time that Jacobi chose to restrict the extension of the term 'person' to the category of human individuals so that its application to the Godhead would be merely anthropomorphic. The trend he thus inaugurated was followed by a number of thinkers of the nineteenth century and influenced the translators of Sanskrit works towards the turn of the twentieth century. In their hands Śaṅkara's distinction between the qualityless Absolute (*nirguṇa Brahman*)—equivalent to the *Deus simplex* of Christian theology—and the anthropomorphic qualified Godhead (*saguṇa Brahman*) became the distinction between the impersonal and the personal *Brahman* or between the Absolute (*Brahman*) and God (*Īśvara*). Today it is practically impossible to convince the Hindus that the personal God of Christianity is really the Absolute and as a rule the nondualists among them consider that the Christians have inherited only an anthropomorphic conception of the Deity.

Against this background it becomes understandable that modem Indian thinkers have hardly been attracted by the person as a topic for reflection or have perceived its interest only on the level of the human individual as treated in the various brands of modern humanism. Yet the materials for an Indian recognition of the person are present both in the theologies and in the various anthropologies of the Indian tradition and it will now be our task to explore them and to discern their value.

1. The Integrated Individual of Vedic Times

In Vedic society an individual enjoys the full dignity of man only in so far as he is a *yajamāna* (sacrificer), i.e. is entitled by his *varṇa* (caste-rank) to employ priests to perform sacrifices (*yajña*). The prototype of *yajña* is the primordial sacrifice of the Great Male or Man (*Mahā-puruṣa*) through whose ritual dismemberment the universe in all its parts and categories of beings has come to be, as recalled in *Ṛgveda*, 10, 90, and to be established spatially and temporally in its perfect order called *Ṛta*, the Truth. What man experiences as untruth (*an-Ṛta*) is the deterioration of this order manifested in droughts, diseases and other derangements of nature. Sacrifice is the special technique by which he is able to overcome this deterioration and restore the whole (*sarvam*), including himself, in its orderly integrity. By correctly performing the daily and other sacrifices, he feeds and duly praises the 'gods' (*devas*) who are, as it were, the cosmic engineers who keep the universe in perfect running order, and thus he secures anew the original wholeness and wholesomeness (*sarvam bhavati*) for himself, his family, his society and his world. He is never a mere individual, insulated by his empirical limits or by any hankering after self-sufficiency, but the centre of a network of links with the beings of the three worlds. Prolonged by his wife, children, cattle and pasture lands, hierarchically complemented by the members of the other *varṇas*, he is the ally of the gods and the friend of a world the secret of whose regulation he possesses in the knowledge which he calls *Veda*.

The Vedic seers incline increasingly to derive the universe not from blind Necessity but from a personal Originator and

Ruler whose mysterious nature and agency they grope towards imagining. In these gropings lies the dawn of metaphysics. Unfathomable, abiding before and beyond the being of his creatures and the non-being of their temporal causes, alive (breathing yet windless) by his own energy, he is the unnamed 'that One' (*tad-ekam*) though given many a title. In the search for an expression of his creatorship, all the modes of production known to the Vedic man are tried and found wanting: the weaver's yarn-stretching (*tan-*), the builder's foundation-laying (*dhā-*), the blacksmith's forging (*takṣ-*), the architect's measuring (*mā-*), the bird's brooding (*tap-*), the mammal's semen-emitting (*sṛj-*), the lord's commanding (*vāk-*) and the priest's sacrificing (*yaj-*). The very plurality of these approaches which cancel one another secures the transcendence of that Father and Lord of the creatures (*Prajā-pati*) who encompasses them all. In his mysterious Personality man finds the source of his dependent being, the support of his life and the security of his well-ordered world. A centre through this Centre, a subsistent through this Subsistent, he also finds in him the dealer of his *varṇa*-status and the weaver of his complementarities.

Never will the conception of man in this subcontinent again be so holistic and attentive to his many-relatedness. Analysis with its sharp tooth will tear it to pieces and an astonishing variety of anthropologies will vie to displace it. Yet even today it appears to survive below the level of sophistication especially in so far as the caste-system continues to regulate the relations and interactions of Indian people and their religiosity remains focused on both the *devas* and the transcendent One. Indeed, the enduring presence of this conception is the basic datum discerned and analysed by the modern anthropological study of man and society in India.[2]

2. Man, the Meeting-place of the Cosmic Powers in the Brāhmaṇas and Upaniṣads

The interrelated but opaque man of the Vedas was destined to be analysed and almost split up during the next centuries, a fate not unlike that of the atom of modern physics. The process started with the equivalence discovered in the *Brāhmaṇas* and *Āraṇyakas* between the sacrifice, the cosmos and man the microcosm in the light of the myth of the self-sacrificing universal *Puruṣa.* The selfsame *devas* fed through the sacrifice had to be not only the great functionaries of the macrocosm but also the internal powers at work in man. His vital energies (*prāṇas*) and his psychological functions (*indriyas*) had to be deities (*devatās*) competing within him for their hierarchical ranking but not different from the power wielders of the macrocosm. Like the ritual sacrifice, he himself was their meeting place and he could through introspection develop a new Vedic knowledge of the henceforth internalized sacrifice by which he would discover in himself the very Power that gave efficacy to the sacrifices, the mysterious *Brahman.*

In the Upaniṣads, the search is on for this *Brahman* as the innermost *Ātman* of man and of every contingent being. Every layer of man, the material, the biological, the psychological, the intellectual, in turn yields some great entity (a *puruṣa* or an *ātman*) which is measured up to the ideal of greatness, supremacy of power and absoluteness conveyed by the *brahman*-idea. Even beyond pure Consciousness reflection attains remarkably the ultimate transcendence of Bliss (*Ānanda*). These two together constitute the earliest adequate definition of *Brahman: Vijñānam ānandam brahma, Brahman* is Consciousness, Bliss (*Bṛh. Up.* 3, 9). Uppermost as well as innermost it stands at the apex of everything in the transcendent simplicity of its fullness. Of man and the universe it is the Essence (*svarupa*), not in the sense of what they are but of that from which they are: "That from which these beings are born, by which once born they live, into which they enter when they die, that is what you must try to understand, that is *Brahman*" (*Taitt. Up.* 3, 1). Ground, support, inner witness and ruler, goal of all contingent beings, it is most immediate to them, their highest *Ātman* indeed, yet it surpasses them all. If we try to name it by any one of their names, it shakes it off and we must say, "*neti neti*, it is nor thus, not thus" (*Bṛh. Up.* 4). For it is non-dual (*advaita*) and in it "there is no disjunction between seer and sight" (ibid.).

It is therefore understandable that if one wishes to coincide by a direct awareness with this inmost Absolute, one should begin with mortification (*tapas*) and train oneself to apophatic self-denial. This is the doctrine of Bhrigu who mortified himself and attained to the successively better realisations that the *Brahman* is the matter from which all food derives, or better the breath of all life-breath, or better still the mind of all minds, or higher than that the Consciousness of every discerning consciousness, and finally the Bliss shadowed in every bliss (cf. *Taitt. Up.* 3, 2-6). There is a direct connection between this doctrine and the desire for renunciation which becomes frequent in the Upaniṣads:

> Once Brahmins have come to know this *Ātman* who transcends hunger and thirst, sorrow, confusion, old age and death, they rise above their desire for sons, riches, etc., and wander forth to lead a beggar's life. They, first, lead a childlike life (*bālya*) in learning (*pāṇḍitya*); then, they reject these two and become silent sages (*muni*); lastly, they put away both silence and its opposite with disgust, and become *Brāhmaṇas* (knowers of *Brahman*). (*Bṛh. Up.* 3, 5).

According to all this, the Upaniṣadic man is no longer a solid organism externally related to the beings of the three worlds but a complex assembly of a whole scale of cosmic powers apart from which he seems to be nothing. He is not exactly their host or even their meeting-place but rather the very form of their active encounter, not their containing shell but a particular shape of their manifestation. On a higher level of introspective analysis even those powers are swallowed up by the mighty *Brahman*, and in their humiliation man finds both his most complete self-denial and his highest exaltation for he is driven to say, I am not this body, nor these senses, nor these higher powers, I am not even this individual ego, but I am *Brahman* (*ahaṁ brahmāsmi*).

This is not a proclamation of pantheism for *Brahman* is not identified with anything finite, and nor even of acosmism for the finite as such is not denied altogether, but it is the entrancing discovery that the Absolute stands transcendingly in the heart of man and of every contingent being. Man is not absolute but the Absolute is within him. Man is no longer the solid centre of many outgoing relationships but he has found the inner relationship of total dependence on the firmest and most solid Existent (*Sat*) from which he receives his whole existence and of which he is but a contingent manifestation. He is no longer a focus but an irradiation. The whole universe is the great wheel of *Brahman* (*brahmacakra*) in which all things get life and subsistence; in this wheel man is like a wild gander fluttering about till he recognises the Impeller of the wheel; then, blessed by him, he goes to immortality (cf. *Śvet. Up*. 1, 6).

The permanent value of this Upaniṣadic anthropology lies in this, that it roots man most ontologically in the divine Absolute and establishes for the centuries to come the creaturely dimension of his personality. It was, however, pregnant with an ambiguity of wide consequence. Indeed, it could be developed in two opposite directions: either as a valuation of man as a wonderful creature of the perfect Absolute and a manifestation of its splendour, or as a devaluation of man who is like nothing compared to the fullness of being of the *Brahman-Ātman*. But already the Upaniṣads inclined to the latter. Helped by the growing popularity of the discipline of renunciation (*saṁnyāsa*) this became the chief trend of Upaniṣadic interpretation, not, however, without some sporadic manifestations of the other alternative especially in the Vaiṣṇava or the Śaiva theologies.

3. Man as the Renouncer

The *saṁnyāsin* undertakes deliberately to be the opposite of the Vedic householder. He withdraws through a radical decision from the ties of family and the bonds of society, frees himself from the duties and rights of his *varṇa*-status and sets himself in the margins of society and its hierarchical framework. Turning away with a shrug of contempt from the honoured triad of human goals, wealth (*artha*), love (*kāma*) and duty (*dharma*), he devotes himself exclusively to the pursuit of a new and supreme goal, *mokṣa*, the complete liberation from the round of rebirths (*saṃsāra*) and its cause, action of all kinds, good as well as evil. His ideal is *nivṛtti*, studied passivity, as opposed to *pravṛtti*, the goal-seeking activity of the caste-man. He is dead to the world, desireless, indifferent, beyond good and evil.

What he represents is not exactly spirituality but transcendence of which he is the living symbol. It is not the spiritual character of intellectual knowledge which judges of all things but its power of abstraction which can ultimately dissolve all concreteness and take its stand in pure consciousness. It is not man's sovereign will to act as he decides but his more radical freedom to break asunder all his ties and even the meshwork of his ensnaring ego. The *saṁnyāsin* is the hero of pure transcendence. He witnesses to this dimension of intellectuality of our 'freedom from' which is usually hidden by the commitments of our 'freedom to.' He has isolated it like a live wire, dangerous but fascinating. However, by isolating it he has also deprived it of its essential accompaniments within the riches of human personality. Fortunately, *saṁnyāsa* will be confronted by other trends and from their interaction new insights will be born which will compensate its austere narrowness.

4. The Man of the Caste-system

During the same period when renunciation became the chosen mode of life of many, Indian society reinforced its *varṇa*-organisation into a caste-system. To the *dharma-sūtras* (law-guides) which belonged to the Vedic *śruti* (revelation) there were now added *dharma-śāstras* (treatises of law) exemplified by the famous Laws of Manu. These belong to *smṛti* (tradition) and were elaborated essentially from the standpoint of the Brahmins, in order to codify in exact detail the hierarchical framework of the castes, the rights and obligations of each caste and, within the caste, of individuals as members of joint families (joint in the community of habitation, commensality, cult and ownership) and exogamic *gotras* (clans); the multitude of prohibitions arising from the polarity between ritual purity and impurity, and the categories of delicts and punishments.

In the exacting bonds of this caste-system, man finds the security of stability, but his freedom is severely curbed from birth to death. Social mobility almost disappears and social conformism determines even his most private acts. The system, while satisfying to the extreme the social requirements of the human person, leaves no scope to his individualistic tendencies or only an exceptional one. This unavoidable exception concerns *saṁnyāsa*. Renunciation, indeed, though it contradicts the whole system as an escape from it, is reluctantly permitted and the countersocial goal it pursues, *mokṣa*, is allowed as an addition to the three traditional 'ends of man' (*puruṣārtha*). Although permitted, renunciation is carefully regulated. It is only at the end of his useful social life, after he has begotten children, given them in marriage and settled everything for their welfare that a man is allowed to leave his sacrificial fire and, with or without his wife, retire to the seclusion of the forest and eventually wander forth homeless, tieless and utterly free.

This is a compromise devised to contain the dangerous spreading of the way of renunciation by confining it in that part of man's life when he becomes a burden on society. The fact that it remained largely theoretical because it was overruled by the absolute claim of the great representatives of *saṁnyāsa* does not withdraw its signification. It proved that the human person cannot be reduced to its social dimensions and that no amount of regulation can smother its deep-seated desire for emancipation.

5. The Monadic Man of Jainism and Sāṁkhya

In this world of caste-men and renouncers, Mahāvīra Jina gave a new life to a probably older form of renounced life. With him, man as a monadic individual is exalted in the transcendency of his spirit. Ignoring (and probably ignorant of) the Upaniṣadic *Brahman*, ground of the world and inner ruler of man, and, as a characteristic renouncer, the claims of the caste-society, he proclaims the eternity, inherent consciousness and potential omniscience of the *jīva* (living one), the monadic soul-substance which he affirms to exist not only in man but in every possible aggregate of matter (*pudgala*). We may note the egalitarian aspect of this affirmation. Inequality, however, though unnatural, is very much a fact of the mundane existence of the *jīvas* through the round of their rebirths (*saṃsāra*). Encapsulated in a diversity of envelopes made of gross matter (called *ajīva*, non-living, non-soul), the *jīvas* share their variety in shape, weight, size and organic modifications; they are subjected to their temporality and all their limitations; and the opacity of matter obscures their natively perfect sight and maintains them in parviscience. Graver still, their embodiment exposes them to the evil effect of activity whether of body, mind or speech. Actions, indeed, affect the soul through a more penetrating kind of materialisation. Like dyes permeating a cloth they colour it, each one in its own shade, and this tainting obfuscates their knowledge most internally. This conception of action, *karman*, as a dye-stuff (made of eight kinds of atoms of subtle matter) has puzzled many, yet it is logical enough once the distinction of the spirit from all non-spirit (including action) is admitted as an ontological difference between heterogeneous substances. What is less logical is the admission of a contamination of the one by the others.

This view of man commands a discipline of dematerialisation and, to coin a word, of 'dekarmanisation' accessible to all regardless of their caste and culminating in monastic renunciation. The laity must begin with the five vows (*vrata*) of non-killing, truthfulness, non-stealing, chastity and non-coveting. These are practised with the help of three restraints (*gupti*) and ten pious duties (*dharma*) including fasts and other mortifications. Those who feel fit for perfect renunciation then enter the monastic life which frees them from all duties to society except preaching the 'way of the Jinas.' They live a life of extreme asceticism, minutely regulated, and aim after the highest purification which some of them anticipate symbolically by a state of permanent nakedness. If their death, which may follow upon a complete fast undertaken voluntarily, coincides with utter freedom from karmanic matter, they attain the release of *nirvāṇa* (going off, like a flame that ceases to burn). Their *jīva* no longer weighted by any atom of *ajīva* and cleansed of any taint of *karman* ascends to the summit of space and recovers the blissful omniscience and freedom of the pure spirit. Godlike (in a universe void of God) but individual, it stands forever in the self-sufficiency of its all-knowingness.

Non-theistic Sāṁkhya resembles Jainism but is more radical in its conception of the individual spirit. The latter, called *puruṣa* (man) or *jña* (knower), is never really but only apparently embodied. Hence, it is never really affected by matter nor tainted in any way by activity which is the exclusive province of unconscious matter (*pradhāna* or *prakṛti*). Its illusory feeling of repeated embodiments in the sorrowful round of births is due to its own reflection in the mirrorlike density of matter. It is a mere fallacy which the Sāṁkhya teaching suffices to dispel, apart from any asceticism, by the finality of its demonstration of the inamissible purity of every *puruṣa*. Whenever this truth is grasped by a *puruṣa*, he at once recovers the untroubled awareness of his isolation (*kaivalya*). Pure, unrelated, he is then neither omniscient nor parviscient but a solitary light shining upon nothing, indifferent and serene.

The relevance of these twin conceptions to an integrated Indian view of personality lies perhaps in this that they have obeyed man's urge to reach his spiritual core with the dangerous fearlessness of any intellect fascinated with the purity of abstraction. Analysis here is completely cut off from synthesis. The fullness of its starting-point, which is necessarily the whole 'phenomenon of man' taken in the concreteness of his very much 'incarnated' activities and experiences, is so impoverished by the analysing process that there is no real accounting for it at the end. This, indeed, is not simply a process of sifting by which the more precious element is distinguished from the others but a process of utter rejection of the non-spiritual. Further, the spiritual itself is hypostatised into a pure ego and thus is a solidified abstraction unlike the transcendent and universal *Ātman* of the Upaniṣads.

6. The Evanescent Man of Early Buddhism

Analysis again is very much at work in the teaching of Buddha, but he shuns entirely the tendency to turn abstractions into substances. What captivates his attention is the mobility and constant changingness of the human phenomenon. The paradigm of reality is not substance but action which is instantaneous and followed immediately by its consequence. Man is like a stream of five conjoined currents (called the five *skandhas* or aggregates) corresponding to what we normally conceive as matter, sensations, perceptions, mental constructs and consciousness. No abiding support underlies this stream to give it ontic continuity, neither *jīva* nor *puruṣa*, nor *ātman* of any kind. "Physical forms are like foam; sensations like bubbles; perceptions like mirage; mental constructs like the flimsy trunk of a banana tree; and consciousness like phantoms" (*Saṃyutta Nikāya* 3). "What is called mind, or thought, or consciousness, is produced and disappears in a perpetual revolving of day and night. Just as, O monks, a monkey sporting in a wood seizes now a branch and then another, so also what is called mind is produced and vanishes in a perpetual passing from day to night" (ibid. 2).

When we perceive ourselves as permanent ego, we are as deluded as the child who takes a spreading flame for a swift-running animal. The end of this illusion is *nirvāṇa*, the blowing out of the imagined ego.

> As a flame blown out by the wind disappears and cannot be named, even so the monk when released from name and body disappears and cannot be named—He who has disappeared, is he non-existent?—No measuring is there of him that has disappeared whereby one might know of him that he is not; when all qualities are removed, all modes of speech are removed also. (*Sutta-nipāta* 1075-6)

Buddha's teaching is curiously reminiscent of modern physics, his flame-man of its bodies, dances of electrons, but physics does not pretend to be an ontology. As Śaṅkara will show, he leaves out of account the resisting fact of the *cogito* which is the door for the reintroduction of spiritual subsistence. But he stands forever as a warning against any facile solidification of man according to the constructs of his desires and instinctual drives. Only the ego belongs to the realm of naming, the true person cannot be reached by the modes of speech. Whether this apophatism did imply in Buddha's mind beyond a rejection of predicamental personality even a denial of any postpredicamental person remains a matter of dispute, but as apophatism it is salutary.

What also deserves to be emphasised is Buddha's contribution to the humanisation of man. While he rejected any Jaina-like extreme asceticism he preached a way of non-violent morality (*śīla*), meditational concentration on selflessness (*samādhi*) and devotion to wisdom (*prajñā*) which transformed the ways of the people of India and of the successive waves of their invaders. In his own life he exemplified a pattern of most attractive virtues (mildness, kindness, compassion, moderation, wisdom) which later legend expanded and hieratised so that he became more and more an ideal Personality (called significantly *mahā-puruṣa* and *bhagavān*) emulated by his monks and venerated with loving devotion (*bhakti*) by the masses of the laity. Thus on the level of transcendence a new ideal of personality was slowly taking shape on the very ruins of the ego tainted conceptions he had so successfully contradicted.

7. The Open Person of the *Bhagavad Gītā*

In order to understand the genius of the author of the *Gītā* as manifested peculiarly in his renovated conception of personality, it is essential to realise that all the above anthropologies were alive and in conflict when he undertook his creation. Their conflict was felt most keenly in the opposition between the fast gaining conceptions of the Buddhist and other Renouncers and the resisting Brahmanic views of a society which defended its caste organisation and its sacrificial tradition. If their tension was to be overcome otherwise than through their sterile effort of mutual destruction, a bridge had to be built, a synthesis formulated which would reconcile their respective value. This is why the *Gītā* was composed.

The first element of this synthesis is the unpromising dualism of Sāṁkhya: man is an embodied spirit (*dehin*) in a body (*deha*) pertaining to material nature (*prakṛti*). Whatever changes happen to him, whether birth, death, activity or suffering, happen to this body only whereas the *dehin* is an impassible knower. "Never is it born nor dies: unborn, eternal, everlasting, primeval; it does not slay nor is it slain: weapons do not cut it nor does fire burn it, the waters do not wet it nor does the wind dry it" (cf. 2, 16-25). Yet lodged in *prakṛti* it experiences the changes that take place in it as if they were its own and thus has the feeling of revolving through the round of births and deaths, but the knowledge of not being at all an agent suffices to deliver it from sorrow.

This dualism provides as it were two separated spans which must be linked if the bridge is to be constructed. Not unlike Descartes who secures the unity of man's thinking self with his body through an indirect recourse to the truthful God, the author of the *Gītā* overcomes his *dehin-deha* dualism through his well-articulated monotheism. Kṛṣṇa, the divine *Puruṣottama* (supreme Person), is the universal *Paramātman* and, as such, the absolute basis (*pratiṣṭhā*) of the *Brahman* (14, 27). This *Brahman* is threefold: it is the *Brahman* of the sacrificers, it is the perfect stillness which the renouncers emulate, and it is the 'great *brahman*' (*mahad-brahman*) of the universe. The latter stands for the totality of *prakṛti* which comprises both material nature (i.e. the *prakṛti* of Sāṁkhya) and all the *ātmans* or *dehins*, or *jīvas*, i.e. all the conscious entities. These, indeed, constitute the higher (*parā*) as opposed to the lower (*aparā*) *prakṛti*. This complete *prakṛti* 'is mine,' says Kṛṣṇa. It is the same as *mahad-brahman*. Now, "great *Brahman* is to me a womb, in it I plant the seed: from this derives the origin of all beings. In whatever womb whatever form develops, of those great *Brahman* is the Womb, I the Father, giver of the seed" (14, 3-4).

An often misunderstood simile extends this teaching from the origin to the whole activity of beings: "in the region of the heart[3] of all beings dwells the Lord, twirling them hither and thither by his uncanny power [like puppets] mounted on a machine" (18, 61). The machine, indeed, is the lower *prakṛti* in which the *dehins* are inserted by their bodies. Thus they share in activities which appear to be their own but which are really the Lord's. Now the Lord's activity is always disinterested (*niṣkāma*) since its fruit can be no gain for him and is produced only for the benefit of beings. Once man understands this, he can easily be converted to *niṣkāma karma*, i.e. cease to desire the fruits of actions and yet accept his role as the instrument or occasion (*nimitta*) of those actions willed by the Lord and produced through the Lord's *prakṛti*.

The traditional Vedic view that man is a sacrificer by divine ordination finds here its point of reinsertion. All obligatory duties can now be considered as sacrifices and ought to be performed as such; and the Lord Kṛṣṇa is not only the ordainer but the recipient and proper object of all sacrifices (5, 29; 9, 24; etc.). Once action is thus reinterpreted as sacrifice, it becomes immune from any charge of binding man through fetters of selfishness or self-centeredness. Man restored as sacrificer, loses all ego-rooted desire and lives beyond fear in serene freedom.

The superiority of the Gītākāra's conception may be expressed comparatively by a short apologue. It has been said that Jina, like a dog, attacked the arrow (*karma*) that tortured him thus increasing his pain (through austerities) whereas Buddha, like a lion, attacked Desire, the shooter of the arrow. Buddha, however, saw no final liberation except through monastic renunciation and contemplative inactivity. Kṛṣṇa while disarming the hunter Desire did not confine the lion to a cave but gave him the freedom of the forest to pursue all his natural and traditional activities.

For him, indeed, man though essentially a passive knower and experiencer is related to action in a very special way. Unable to escape it owing to his link with *prakṛti*, he is faced with two possibilities, either to pass into its bondage by greedily desiring its fruits or to find his very freedom by assuming it disinterestedly. The latter demands that he recognise all activity as but the actuation of divine will and accept sharing in it as in a pure sacrifice, thus imitating the transcendent disinterestedness of the Lord. If he does this, he finds the authenticity of his engagement in history. History, indeed, far from being a senseless succession of changes, has an immanent purposiveness since through it God works unceasingly to procure the welfare of his creatures. Man by identifying himself with this work becomes himself an agent of this purpose.

The very fact that there are two possibilities implies man's freedom of will. After instructing Arjuna in all this, Kṛṣṇa exhorts him to do as he chooses. Arjuna is called, not obliged, to take his refuge in Kṛṣṇa. If he takes this first step through a deliberate surrender in faith, he begins to tread the path of loving devotion (*bhakti*) which will transform his historical existence into a dedication to God through serving his creatures. Beyond this *bhakti* of selfless service which Kṛṣṇa deems inferior still (*aparā*) he will reach the highest (*parā*) *bhakti* which is unitive love in eternity.

Thus the *Gītā* conception of man is highly personalistic notwithstanding its unpromising Sāṁkhya basis. Man in dependence upon his Lord is an agent, a sacrificer, a being capable of free choice, of selfless commitment to meaningful history, of religious faith and love, of acceptance of divine grace, of personal surrender to the supreme Person. This exalting personalism marks even the *Gītā* conception of the Deity. None of the great teachings of the Upaniṣads concerning the absolute *Brahman* is neglected but the notion of *Brahman* or even *Paramātman* is itself transcended insofar as it is said to have a basis. This basis is Kṛṣṇa as the supreme *Puruṣa* (*Puruṣottama*), the Absolute as Person, *Bhagavān*, Dispenser of grace, not only loved but Lover in the eternal union of perfect mutual *bhakti*. This view inaugurates the personalistic monotheism which will characterise the religion of *bhakti* of the succeeding ages.

8. The *Bodhisattva* as the Ideal Man in Mahāyāna Buddhism

After the innovations of the *Gītā* concerning both God and man, Buddhism itself could not remain the same. The masses were now presented with a better Bhagavān than Buddha, for Kṛṣṇa was not only a rival human teacher of liberation but God himself manifested as a man without any loss of his infinite power and wisdom. The way he taught was not an unnatural path of withdrawal from secular duties in order to secure complete renunciation but a way combining active commitment with indifference to its fruits in a sacrificial spirit of single-minded devotion to God and his work. Further, instead of a denial of any *ātman*, the embodied spirit of man was assured of eternity and called to a bliss of mutual *parābhakti*.

Without betraying the essentials of their doctrine, the Buddhists succeeded in opening up a 'great career' (*mahāyāna*) which would in some fashion emulate these attractive developments.

In Mahāyāna we observe a fast mutation of buddhology towards apophatic monism. A sort of gnosticism exalts the supramundane (*lokottara*) nature of the Buddha at the expense of his historical birth. In the *Lalitavistāra* he is made to declare: "I am the God who transcends gods (*devātideva*) ... but I shall conform myself to the world.... Gods and men in unison will proclaim, 'He is God by Himself only' (*svayam eva devaḥ*)." Increasingly, his historical existence is conceived as purely apparitional (*upapāduka*) and his human body as a mere accommodation to the world (*lokānuvartana*). What matters henceforth is his *dharma-kāya* (law-body) which is made of the five features of his teaching: morality, concentration, wisdom, liberation and his awareness of this liberation; it is in this *dharma-kāya* that men are invited to take their refuge. By the year AD 400 this conception has reached its full expression in the works of Asanga. The *dharma-kāya* is simultaneously the true doctrine of the Buddhas, their spiritual body, their proper nature, and the absolute of reality. Hence, it is the transcendent, absolute, eternal and infinite essence of all things. However, the very purity of this essence is expressed in terms of void (*śūnya*) through a persistent denial of all substantiality. Though it has become a homologue of the Upaniṣadic *Brahman*, it is never conceived as fullness (*pūrṇa*) but only as the apophatic opposite of all our positive conceptions.

Nevertheless, if it is the deepest essence of beings, then everyone has in himself the 'germ of Buddhahood' (*tathāgata-garbha*); which means that the 'great career' (*mahā-yāna*) of a Buddha is open to all. Whoever enters it is a *bodhisattva*, one who has his being in enlightenment, and stands as the concrete ideal to be imitated by all men, for he conquers successively the ten perfections. His career is described minutely. He is born with an inclination to accept the true doctrine and easily becomes a beginner. Thence arises in him the thought of enlightenment in the form of two wishes, namely, to obtain enlightenment and to lead all beings to it. He then commits himself by a vow before an elder *bodhisattva* to fulfil these wishes which he does through preaching, meditating, honouring the Buddhas with a ritual cult, cultivating the ten perfections and even transferring upon others his acquired merits. Thus he becomes not only a hero of charity, morality and wisdom but a merciful saviour. Yet, he is not simply to be revered, trusted and invoked, but actually to be emulated. Indeed, he is not a Platonic ideal of an inaccessibly divine goal but he is in his own way what each one is really able to become. How to characterise his humanity? Not only by utter selflessness which is the renouncer's ideal but by the most universal and unrestricted service of others. Personality here breaks forth beyond the 'ego-barrier' not, however, to become lost beyond any reach but rather to become open to all and to encompass them with boundless wisdom and compassion.

9. Man as the Reflection of the Absolute according to Śaṅkara

It is common knowledge that Śaṅkara teaches that *Brahman*, the Absolute, is the supreme *Ātman* of the individual or, as he says, of the knower-agent-and-enjoyer. The latter alone is the ego that says 'I' and 'mine.' But is this ego some kind of entity and which one? In *Upadeśasāhasri* 18, Śaṅkara provides the following answer:

> The appropriator is the ego-sense which always stands in proximity to this [absolute Consciousness] and acquires a reflection of it.... Only when

> there is a reflection (*ābhāsa*) of the inner Witness can words like 'I,' 'thou,' etc., by referring to the reflection, indirectly indicate the Witness. They cannot designate the latter directly in any way.... Because the ego-sense bears a reflection of the *Ātman*, it is designated by words pertaining to the *Ātman*; just as words pertaining to fire are applied to torches and the like though only indirectly....
>
> The reflection of a face is different from the face since it conforms to the mirror; and in turn the face is different from its reflection since it does not conform to the mirror. The reflection of the *Ātman* in the ego-sense is comparable to the reflection of the face while the *Ātman* is comparable to the face and therefore different from its reflection. And yet ordinary knowledge fails to discriminate them.

What is the ontological status of this ego-like reflection? The reflection of a face in a mirror is not a property either of the face or of the mirror or even of both together since it depends only on a certain relation between them. Further, due to this very dependence, it is not a reality in its own right (*vastu*); rather its 'true reality' is the face compared to which it is 'unreal' (*asat*). All this applies to the human ego which exhibits the marks of the *per se* Consciousness it reflects but is in itself dependent, contingent, and as unable to support itself as any reflection apart from its prototype.

Yet, the awareness that the ego is merely a reflection of the *Ātman* is not only "the only door or bridge (*dvāra*) by which we can pass from the ordinary meaning of 'I' or 'thou' to what they mean indirectly, namely, the *Ātman*," but is also the key of any correct anthropology. Śaṅkara's comment on *Bṛh. Up*. 4, 3, 7 shows clearly the instrumental role of the ego-reflection in the integration of the human person:

> As an emerald dropped for testing into milk imparts its lustre to it, so this Light of the *Ātman*, through being within the heart, i.e. the *buddhi* (intellect), because it is more subtle than it, unifies (*ekīkṛ-*) and imparts its lustre to the body and the organs including the heart.... The *buddhi* being diaphanous and next to the *Ātman*, puts on a reflection (*ābhāsa*) of the Consciousness-Light of the *Ātman*; this is why even discriminating men happen to identify themselves with the *buddhi*, first. Then the reflecting Light of Consciousness falls upon the *manas* (mind)... then on the sense-organs... and lastly on the body.

Or as he says when explaining *Gītā* 18, 50: "The *Ātman* is extremely pure. And the *buddhi* being almost as pure, can put on a reflection of that aspect of the *Ātman* which is Consciousness.

And the *manas* can put on a reflection of the *buddhi*, etc. Hence, worldly men see the *Ātman* in their body only."

Thus in conceiving the human person as an aggregate but internally unified by the absolute *Ātman* via the reflection-like ego, Śaṅkara integrates the great utterances of the Upaniṣads without consenting to either pantheism or acosmism. Unfortunately, his anthropology did not gain the attention it deserved and many among the later Vedāntins, even of his own school, veered towards either of these very directions which he had so carefully avoided.

10. Conclusion

It is not possible within the compass of these pages to sketch out any more of the other views of man or God elaborated in India. Those outlined here are sufficiently typical to provide features which seem characteristic of the approach to the mystery of the person in this ancient but ever alive culture.

There is obviously a tension at work between the two aspects of active transcendence and cosmic-social relatedness. Secular thought, whether Vedic or Dharmaśāstric, attempts to resolve it into an equilibrium but this remains unstable because of the radical demands of the renouncers in favour of complete transcendence. To many of them this means the transcendence of the pure spirit in man, illusorily enmeshed in nature but able to recover its purity through the escape of a total isolation (*kaivalya*) from nature. To others the transcending element is not even a spirit but mere spiritual dynamism beyond any substance-like ego and in regard to which the whole world is like a mirage while from the standpoint of the world it itself appears utterly evanescent. To others still, the transcendence which affirms itself within man is to be viewed as itself transcended by a spiritual Absolute which escapes any classification. Whether *Brahman* or *Dharmakāya*, this Absolute is ultimate and commands a reordering of all other conceptions.

Paradoxically, while the discovery of such an Absolute relativises all the transcenders it transcends, it has also given rise to a new kind of anthropologies less cut off from the world and, we may even say, open to it though fully imbued with the sense of spiritual evaluation inculcated by the renouncers. There is indeed a remarkable affinity between the conceptions of the *Gītā*, of Mahāyāna and of Śaṅkara insofar as their very focusing on an ultimate Absolute (though the latter be differently conceived) allows them as it were to turn compassionate eyes to the world and to adopt a humanistic stance within their religious perspective. This is obvious in the case of Arjuna or of the *bodhisattvas*, less so in the case of Śaṅkara. Even apart from his exhibiting the humanity and virtues of the merciful teacher and from his upholding the relative validity of the empirical world and its *pramāṇa*, we find in his theory of the ego as arisen in the image and semblance of the *Brahman-Ātman* and of the integration of the whole human aggregate around this reflection-ego a more holistic conception of the human person than in the Absoluteless doctrines.

It seems then that in India human personalism is bound to be very meagre unless it is lit up and supported by a religion of the Absolute which itself tends to be a personalism of the Divine beyond all anthropomorphisms.

* * *

Bibliography

The following list is a fair representation of recent writings by Indian authors concerning the Person. It comprises those available at the Centre of Advanced Study in Philosophy of the University of Madras (with acknowledgement to the Library Assistant, Mr Abdul Rawoof). Simply reading their titles will reveal much of the background allegiance and standpoint of their writers.[4]

BOOKS

Concept of Man. S. Radhakrishnan and P.T. Raju. London: Allen & Unwin, 1960.

Concept of Self. Kamala Roy. Calcutta: Firma K.L. Mukhopadhyay, 1966.

East-West Studies of the Problem of the Self. P.T. Raju and Albuney Castell, eds. The Hague: Nijhoff, 1968.

Idea of Personality. P.N. Srinivasachari. Madras: Adyar Library, 1951.

Individuals and Societies. D. Chattopadhyaya. Bombay: Allied Publishers, 1967.

Ramakrishna-Vivekananda Vedanta and Human Personality. Coimbatore: Ramakrishna Mission, 1966.

Nature of Self. A.C. Mukerji. Allahabad: Indian Press, 1938.

Personality. Rabindranath Tagore. London: Macmillan, 1961.

Philosophy, Logic and Language. Kalidas Bhattacharyya. Bombay: Allied Publishers, 1965, pp. 116-154.

Sankhya Conception of Personality or a New Interpretation of the Sankhya Philosophy. Abhay Kumar Majumdar. Calcutta University, 1930.

The Subject as Freedom. K.C. Bhattacharyya. Amalner: Malkani, 1930.

Towards the Universal Man. Rabindranath Tagore. London: Asia Publishers, 1962.

Vedanta: Its Doctrine of Divine Personality. K. Sundarama Iyer. Srirangam: Vani Vilas Press, 1926.

Way of Humanism, East and West. Radhakamal Mukerjee. Bombay: Academic, 1968.

Concept of Mind in Indian Philosophy. Sarasvati Chennakesavan. Bombay: Asia Publishers, 1960.

Our Knowledge of Other Selves. Margaret Chatterjee. Bombay: Asia Publishers, 1963.

ARTICLES

"The Concept of Person in Strawson and Vedanta." C. Sampurna. *Indian Philosophical Annual* **6** (1970) 181-188.

"The Concept of Self in Buddhism." Kalidas Bhattacharyya. *The Philosophical Quarterly* (India) **34** (1961) 77-87.

"The Dynamism of Personality." S.N. Roy. *The Philosophical Quarterly* (India) **24** (1951) 35-40.

"Early Trends in the Indian Understanding of Man." R.V. De Smet. *Philosophy East and West* **22** (1972) 259-268.

"God as Personal and Impersonal." H.M. Joshi. *Pathway to God* **7** (1972) 60-68.

"Humanism and Indian Thought." A. Chakravarti. *Journal of the Madras University* **9**/1 (1937).

"The Role of Man in Hinduism." R.N. Dandekar, in K.W. Morgan, *The Religion of the Hindus.* New York: Ronald Press, 1958.

"Man in Hindu Thought." R.N. Dandekar. *Annals of the Bhandarkar Oriental Research Institute* **43**/1-4 (1963) 1-57.

"Humanistic Transformation." P.T. Raju. *Aryan Path* (June 1951).

"Identity of the Self." S.C. Chatterjee. *The Philosophical Quarterly* (India) **24** (1952) 217-224.

"Individual and Society in Indian Social Thought." N.A. Nikam. *Indian Philosophical Annual* **6** (1970) 41-43.

"Individualistic Trends in Gandhian Thought." Kanak Khanna. *Indian Philosophical Annual* **5** (1969) 160-165.

"*Karma* and *Avatāra*, a New Direction to the Doctrine of Incarnation in Hinduism." K.R. Sundara Rajan. *Saiva Siddhanta* **3** (1968) 146-148.

"*Karma* and Grace." C. Ramalinga. *Saiva Siddhanta* **3** (1968) 5-8.

"Mind and Consciousness, a Comparison of Indian and Western Views." Sarasvati Chennakesavan. *The Philosophical Quarterly* (India) **26** (1954) 247-252.

"Phenomenological Approach to a Metaphysics of Personality in the Light of Advaita." Debabrata Sinha. *The Philosophical Quarterly* (India) **29** (1956) 83-86.

"Self and Others." Kalidas Bhattacharyya. *The Philosophical Quarterly* (India) **31** (1958) 145-156.

"Self and the Body." K.C. Gupta. *The Philosophical Quarterly* (India) **32** (1959) 43-48.
"Self and the Ego." Bhasker S. Naik. *The Philosophical Quarterly* (India) **7** (1931) 171-176.
"Self, Reality and Salvation in Christianity and Buddhism." Mervyn Fernando. *International Philosophical Quarterly* **12** (1972) 415-425.
"Some Implications of the Concept of Personality in Social Philosophy." S.H. Kelshikar. *The Philosophical Quarterly* (India) **31** (1958) 11-18.
"The Theistic Concept of Progress." V.A. Devasenapathi. *Saiva Siddhanta* **2** (1967) 6-8.
"Towards a Philosophy of Transcendental Personalism." S. Vahiduddin. *The Philosophical Quarterly* (India) **23** (1950) 17-21.

Notes

[1] [First published in *Contemporary Indian Philosophy*, Series II, Muirhead Library of Philosophy, ed. M. Chatterjee (London: Allen & Unwin, 1974) 51-75. Paperback edition by Motilal Banarsidass (Delhi, 1998) 51-75.]
[2] Cf., for instance, D.G. Mandelbaum, *Society in India*, 2 vols. (Berkeley: University of California Press, 1970).
[3] [The 1974 text reads "in the religion of the heart"; corrected in the 1998 text to "in the region of the heart".]
[4] [I have retained De Smet's ordering of the bibliography, which is generally alphabetical according to title, but not always.]

10

ĀTMAN AND PERSON Contributions to the *Marāṭhi Tattvajñāna Mahākoṣa*[1]

1. *Ātmavāda* / Doctrine of *Ātman*[2]

Ancient man believed that in every man there was a power controlling his life and deeds. From a gross point of view, it was thought that this power was a subtle form of the individual [*vyakti*] himself, which left the body at the time of death. This idea of a replica of the individual [*prativyakti*] within the individual [*vyakti*] is the beginning of the idea of *ātman* in the history of mankind.

The concept of *ātman*. The concept of *ātman* has a certain logical purpose. The experiences of an individual are fluid. A variety of wishes, desires, memories, sensations follow one upon another. Despite such transformations, the individual remains the same. Our intellect presumes that there must be some stable principle at the root of such changing experiences. Such an enduring principle is what is indicated by the concept of *ātman*. As the concept of *ātman* is employed to indicate the identity underlying experiences, so also it has the task of unifying the experiences of the individual. Experience is multi-faceted. Seeing and hearing, liking and being surprised, many such experiences occur in a single moment; but the one who experiences is one and the same. The unity underlying a multiplicity of experiences is also expressed by the concept of *ātman*.

Experience of the *ātman*. The question arises whether the *ātman* is merely a logical concept, or whether it can also be experienced. The Buddhists and David Hume maintained that there is no experience of any element called the *ātman*. However much one peers into consciousness, one finds only modifications of consciousness [*citta-vṛtti*]; the 'I' can never be found. Happiness and pain, joy and grief, yellow colour or blue and other such experiences keep arising one after another, but there is never any experience of an 'I.' Therefore there is no such thing as 'I' or *ātman*.

But how then do we distinguish between my experiences and the experiences of others? Is it possible to mistake one's experiences for those of another, like people bathing in a river sometimes mistake one another's clothes? Does confusion ever arise about whether an experience is mine or that of someone else? How is it that I am able to perceive the identity between the 'I' who slept the previous night after switching off the lights, and the 'I' who got up yawning this morning? Hume's answer to such questions is that the prior perception is the cause of the next, and that since these two perceptions are contiguous in time, they are also similar. As a result we class them together and mistakenly imagine that underlying them all is a stable substance called 'I.'

After examining one's stream of consciousness, it is clear that not everyone can agree with Hume's analysis. When I become conscious of anything, I am also conscious that that experience is mine. Every single one of our experiences bears the stamp of 'I' and 'mine.' When I am conscious that I am unhappy, I am conscious not merely of unhappiness but of my unhappiness. In affirmations such as 'I am happy' or 'I feel insulted,' it can be said that the 'ego' [*aham*] or 'I' is experienced.

The Ātmavādin will suggest that the 'I' that is experienced be called *jīva* or *jīvātman* rather than *Ātman*. The *jīva* suffers grief and is elated by happiness. It can be experienced as the 'ego.' Moreover, all the things that we label as 'mine,' such as body, house, money, sons and fame, are included in this 'I.' This 'I' is the object of knowledge.

Self-knowledge [*ātma-vijñāna*]. The one who knows the 'I,' however, is the *Ātman*. This *Ātman* is not the object of knowledge. It is the pure 'knower.' The one who knows 'I am deceitful' is still the 'I.' But the 'I' that is deceitful and the 'I' that knows that deceitful 'I' are not one and the same. The knowing 'I' is the *Ātman* or knower [*vijñāta*]. That *Ātman* cannot be known as an object of knowledge. "*Vijñātaram are keṇa vijānīyat*?' ["Who indeed can know the knower?"]

Because the *Ātman* is not an object of knowledge, its nature does not possess attributes [*upādhi*]. It cannot be said to be 'smaller than this one,' 'bigger than that one.' It is not possible to attribute to it spatial limitations such as 'it is here, but not there.' It is not possible to ascribe to it temporal attributes such as 'it is today,' 'it was yesterday.'

The self-luminosity of the *Ātman*. Though this *Ātman* without attributes cannot be known as an object of knowledge, still its existence cannot be doubted, for it is self-conscious or self-luminous. Since it is self-luminous, there is no need of establishing its existence, nor is it possible to do so. In contrast, if we want to prove the existence of a piece of gold in a safe, it is necessary that someone should have knowledge about it. The proof of its existence is dependent upon knowledge. That existence is not self-established [*svapratiṣṭha*]. It is possible that there is no gold piece there. On the other hand, even when saying 'I am not,' the speaker remains. In the very process of saying 'no' he manifests himself. This manifestation is itself his existence. The 'I' in 'I am' is there for the sake of grammar. The pure 'am' that remains when the 'I' is removed is the self-luminosity of the *Ātman*. The existence of the *Ātman* is self-established. The existence of a gold piece is different in kind from this. In order to prove its existence, it is necessary for it to be known by a knower that is distinct from it. The gold piece is what is seen [*dṛśya*]. The *Ātman* is seeing [*dṛk*]. In the relationship between seeing and what is seen, the existence of what is seen is dependent on the seeing. The existence of seeing is self-established. In his assertion, *Cogito ergo sum*, Descartes had actually established the self-luminous *Ātman*. He thought, however, that he had established the existence of the 'I' with attributes or *jīvātman*.

Cidvilāsvāda. Many things can be seen in the world; they are objects of knowledge. That is to say, their existence depends on the *Ātman*. Because the *Ātman* exists, they exist. If this *Ātman* were not, then *jagad-andhakāra-prasaṅgaḥ*—there would be only darkness. Such a doctrine is called Ātmavāda. It is not that Ātmavāda has to reject the existence of the world. All that Ātmavāda says is that the *Ātman* is the source of all that is in the world. Jñāneśvara's Cidvilāsvāda, which maintains that the whole world is the play of the *Ātman* (*jaga asaki vastuprabhā*) is really one of the forms of Ātmavāda.

Berkeley's idealism. Ātmavāda can be compared to Berkeley's idealism. According to Berkeley, whatever exists has to be perceived. Now everyone will agree that there are many things that are not perceived by me. So Berkeley resorts to the Supreme Self in order to account for their being perceived, and says that all the things of the world are in existence only because they are perceived by it. In contrast, in the Ātmavāda described above, one begins from the self-conscious existence of the *Ātman* in order to base visible things (or Berkeley's perceptions) on it.

'Ātmavāda' can have two other meanings. (1) Just as there is a self [*ātman*] within the individual [*vyakti*], so also there is a self principle [*ātmatattva*] within the universe; this is the Upaniṣadic point of view regarding the universe. The teaching of the Upaniṣads, that the self of the individual and the self principle at the root of the universe are one [*ekarūpa*], is called Ātmavāda. Since the word *ātman* is a pronoun denoting agency, it seems to indicate human individuality [*vyaktitva*] in the form of a composite consisting of several different layers or sheaths. In the analysis of such a composite, it is necessary to begin from the gross body (*annamaya kośa*) and proceed in an orderly manner through the different inner sheaths till one reaches the blissful abode [*ānandamaya adhiṣṭhāna*]. Such an analysis that goes from the effect to the cause, from the gross to the subtle, from the outer to the inner, from the inferior layers to the excellent, from what is supported to the support itself, from the outer expression to its inner seed or ground, is an evaluative analysis that can be called discrimination [*viveka*]. The principle against which such evaluation is done is such that what is subtle, interior, pervading, inspiring, or, in short, '*pratyagātman*,' is more profoundly being, more deeply true, eternal and immutable. Many alternative series of selves have been proposed on the basis of the *viveka* or evaluative analysis carried out by the Upaniṣads. For example, in the answer given to Gārgī's question, 'With what yarn is the cloth of this whole universe woven?' a whole series of universal principles is presented, beginning from earth, water, wind and space, and going up to

Brahmaloka and the indescribable nature of *iśvara* (*Bṛh. Up.* 3, 6). Then in 3, 7 we find Yājñavalkya's sublime teaching about the *pratyagātman* that is indwelling, immortal, that has its abode in earth, water, etc., that is different from them, is unknown to them, and that directs them. In the *Kaṭhopaniṣad* (3, 10-11) we find the presentation of a pre-Sāṁkhya series of elements such as visible things, mind, intellect, the *mahadātman*, the unmanifest [*avyakta*], and the *puruṣa*. Commenting on this series of elements, Śaṅkarācārya has said that each term in this series "being the '*pratyagātman*' of the previous term, is more excellent, more subtle and greater than that previous term." Of this series, '*puruṣa*' is "the final state of the creation [*paramotkarṣa*] and dissolution [*paryavasāna*] of the utter limit, the culmination, the climax of subtleness, greatness and inner-selfhood." ("*Sūksmatva-mahatva-pratyagātmātvānāṃ sa kāṣṭhā niṣṭhā paryavasānaṃ.*")[3] In such series of principles, a class of lesser selves is first presented, and then a supreme self is proposed. This supreme self, it is pointed out, is none other than *Parabrahman*. In several places, it can be seen that the *mahadātman*, elsewhere called '*jīvātman*,' is also given a place of prominence in comparison to other elements.

(2) The name Ātmavāda can also be given to the conviction that there is certainly a substance called *ātman* that unifies, by its own witness [*sāksitva*], the different experiences that keep arising in us, and that underlies them in a stable way. The rejection of such a stable principle is called 'Anātmavāda.'

References: V.D. Gokhale, ed. *Srijñānadevavircita anubhavāmṛta* (Pune, 1968); Śaṇkarācārya, *Ātmabodha*, in *Srī Śaṇkarācārya's Miscellaneous Works*, vol. 4, ed. A. Mahadevashastri and K. Rangacharya (Mysore, 1899); W. James, *Principles of Psychology*, 2 vols. (New York, 1950).

* * *

2. *Ātmā – Ihetara Jīvana* / Soul – Afterlife[4]

Anthropologists have collected convincing evidence regarding belief in life after death, rebirth, reincarnation, immortality, etc., and have concluded that some kind of belief in immortality was prevalent among even in primitive societies.

Often such belief was not connected to morality. However, the Egyptians, the Iranians and Vedic Aryans did link it to rewards and punishments in the afterlife. Although the first philosophical inquiry regarding evidence for this belief is to be found in Naciketa's third question to Yama in the *Kaṭhopaniṣad* (1, 20), it is nevertheless vaguely present also in the earlier Upaniṣads. The Upaniṣads came to the conclusion about immortality on the basis of the conscious nature of the self. The important truth that they discovered is that the true nature of the self is beyond space and time, that its relationship with the material and changing world is temporary and in a sense false, and that hence the self is immortal. From this it follows that, just as the self is without end, it is also without beginning. Because of this it becomes difficult to distinguish between the eternity of the *ātman* and the divine eternity. In the same way it is difficult to say whether the self is a limited self [*jīvātman*] distinct from the supreme Self [*paramātman*], or whether, being identical with the supreme Self, the limited self is intellect alone, or the combination of intellect, ego-sense and mind, or else the subtle body [*liṅga-śarīra*]. Generally it is held that, since this limited self is under the rule of *karma*, the true self of the nature of consciousness is in a motionless state that is eternal, without attributes, and free of all desires, and that it knows neither space nor time nor death. As described in the *Māṇḍūkyopaniṣad*, we can get an idea of this from the *turīya* state of cognition, in which the mundane world is destroyed. The supremely free swan [*haṁsa-paksī*] is the emblem of this self.

The thinking of Western philosophers. Plato and Aristotle have given similar replies to the foregoing questions; only, they did not proceed to the identification of individual self and the Supreme Self.

While the materialist Epicureans and the early Stoics did not accept individual immortality, Cicero instead did. The later Biblical Jews, and the Christians after them, carried it further. They also accepted that, after death, there would be a resurrection of the body by means of divine power. The early Zoroastrians and later the Muslims also accepted this belief. Avicenna expounded the immortality of the soul. Averroes, on the other hand, admitted only the eternity of the universal intellect. The medieval Christian thinkers further developed the doctrine of the immortality of the soul. The major support for this comes from the epistemological and the metaphysical arguments flowing from the nature and activity of the soul, while the minor support comes from the ethical argument that good and bad deeds must get their just reward. Spinoza rejected individual immortality, Leibniz accepted it on the basis of his eternal self [*atyuttātmā*], and Kant considered it to be an ethical axiom. Hegel is uncertain about immortality, while Schopenhauer rejects it. In the first half of the twentieth century the Marxists, the empiricists and the neo-empiricists either rejected immortality or else questioned its validity. Bergson and other French philosophers of consciousness, along with the neo-Thomists and other Christian thinkers, have upheld the doctrine. In 1945 W.E. Hocking challenged scepticism by calling it 'mental lethargy.' Without accepting a conscious and therefore immortal self or an eternal God, and on the basis of empirical processes alone, it is impossible to distinguish between truth and untruth. This makes the unbelief of the naturalists unacceptable. If it is held that there is only one self or conscious principle, the difficulty arises that truths or untruths have to be regarded as the thoughts of this single consciousness. Therefore a single consciousness must be regarded as self-contradictory, because a struggle would be going on within it between knowledge and ignorance, good and evil. To call this state indescribable is to regard it as beyond the scope of thinking and of philosophy.

The thinking of Indian philosophers. In India, ethical thinking links the doctrine of immortality with the belief about rebirth based on the doctrine of *karma* (Upaniṣads, Jainism, Buddhism). It is accepted without discussion that the fruits of *karma* have to be endured, and that one has to undergo many different rebirths. In these births, the fruits of previous actions [*karma*] are exhausted, and new actions are performed which again become the seeds of rebirth. All this is described briefly in the *Bhagavad Gītā* (2, 22). It is not assumed that the pure self is the link between two births, for there is no personal [*vyaktitva*] element in the self. The link between two births is understood to be something else that is either the *liṅgaśarīra*, or the *jīvātman*, or the *manomaya* (which governs soul [*prāṇa*] and body) or the mind or the *ahaṁkāra*, or the *jīva* or the *liṅga* (on this point the Vedānta, Yoga and Sāṁkhya schools differ, see *Sāṁkhyakārikā*

42), or just plain action (in Buddhism which upholds Anātmavāda). On the other hand, Jainism, Nyāya and Vaiśeṣika consider the self itself as the link, but their ideas about the self are different. In Buddhism the one liberated from *karma* is free of all desires, while in Hindu philosophy he is under the control of God. The Nyāya-Vaiśeṣikas tend to bring the *karma-siddhānta* under the control of God. Śaiva philosophy made his nature gentle with the help of divine compassion and mercy. Śaṅkarācārya brought him completely under the direction of God. He also clarified that the idea of rebirth cannot be proved by any other means except *śruti*. If Śaṅkarācārya accepts the value of the doctrine of rebirth as a possible explanation of the state of affairs in the present birth, he has also noted that there is neither memory nor knowledge that might be able to link two births.

If belief in rebirth is accepted by all within the Hindu *dharma* (although there is no agreement on the matter among the Sikhs), very few have accepted it outside India. It may be encountered in the philosophies of Orphism, Pythagoras, Empedocles, Plato (though only as a corollary), neo-Platonism (Philo, Ammonius Saccas, Origen, Plotinus), the Kabbalah, some Sufis (Rumi?), Bruno, Lessing, the Theosophists, and in some modern philosophers such as A. Huxley and J. McTaggart. Those who are willing to accept this idea in the Western world today believe that individuality is retained in rebirth; but it is precisely this that the Hindu mind is afraid of, and hopes for liberation from it by means of *jñāna*, *karma* or *bhakti*.

Modern arguments. Modern arguments in support of rebirth are as follows. (1) Just as there is transformation in nature so there is transformation in conscious being. (But then there is no meaning in *mukti*). (2) Several births are necessary in order to express all human potentialities. (Are these rebirths of the same individual, or instead of many individuals of the same class? Or does *śruti* teach that progress is in one and the same direction?) (3) Rebirth explains the differences between individuals. (Perhaps; but is this explanation necessary and sufficient? There are many other competing explanations). (4) The doctrine of rebirth ensures the enjoyment of the fruit of action. (Yes, but this series of enjoyments has neither beginning nor end, so disorder and confusion arises. Moreover, in many religions the enjoyment of fruit is assured without recourse to the doctrine of rebirth).

Indeed, even in Hinduism, thinking about the other world is not connected only to rebirth, for it is held that *mukti* is beyond rebirth and the field of *karma*. In other religions it is held that in the life after death there is a limited punishment in the nether world [*pātāḷa*] and a longer punishment in hell. Entry into paradise or heavenly bliss are the rewards after death. This heaven is believed to be complete union with the one God. Whether the doctrine of rebirth is accepted or not, the religiously accepted concepts of immortality and eternal bliss carry human history into a world that lies beyond. In the same way they engender hope in a life beyond the limits of this-worldly progress and the wheel of time, and uphold the value of history. Such a philosophy of history has been proposed by a Muslim philosopher (M. Iqbal) and a Hindu philosopher (Aurobindo), and a synthesis of science, philosophical introspection and faith by a Christian philosopher (Teilhard de Chardin).

References: F. von Hugel, *Eternal Life* (Edinburgh, 1912); A.S. Pringle-Pattison, *The Idea of Immortality* (Oxford, 1922); J.G. Frazer, *Man, God and Immortality* (London, 1927); S. Radhakrishnan, *An Idealist View of Life* (London, 1932; revised 2nd ed. 1937); Aurobindo, *The Problem of Rebirth* (Pondicherry, 1952).

* * *

3. *Jīva (Jīvātman)* / Individual Self[5]

It is generally agreed that the *ātman* is an inner life principle. It can be vegetative (in trees), sensitive (in animals), or intellectual (in human beings). The Sarvacidvādins (e.g. the Jains) hold that there are selves even in inert substances.

The nature of the self. At first, the self was thought to be the same as the breath (*prāṇa*) that is the sign of life (the *Ṛgveda* mentions *prāṇa*, *ātman* only four times), or as a material principle such as a multitude of atoms (Democritus, Empiricus); or else it was considered to be a subtle light (the Stoics). Following this line of thinking, Hobbes, Lemaitre and other positivist philosophers held that the self was a unity of apperceptions, or a phenomenon or epiphenomenon. Others within this line of thinking considered the self to be something fictitious (the Buddhists and Hume). Generally, the nature of the self is considered to be spiritual, i.e. intelligent and free (at least in human beings). Socrates propounded this spirituality mainly with the help of moral reasons. Plato, Aristotle, Plotinus and the Christian thinkers expanded this idea. A similar development regarding the concept of self took place in India from the Upaniṣads to the darśanas. Plato considered the soul to be naturally a purely spiritual form, which accidentally happens to be related to a body within a series of births. Descartes, Malebranche, Spinoza (parallelism of thought and extension), Leibniz (pre-established harmony of intelligent monads) carried forward this dualist doctrine regarding body and soul. Aristotle thought the soul to be 'form' or 'act' (dynamic energy). As a consequence the human soul itself gives form to prime matter, and from the unity of these two co-principles arises the substance that is body and intelligence [*cetana*]. This substance alone is the complete individual or *jīvātman* that is man. St Thomas Aquinas developed this concept and it went on to become a central doctrine of Catholic philosophy. St Augustine before him had only mentioned the natural unity of soul and body. Some of the elements of this idea were restated by N. Hartmann and G. Marcel. Plotinus thought it necessary to think of the human soul as having two parts, a lower (*psychê*) and a higher (*nous*). Because of this, Aristotelian philosophers began to think of *nous* as an independent and universal 'agent intellect' (Alexander of Aphrodisias, Avicenna, Averroes). Aquinas and R. Bacon admitted the need of a higher agent intellect and held this agent intellect to be identical with the God without attributes; still, Aquinas maintained that the soul had its own active, finite agent intellect. In Western philosophy it is generally held that senses, imagination or ego-sense or common sense, memory, sensitive passions, intelligence, intellectual passions or volitions are functions or potentialities of the soul. In India, in the *Kaṭhopanisad* (6, 7-8) the self is first analyzed in the following manner: sense-organs, mind, *sattva* (i.e. *buddhi*); *mahānātman* (i.e. *jīvātman*), beyond which are only the *avyakta* (i.e. universal *prakṛti*) and the divine '*puruṣa*.' In the *Bhagavad Gītā* (3, 42) this analysis is repeated up to the '*mahānātman*.' Only, in verse 43 this *mahānātman* is referred to simply as '*ātman*.' Early

Sāṁkhya introduces the element of *ahaṁkāra* between mind and intellect (*mahat*); but this darśana considers all these elements of material creation arising from *prakṛti* as distinct from *puruṣa.* This '*puruṣa*' is similar to the *mahānātman* or *ātman* described above; but being pure, undivided, devoid of action, and disinterested consciousness, it is not related to the ultimate *avyakta* or divine '*puruṣa.*' On the contrary, Śaṅkarācārya believes the *jīvātman* to be of the form of consciousness (*cit-rūpa*); but the *jīvātman* is not pure consciousness; perhaps pure consciousness, i.e. *paramātman* (*Brahman*), is its ground. The *paramātman* is greater and more interior than the *jīvātman.* It is itself the inspiring force of all *jīvātmans* (*sarvātman*). Therefore from the viewpoint of the *paramātman*, the *jīvātman* is a super-imposition (*upādhi*) that is name and form, of the nature of action, and like a veil. Only when we go beyond its finite nature and outer freedom are we able to see and experience its ground and abode that is the eternal [*kevalasvarūpi*] *saccidānanda Brahman* in its nature that is one without a second. Comparing Sāṁkhya and Advaita, Ramanūjācārya regards the *jīvātman* not as an *upādhi* but as a 'mode,' i.e. a part and *śeṣa* of '*Viśiṣta*' *Brahman.* According to Madhvācārya, although the *jīvātman* is eternally different from and co-existing with *īśvara*, it is nevertheless a projection [*ābhāsa*], reflection [*pratibimba*] and part of *īśvara.* From the viewpoint of the Naiyāyikas, since the *ātman* is an independent substance it possesses properties. Some followers of Śaṅkara who interpret his teaching as pure *māyāvāda* or acosmism, maintain that only *Brahman* has being and that *jīva* or *jīvātman* has no being.

The origin of the *ātman*. Various theories have been suggested about the origin of the self: that it has existence from the beginning (pre-existence) and is eternal (Plato, Plotinus, pantheists, Kant, Indian spiritualists), or that it arises from material substances (materialists), or that it is generated by the father and the mother (Tertullian), or that it is inducted from the 'outside' (Aristotle), or that it is created by God (Aquinas, many Christian thinkers, Descartes, Leibniz, orthodox Muslims). Apart from Sāṁkhya, Yoga, Jainism, Nyāya, Vaiśeṣika and Madhvācārya, other Indian spiritualists believe that, though the soul is eternal (and because of the doctrine of *karma* it is impossible to think otherwise), and though it does not emerge from *prakṛti*, still it originates from *Brahman* in one way or other, either by *pariṇāma* or by *vivarta*.

The 'self' ['*sva*'] or *jīvātman*. The meaning of these terms is construed in different ways in India and in the West. In India, these terms are generally considered synonymous with the terms related to the *ātman* (*jīva*, *jīvātman*, the '*puruṣa*' of Sāṁkhya, etc.); only, a distinction is often made between '*sva*' and *jīvātman*. In such a situation, since the '*sva*' is the *ahaṁkāra* or individuality (thought by many to be merely fictitious) arising from the *ātman*, it binds the *ātman* to selfishness and its bad effects. In Western countries the words '*sva*' and '*jīvātman*' are considered to be similar in meaning to 'individual,' and they refer to the union of the human body and soul or to the human spiritual soul as the bearer of personality [*vyaktimatva*]. This *jīva* stands before other individuals [*vyaktis*]. According to theists, it stands before its source and ground—i.e. God. Because of this, selfishness is not an inevitable constitutive factor. There has been much discussion about the 'I-thou' relationship.

References: F. von Hugel, *Eternal Life* (Edinburgh, 1912); A.S. Pringle-Pattison, *The Idea of Immortality* (Oxford, 1922); J.G. Frazer, *Man, God and Immortality* (London, 1927); S. Radhakrishnan, *An Idealist View of Life* (London, 1932; revised 2nd ed. 1937); Aurobindo, *The Problem of Rebirth* (Pondicherry, 1952).

* * *

4. *Mānavavāda* / Humanism[6]

Rarely used before 1870, this term has two accepted meanings: (a) the humanist ideal of human culture during the period of the European Renaissance, to be attained with the help of art and the study of Ancient Greek and Roman literature; (b) the tendency to give man first place in philosophy, or to regard man as 'the measure of all things' (Protagoras). The different ideas about man are simply different forms of this theoretical humanism. Since generally naturalism and monism are opposed to humanism, when discussing metaphysics or the cognitive meaning of propositions, it rejects abstract logic which tends to neglect their particular background, context and motives. This is especially applicable to 'closed' humanism. Closed humanism emphasizes man's self-sufficiency and is mostly atheist. This attitude is accepted by many tendencies of thought.

(1) **Rationalism** tends to derive all philosophical truths from elements that are prior to experience, e.g. the human intellect from internal elements, and maintains the total autonomy of this internally constituted intellect. Thus, e.g., Brunschvicg rejects all the forms of data and derives everything with the help of developing knowledge. He believes that the human mind, being an autonomous power that is able to engage in research and obtain freedom, is the source of new values, and that man is the authentic witness and the only agent of this creative evolution.

(2) **Marxism**. By means of naturalism, and making use of dialectical materialism, Marxism seeks to abolish everything that goes against the true nature of man. It believes that in a classless society, harmony will be established between thought and action, individuals and society, dialectical development and history, man and nature, and a new and liberated human species will thus emerge.

(3) **Pragmatism** examines the value of knowledge from the human point of view. It was William James who brought out the humanist meaning of pragmatism. This interpretation was, however, completely rejected by C. Peirce, the father of pragmatism. The popularity enjoyed by pragmatism at the beginning of the twentieth century is very much on the wane.

(4) **Atheistic existentialism** is a 'closed' type of humanism. According to Sartre, for example, man is thrown before a nature (pure being) that is totally alien, and embracing an irrational freedom he himself creates life values and morals, to be considered merely as means; but in the end all this is swallowed up in the meaningless event called death.

(5) **Indian materialism (*Ājīvikas* or *Cārvākas*).** This was a 'closed' type of humanism. Jainism and Buddhism can also be included in this type, even if we take into account their asceticism and devaluation of the world. Not only these, but also Pūrva-Mīmāṁsa, Vaiśeṣika, early Sāṁkhya and some forms of Yoga are humanist, because their only interest is in human welfare or final liberation (*mukti*). These darśanas are 'closed' because they indicate the hope of attaining their objectives by means of techniques (sacrifice or *yoga*) or by the kind of

knowledge of 'truth' that does not take the divine element into account. On the other hand, 'open' humanism, while not rejecting any of the constructive elements of the above darśanas, embraces those elements neglected by them. Man must not be confined within the bounds of his own humanity; he must be helped to go in all the directions leading beyond his humanity. The world transcends man in some respects, and the God who is consciousness without attributes also transcends man, and without him it is not possible for man to attain liberation (*mukti*). Among the theistic systems, many, both from outside India and within, have accepted the humanist viewpoint. When, however, they do not sufficiently recognize human values within this world, their humanist tendency remains somewhat incomplete; but the title 'humanism' is given, especially in Europe, to the following Christian philosophies that have arisen in the last 80 years: (1) Blondel's philosophy of action, characterized by faith in the immanence of God and in the human possibility of attaining the supernatural; (2) the integral humanism of the Neo-Scholastics, especially that of J. Maritain; (3) the 'philosophy of the spirit' of Lavelle, Le Senne and others; (4) the 'philosophy of hermeneutics' of Ricoeur and others; (5) the integralism of Sciacca, with its widespread influence in Italy. In contemporary India, in addition to the open humanism of the Bhakti tradition and the Vedānta, we have to take note now also of the 'closed' humanism contained in government-sponsored secularism, the technologically-based social reform movement, the militant humanism of M.N. Roy and the various forms of political Marxism.

References: H. de Lubac, *Drama of Atheist Humanism* (London, 1949); J. Maritain, *True Humanism*, tr. M. Adamson (London, 1939); W. James, *Pragmatism* (London, 1907); F.C.S. Schiller, *Humanism* (London, 1903); J.S. Huxley, *The Humanist Fame: Essays* (London, 1961).

* * *

5. *Vyakti* / Person[7]

In the beginning the term 'person' signified the masks of the actors on the Greek and Roman stage. Later the same term was used to denote the roles of the actors on the stage, or the characters in the play, or the hero. The Stoics employed this term to refer to man playing the role allotted to him by God on the world stage. Roman courts used this term to signify someone having legal rights and duties, the opposite of the term 'slave.' The early Christians accepted the term in the sense of man expected to respond responsibly to the merciful love offered by God in the form [*rūpa*] of Jesus Christ. They also found this term useful for denoting both the ontological unity of Christ in whom the divine and the human natures exist together, and the concomitant distinction between the three divine persons, Father, Son/Word and Holy Spirit. Boethius suggested the definition of person as any independent rational substance.[8] The Schoolmen improved upon this definition in order to use the term for consciousness on both divine and limited levels of perfection. They emphasized the following points: intellectual self-awareness, self-consciousness, existence, integrity or completeness, freedom of action and self-accountability, impossibility of being otherwise, consciousness of unity, dignity in the sense of being an end in itself and the consequent rights, unconditional openness towards others.[9] In short, the term 'person' came to mean a being that is complete, self-subsistent, intellectually aware, free and possessed of the consequent qualities. Many modern philosophers found it difficult to retain all the characteristics mentioned in this definition. Descartes objectified only the intellectual essence in man. Locke defined 'person' as one who is constantly conscious of his identity; he also placed limits of time and place upon the term. Lawyers applied the term to beings that enjoy legal rights and duties, i.e. those that are subject to procedural laws. Kant reminded us that persons, being intentional, are the source of values, and so expanded the meaning of the term; but F.H. Jacobi, the vindicator of faith, interpreted the term as 'empirical being' ['*sattā-vitti*'], and following him, many nineteenth-century Protestant philosophers restricted the meaning of the term to human beings alone, thinking that by referring to God as person they ran the risk of attributing human characteristics to God. Their particular religious opinions influenced the great translators of Sanskrit works at the close of the nineteenth century, who connected 'personal' to *saguṇa* and 'impersonal' to *nirguṇa*.

Difference between India and the West: Since 'person' is not a term with roots in Indian philosophy, there is no satisfactory equivalent for it in Sanskrit. In its original Western meaning, this term can be applied properly and non-metaphorically to God, indicating absolutely free and perfect intellectual essence; on the other hand, terms such as *vyakti* and *puruṣa* seem to bring in limitedness and qualities into the Supreme Being that is simple and without attributes. As a result most Indian philosophers fail to notice that in the orthodox Christian faith, the term 'personal God' is used to denote a God without attributes who is simple [*akhanda*, *nirguṇa*], pure undifferentiated Truth [*sad-eva*]. As a result of this ambiguity they misunderstand many references to the 'personal God' in Western philosophy. Fortunately the recent discussion of the term 'personal' by British analytical philosophers may be helpful in doing away with this ambiguity. In his book *Individuals*, P.F. Strawson has unknowingly brought together again many characteristic qualities of the person that were known to the Schoolmen but neglected by subsequent philosophers. Distinguishing between M-predicates and P-predicates (signifying material things and persons respectively), he has shown that P-predicates do pervade M-predicates but are also beyond them, and that therefore the term 'person' cannot be limited to persons with physical bodies. He also shows that it is not possible to analyze persons into further component parts, and that as a consequence persons are indivisible fundamental forms. On the other hand, existentialist philosophers have emphasized freedom as the characteristic of persons, as also the totally new relations that persons may establish among themselves. The thinking of the existentialists has been greatly influential in the importance that is today being given to dialogue both as a fundamental attitude as well as an encounter between persons. (N.B.: the meaning of the term 'person' is not very closely related to the basic term 'personality' in psychology.)

References: F. Max Müller, *Collected Works of F. Max Müller*, vol. 10, *Persona* (London, 1912); P.F. Strawson, *Individuals* (London, 1949).

* * *

6. *Vyaktitattva* / Principle of Individuation[10]

Just as from a logical point of view the word 'particular' is opposed to 'universal,' so also from a metaphysical point of view the word 'individual' is opposed to 'genus' ['*samūha*']. In order to be an individual, a being must be "one in itself and distinct from all other beings." To ask about the principle of unity and distinctness in such a being is to ask the metaphysical question about the principle of individuation. From the viewpoint of the supreme principle, God is individualized by his inherent perfection and transcendence, and because he has no qualities he is different from all beings with qualities. If there exist beings that are pure forms, they are individualized by reason of the perfection of their limited nature or formal essence. The question emerges in a particular way when many physical beings are included in a single species. They are not individualized by reason of their essence, because this essence is realized in each member of the species. Aristotle and Aquinas answered this question by saying that physical things are individuated by means of prime matter. Since prime matter is pure potency and so basically indeterminate, it cannot exhaust the form. An element of imperfection remains in its reception of the form. The result of this is the particular individual. For example, a horse does not exhaust 'horseness' but rather participates in 'horseness'; a man does not exhaust 'humanity,' etc. Therefore, 'horseness' or 'humanity' have determination [*bhāvarūpatva*] by reason of their form, but particularity and inexhaustibility by reason of prime matter. Because he failed to distinguish between these two elements, Duns Scotus held that individual particularity was the cause of formal individuality. As for Ockham, Suarez and Leibniz, they, in a way similar to the Indian philosophical understanding of the individual, regarded the complete being as the principle of individuation. The Vaiśeṣika school also regarded the distinct category of '*viśeṣa*' as the principle of individuation. Buddhist philosophy regarded the visible and subtle series of events as the principle of individuation, while illusionistic [*māyāvādi*] Vedānta explained individuation in terms of false knowledge arising from ignorance.

Recently P.F. Strawson has taken up the question of particularity and individuality, but he has dealt with this question solely from the epistemological viewpoint, asking how we are able to recognize individuals and particulars. This question is not the same as the metaphysical question about the ultimate ground of individuation. The new answers of contemporary philosophers have not been able to supersede the answers given by classical philosophy to this ultimate metaphysical question in terms of prime matter and substantial form.

References: F. Copleston, *A History of Philosophy*, 8 vols. (London, 1946-66); P.F. Strawson, *Individuals* (London, 1949).

* * *

7. *Vyaktivāda* / Personalism[11]

Although many philosophers have discussed the nature of 'person,' the discussion of the term 'personalism' is rare before 1900. After this, we find the French philosopher Renouvier (1903), the German philosopher Sterne (1906), the American philosopher Bowne (1908), and others using this term. Personalists maintain that 'person,' being a basic and ultimate metaphysical term, can be used of both man and God, and that other categories become meaningful only with reference to this concept. Except for J.M. McTaggart, all personalists are theists. However, the personalism of philosophers like Bowne and Brightman is largely humanistic. Persons are explained as centres of cognitive and free activity and sources of values. That is why personalism is related to the theory of value and to the French theory of consciousness. Many Christian and Jewish philosophers are either adherents of personalism or else sympathetic to it. Among these are philosophers such as A. Brunner, J. Maritain, É. Gilson, G. Marcel, E. Mounier, N. Berdyaev, and M. Buber. French personalism gives great importance to social responsibility. American personalism, in the philosophy of W.E. Hocking, seems to be based on unconditional idealism; while in the philosophy of B.P. Bowne, G.H. Howison, E.S. Brightman, and F.J. McConnell, and in that of *The Personalist* under the influence of A.C. Knudson, R.T.

Flewelling and others, it seems to be leaning towards pluralism. Italian personalism has its source in the philosophy of V. Gioberti, A. Rosmini and G. Gentile. Especially in the period between the First and the Second World Wars, personalism flourished in France thanks to the influence of the writings of E. Mounier and through the institute *Esprit* that he founded. Generally speaking, existentialism became the vehicle of this thinking in the period after 1945. It can be said that the writings of Max Scheler made a lasting contribution to this viewpoint. Personalism did not flourish much in India, yet it is possible that Indian writers writing about humanism may have been influenced by personalism.

References: R.T. Flewelling, "The Person," *Twentieth Century Philosophy*, ed. D.D. Runes (New York, 1943); P.A. Bertocci and R.M. Millard, *Personality and the Good* (New York, 1963); J. Maritain, *Person and the Common Good*, tr. J.J. Fitzgerald (London, 1947); N. Berdyaev, *The Destiny of Man*, tr. N. Dadington (London, 1937); E. Mounier, *Personalism*, tr. P. Mairet (London, 1952).

Notes

[1] [First published in the *Marāthī Tattvajñāna Mahākoṣa* (henceforth *MTM*), ed. D.D. Vadekar (Poona: Marāthī Tattvajñāna Mahākoṣa Maṇḍala, 1974). De Smet contributed at least 68 entries to the *MTM*; the 7 entries selected for inclusion in this chapter all pertain in some way to the topic of the person. They have been translated by Ivo Coelho and Nelson Falcao, with the assistance of Tony George, Robert Pen, Daniel D'Souza and Mylin Noronha. The entries were originally written in English, then translated into Marathi, and subsequently retranslated into English so as to give De Smet the possibility of some control over the Marathi translation. Unfortunately, I have been able to trace neither De Smet's originals nor the subsequent English translations of the Marathi.]

[2] [H. Dixit and R.V. De Smet, "*Ātmavāda*," *MTM* **1**:69-70. The *MTM* glossary renders Ātmavāda as 'Doctrine of Ātman, Spiritualism' (**3**:392). "Doctrine of Atman" seems to have been the title of the English original, if we are to go by "Publications of Dr Richard V. De Smet, PhD, SJ" (cf. "Richard V. De Smet, SJ: A Bibliography," no. 697 below). It would seem that the article was written by De Smet (since he lists it in his "Publications") but re-written by Dixit (whose name appears before that of De Smet, despite the alphabetical order). Clearly, it does not always reflect the mind of De Smet.]

[3] [See "*Persona, Ānima, Ātman*" 33 above.]

[4] [R.V. De Smet, "*Ātmā – Ihetara Jīvana*," *MTM* **1**:71-73. Kozhamthadam does not list this particular entry, while Malkovsky translates it as "Soul (Eschatology, Rebirth, Immortality)," following De Smet. The *MTM* glossary translates *ātmā* as 'Entelechy, Self, Spirit' (**3**:392), and *ihetara ātmajīvana* as 'Extramundane Life of the Soul' (**3**:393).]

[5] [R.V. De Smet, "*Jīva (Jīvātman)*," *MTM* **1**:262-263. The *MTM* glossary translates *jīva* as 'Individual Self, Individual Ego, Self, Individual Soul,' and *jīvātman* as 'Ego, Individual Ego, Finite Self, Individual Soul or Psyche' (cf. **3**:401). With De Smet, Malkovsky translates the title of the article as "Individual Ego, Self, Soul." Despite the fact that the MTM glossary renders *ātmā* as 'Entelechy, Soul, Spirit' (**3**:392), I have decided to translate '*ātmā*' as 'self,' except where the context clearly demands that it be translated as 'soul.' The matter is complicated by the fact that one of the sub-headings of the present article uses the Marathi '*sva*', which has clearly to be translated as 'self.']

[6] [R.V. De Smet, "*Mānavavāda*," *MTM* **2**:436-437. The *MTM* glossary does not list the word *mānavavāda*, but does have *mānavatāvāda* which it renders as 'Humanism' (**3**:416). The text of the entry contains *mānavatāvāda* as well as another variant, *mānavyatāvāda*. Following De Smet, Kozhamthadam and Malkovsky both translate the title as "Humanism."]

[7] [R.V. De Smet, "*Vyakti*," *MTM* **3**:97-98. Despite the fact that the *MTM* glossary translates *vyakti* as 'Individual'(cf. **3**:424), the title here is definitely to be translated as 'person,' not only because the Marathi contains the transliterated word 'person', but also because the content of the article matches what De Smet writes elsewhere about 'person': cf. "*Persona, Anima, Ātman*" 25-29; "The Discovery of the Person" 45-47, 51-52, etc. Kozhamthadam and Malkovsky also translate the title as "Person."]

[8] ["*Persona, Anima, Ātman*" 26 above: "*Persona proprie dicitur naturae rationalis individua substantia*," which De Smet goes on to translate as "individual substance endowed with an intellectual nature." "The Discovery of the Person" 52: "any individual substance possessed of a rational nature." Cf. also "The Loss of the Person" 55 above.]

[9] ["The Loss of the Person" 55-58 above: 'subsistent' rather than 'substance,' meaning the whole existent subject rather than only the essence or nature; 'singular' or 'distinct' instead of 'individual'; 'intellectual' instead of 'rational', though Boethius' 'rational' must be understood as equivalent to the Greek *logikos*, 'of the nature of the logos, i.e. intellectual (ibid. 58).]

[10] [R.V. De Smet, "*Vyaktitattva*," *MTM* **3**:98-99. The *MTM* glossary translates *vyaktitattva* as 'Individuality, Individuation, Principle of Individuation' (**3**:424). Kozhamthadam and Malkovsky translate the title of the entry as "Principle of Individuation"; this is supported also by the content of the article.]

[11] [R.V. De Smet, "*Vyaktivāda*," *MTM* **3**:99. Once again, the content of the article makes it clear that *vyaktivāda* is to be translated as 'personalism' rather than as 'individualism.' This is supported by the *MTM* glossary (cf. **3**:424) as well as by Kozhamthadam and Malkovsky.]

11

THE ARISTOTELIAN-THOMIST CONCEPTION OF MAN[1]

Saint Thomas Aquinas, whose 700th death anniversary is commemorated this year, turned deliberately the whole current of thought in medieval Western Europe from a heavy philosophical reliance on Plato to a new confident reliance on Aristotle. We may well wonder why. Was it to appear up-to-date, as the works of Aristotle were then avidly read and studied in successive Latin translations, first from the Arabic and then soon from the Greek itself? But the dedicated truth-seeker that he was, he did not care for either antiquity or modernity. Rather, what conquered him was the philosophical satisfaction he found in Aristotle's method of enquiry and in his understanding of man. The aim of this paper is to throw some light on these two topics.

1. The Method of Enquiry

Aristotle departed—painfully—from Plato because he had found the idealistic method of the latter and his idealistic doctrines unable to answer correctly the host of questions which his own attentive observation of man and world and his critical study of the development of philosophy from the Presocratics to his own time were urgently raising. Raising questions, establishing the problematics of a discipline, took great importance in his teaching and written notes as they would in the teaching and works of his renovator, St Thomas. This may be shown through an outstanding example.

2. A Rich Problematics

In the first chapter of Aristotle's *Peri Psychês* (Concerning the Soul), the following questions are set out:

What is '*psychê*,' what is meant by the word, what is its nature and essence? What attributes and events are peculiarly psychological, and what are also organic? Is any general definition of *psychê*, which will cover all cases and no others, in any way possible, and if so by what method is it to be attained? Is it an 'it' at all, and if so, in what senses: as an independent existent subject (as Plato had implied), or only as a component of such an existent? Or is *psychê* only a qualitative, or quantitative or otherwise secondary predicate of some other existent? Should we attribute *psychê* only to man, or is there an animal and even a plant *psychê*? Wherein precisely do the human and non-human *psychês* converge and diverge? Should we admit a multiplicity of *psychês* in one individual? In what way, if any, can *psychê* be analysed into a number of component parts? Is *psychê* quantitative, divisible, localised? How is *psychê* related to space and time, that I can attribute to it an 'inner' and an 'outer,' a 'before' and an 'after'? If intrinsically divisible, in what sense can it be analysed into parts? If only in terms of potentialities to phenomenal operations, how are these to be characterised and classified? Are we to argue *a priori* from the *psychê* and its potentialities to their operations, or inductively from the latter to the potentialities and to *psychê* itself? Are all the operations and experiences attributed to *psychê* dependent on organic processes, and do all (as some evidently do) involve affect? How is the psychological and the physiological treatment of the same phenomenon to be distinguished? Are there also operations of *psychê* which can be only of the *psychê* and which, even though presupposing organic activities, can in no way be their product but are inherently independent? Must not a *psychê*, capable of activity independent of the corruptible body, be itself incorruptible and capable of independent existence? What should we think of attempts to conceive the *psychê* solely in terms of physical kinetic force as by many of the earlier Greek thinkers? Can *psychê* be identified with, and limited to, consciousness, as by Democritus? Can consciousness itself be accounted for in terms of micro-macrocosmic correspondence, whether in the materialistic form of Empedocles or in the mathematical fashion of the *Timaeus*? If neither dynamic nor quantitative concepts cover all the facts, can they be combined as in the 'self-moving number' of the later Plato? Or can we conceive *psychê* solely in terms of functional pairs of opposites, as perhaps by Heraclitus? Or as a Gestalt, a Harmony of opposites? Or as a wholly independent entity, mysteriously indwelling the body, but with no essential relation to the organism, as by Plato and the Pythagoreans?

For the sake of brevity I omit to cull from the works of St Thomas a parallel array of the problems which the topic of the soul musters up in his mind, though it would be most interesting to compare such parallel lists. But I want to stress the non-artificial character of their problematics. The questions they raise are not meant to fill up some oratorical or pedagogical need. They are called up by the sincerity of their enquiry which considered the whole extent of the phenomenon of *psychê* (or any other phenomenon they have decided to study) and they press upon one another like waves surging crest after crest and moving onwards till they subside in their resolution.

3. From the Totality of the Phenomenon to its Necessary Conditions

A first characteristic of Aristotle's procedure is that he considers the whole extent of the phenomenon he tries to understand and explain. This is a rare feature among philosophers, for too many of them are quickly fascinated by some particular aspect which gains prominence in their view, be it change or permanence, the *cogitatum* or the *cogito*, the *sensatum* or the idea, the analytical plurality or the unity, etc.

With regard to the particular field of *psychê*, Aristotle multiplies his observations, avoiding the premature intrusion of any interpretative concept, and explores it in all its dimensions, physiological, biological, affective, mental, intellectual, volitional, linguistic and historical. The results of this total observation are recorded not only in *Peri Psychês* but in his treatises about *Sensus and Sensatum*, *Memory and Recollection* and many of his other writings.

His observation is analytical and implies a certain amount of classification but he never breaks up the given unity of the phenomenon and keeps in view its totality. This totality defines the field to which he applies the exact method of empirical observation, induction and deduction which he has described and worked out in detail in his *Analytics*.

What is the unitary field of *psychê*? Aristotle insists (e.g. in Book Delta of *Metaphysics*) that the scientific definition of words must be based on common experience and common speech. Now, common speech ascribes '*psychê*' to the living as distinct from the dead. The most elemental of human experiences—life and death—this is what gives rise to the everyday ascription of *psychê* to what is alive, and the denial of *psychê* to what is dead. And what distinguishes the 'live' body from the 'dead' body is movement, change, process. Not any movement, but spontaneous, immanent, self-produced movement. The living being moves or changes not only when acted upon by other agents or forces, but by its own forces it at least nourishes, conserves, repairs and reproduces itself, as in the vegetable kingdom. In the higher forms of life, the animals, come higher forms of self-transmutation—locomotion, sensation, memory, phantasy and corresponding forms of appetites. In man there is also *nous* (approximately, the intellect)—the power of transcending his own mechanically conditioned organism, of forming conceptions which likewise transcend material spatiotemporal limitations, and the conceiving, and arguing to, reality which lies beyond sense-perception entirely—and the forms of desire, volition and conation which correspond to it. All this constitutes the *psychê* phenomenon, the rich field of self-immutation through activities and passivities; as such it is unitary despite its great qualitative variety.

The second important characteristic of Aristotle's method consists in the kind of rational explanation which he devises to account for the well-observed phenomenon. First of all, a rational explanation is demanded because we have no intellectual intuition of the inner nature of any reality. And it is possible because we have at least an intuitive apprehension of those of our activities and passivities which fall under the purview of our sensitive intellectual consciousness. As St Thomas will say, "whenever I know an object, say a stone, I simultaneously know this knowing as performed by me, and the nature of this activity." On the basis of undeniable similarity, I can then extend the knowledge thus gained directly and internally to other activities known only through their external phenomenon or their effects. It is in this two-way fashion that I know, for instance, the whole phenomenon of *psychê* as related to me and not only as conditioned by objects. And I know more than that for I thus apprehend myself as the subject of that phenomenon which is at least partially intuited. Thus, even though I have no pure intuition of the self, I at least know its existence and somehow its nature as subject of the *psychê*-phenomenon. From this can be formulated the first gnoseological principle: The self is known through its activities (and passivities), and, in general, every being is known (by us) from what it does (actively) and undergoes (passively). *Yatha kriyā* (*bhogaś ca*) *tathā kartā* (*bhoktā*), thus may this formula be rendered if we accept to understand *kriyā* as extending even to cognitive activities.

Now we may ask, what is there in the subject-agent which links it so intimately with its activity. This obviously is not a passive or static disposition but a dynamic force, an energy, what Aristotle, indeed, calls *energeia*, from *en* (in) and *ergon* (work, from the same Indo-European root *werg*-). According to him, this *energeia* which characterises the agent acts through the operation (*praxis*, the working process) upon the potency or potentiality (*dynamis*). It actuates this potency according to the latter's limiting dispositions (*pathos*, *exis*, *proairesis*) so that, as a result (*en telei*), there is found in the work (*ergon*) a received perfection similar to that of the *energeia*. As resulting at the end of the process, this perfection is called *entelecheia*, entelechy. But since it derives from the *energeia*, it *a fortiori* pertains to the latter which is, therefore, with even more right called *entelecheia*. The following diagram presents the conceptual field of ENERGEIA and DYNAMIS:

Source-ENERGEIA
= ENTELECHEIA
= "Act", actuating principle
↓
ENERGEIA in PRAXIS
= actuation, activity
↓
ERGON = TELOS ←ENTELECHEIA
= Work End-result as Resulting perfection
↑
PATHOS, EXIS, etc.→ DYNAMIS
= dispositions / = "Potency", potentiality
Principle of receptivity
and limitation.

The ENERGEIA-DYNAMIS couple is inferred by Aristotle through a rational process meant to discover the ontological necessary conditions immanent in every type of activity wherever activity results in a positive change. We may throw light on it if we notice that it reconciles *satkāryavāda* with *asatkāryavāda*. It explains, indeed, that the *sat* of the result, its perfection or entelechy, was causally present in the *energeia* or actuating principle viewed as *entelecheia*, and that the *asat* of the result, its limitation which makes it new, non-identical to its actuating principle, is due to a receiving and limiting co-principle, the potency or *dynamis*. *Dynamis* is not a logical possibility and it is not an ontological nothing though it is a no-thing, a not-yet-thing apart from its actuation by an 'act' or *energeia*. It is the ontological receiving principle in every change, the co-principle of *energeia*. On the lowest and most primordial level of change, it is pure *dynamis* which may be called prime matter (*prôtê hylé*). This is distinct from concrete matter which is already a synthesis of 'act' and 'potency' and, therefore, full of energy and forces (in act) but unstable and liable to change (in potency). *Energeia* and *dynamis* are the contrary but synthesizing co-principles necessarily immanent to any change. The actuality or perfection (entelechy) of the *energeia* is found in the result only in the measure of the receiving *dynamis*. This is why effects are not identical to, but similar-and-dissimilar to, their cause. They only participate in its perfection.

Aristotle's inference of *energeia* and *dynamis* may now appear to be of the *arthāpatti* type. This consists in reconciling two contrary features of a given reality by assuming either a sufficient or a necessary condition of their co-existence. In the first case, a choice between a variety of possible sufficient conditions imposes itself and the principle of parsimony generally determines that choice resulting only in a more or less high probability and revisability. This is the case of all the positive, whether physical or human, sciences. In the second case there is no such choice, but a most penetrating dialectic helped by discerning acumen and insight endeavours to determine not simply the formal but the ontological necessary conditions of the observed state of affairs. Such an endeavour characterises the metaphysical enquiry. The measures of its success are the intelligibility, coherence and adequacy of its conclusions. Being concerned only with necessary and not sufficient conditions, it cannot claim self-sufficiency in accounting for the state of affairs. It only accounts for the radical possibility of the facts and the solution of their apparent antinomies whereas it yields to the scientific enquiry the task of explaining their particular how and contents.

Applying this method to the *psychê*-phenomenon which is the field of all life-activities and passivities from the organic to the noetic, Aristotle determines that its most radical necessary condition must be a first entelechy whose actuating energy synthesizes with the pure potency of prime matter so that their very synthesis is an organic body endowed with whatever degree of life (cf. his definition of *psychê* in *Peri Psychês*, 412a20: "The first entelechy of a natural body in potency to possess life.") This then is the soul in general and there are various types of souls (and organic bodies) from the vegetable to the human since there are distinct levels of bodily life.

By naming this entelechy a soul we seem to hypostatize it and to fall back into Platonism. But no Aristotelian 'soul,' not even the human one, is a substance; for what Aristotle's *arthāpatti* led him to assume is not a separate entity mysteriously indwelling and animating a living body, but a co-principle, the life-providing *energeia*, essentially synthesizing with another co-principle, the prime *dynamis*, equally a non-substance. It is still the *raison d'être* of the body-subjectivity, of its vitality, centricity, and eventually of its interiority and consciousness, but it has no nature of its own apart from these functions. It is not an *ātman*, a *jīva* or a *puruṣa* and neither is it a pure *sākṣin*, *dṛś* or *jña*.

4. The Conception of Man

We may now ask, why was Aristotle so concerned to formulate the *psychê* in terms of pure reason? Why, more precisely, in terms of *energeia* and *dynamis* (act and potency)? What theoretic or practical value is to be found in this insistence, as against Plato, that *psychê* is not a complete 'it' but that 'by which we live' (ibid. 414a5), not an independent entity but the energetic, determining, constituent principle of a living *compositum*?

The answer to these questions lies in his historical situation. As a Greek of the fourth century BC, he felt himself claimed and challenged by two opposing worlds: the changeless world of *nous*, of Pure Thought, of Being, of Changeless Certainty, of 'Is'; and the world of sense-perception, of *Aisthêsis*, of Becoming, Instability, Change, of 'Seems.' On the one side, the world of Parmenides in which man was dissolved into the indivisibility of Being; on the other side, the world of Heraclitus in which man is a mere wave of the flux of change. The strife between the two worlds was no mere academic discussion; it was the initial struggle for the wholeness of man. Was man nothing but a field of opposing forces, and was his aspiration to transcend spatio-temporal processes an illusion? Or was he, contrariwise, nothing but the one Being, strangely involved in the unreal, weary wheel of purposeless becoming, from which his sole aspiration should be liberation?

Plato had inclined heavily towards the latter alternative. Somehow, unaccountably, man was involved in the world of sense perception but his true home was the realm of pure thought and eternal ideas. Man, in short, was not soul and body. Man was soul, and soul was the godlike *Nous*. The body was his unfitting prison-house or, at best, his steed.

Energeia and *dynamis* was Aristotle's rational answer to the dilemma of *Nous* or *Aisthêsis*, of Being or Becoming. It alone provided the terms of reference without which change remained unintelligible. Assumed first of all to make intelligible the changeful *psychê*-phenomenon, act and potency substituted 'Both-And' for the previous 'Either-Or' and preserved its complex integrality. They enabled Aristotle to see psychology on the one hand, and biology and physiology on the other, as concerned neither with two disparate fields of enquiry, nor yet with two purely subjective aspects of the same reality, but as concerned respectively with the determining and the potential constituents of the integral *humanum*. The explanation they command can still enable us to avoid the pitfalls of psychophysical parallelism, of psychological epiphenomenalism, those of a psychology which would restrict *psychê* to conscious mentation, and all *a priori* limitations which would banish the irrational and the unconscious from psychological consideration. As Wundt remarked in his *Grundzüge der physiologischen Psychologie* (4th ed. p. 633), "it is only the *psychê* conception of Aristotle, in which psychology is combined with biology, that issues in a plausible metaphysical conclusion for experimental psychology." Indeed, it enables us to see psychology as concerned with the whole man—as soul *and* body.

It was this vigorous affirmation of the flesh as being of the very essence of man which finally recommended the Aristotelian formula to Catholic Christianity. It was accepted notwithstanding Aristotle's hesitations concerning immortality, the denial—at least by most of his school—of the individuality[2] of *Nous*, and the absence from his later work of the 'other-worldly,' 'religious' qualities of Platonism which made the latter more congenial to Christian faith. Already Tertullian (160-230) in the *De Anima* (esp. ch. 4, 12) and others had in early times seen the incompatibility of Platonic 'spiritualism,' and the relative compatibility of Aristotle's hylemorphism, with the Gospel whose central message was that of man's psycho-physical integrity—the message of health or salvation (*salvus* comes from the same root as Skt *sarva* and Gk *holos*, entire, intact, whole, wholesome, healthy, integral) wrought in and through the flesh and the hope of glory through the full redintegration of man, soul and body. It was finally St Thomas with the Gospel in one hand and Aristotle in the other who could give both their due and show how the former could supply the insufficiencies of the latter.

He retained and secured even more firmly the holism of Aristotle's conception of man but completed it by establishing the 'other-worldly' dimensions of the human soul. Already Aristotle had been compelled by his very principles of Act and Potency to the conclusion, "summing up all that has been said about the *psychê*," that "the human *psychê* is in a sense the whole existing universe" (*Peri Psychês* 431b20). St Thomas expressed the rationale of this in his statement that "the intellect (*nous*) in act is the known in act" (*Summa Theologica* I, 87). In the actuation of thinking both the thinking 'I' and the things 'known' emerge, on reflection, as potencies to one unique and identical act of knowing and being known. Thus by passing from potency into act, the intellect (*nous*) opens up the limited individuality of man to the reality of the universe. And Aristotle consequently places the highest end of man in the perfect understanding and contemplation (*theoriâ*) of this reality. Man's bliss, he thinks, must consist in the highest activity of the soul's highest power, the *nous*, exercised on the highest objects and with the maximum of perfection and permanence "so far as this is possible" (*Nicomachean Ethics* X, 7 passim). But this seems to be a very aristocratic and seldom practicable ideal.

St Thomas preserves and amends the truth of Aristotle's view. There is, he shows, in the dynamic intellect an essential, natural desire (*jijñāsa*) for the perfect intuition of the highest Intelligible and in it of all others. This ineluctable desire plays even the chief role in his best argumentation that this supreme Intelligible exists as the *Deus simplex* (*nirguṇa*), Fullness of Being, Life, Knowledge and Happiness, and free, independent and total Cause of all other realities, whether spirits, or matter. Man's highest end, therefore, can only reside in the fulfilment of that desire for the Absolute which imbues the intellect and impels it to ever higher and higher intellections. But Thomas also shows that this fulfilment escapes the unaided power of man's intellect. Not because its potentiality would fall short of the Absolute but because the Absolute cannot be conquered by a finite intellect. Indeed, it is a constant datum of our experience that our finite intellect cannot pass into act unless it be informed (through the *pramāṇas*) about the objects to be known (*jñeya*). But with regard to the supreme *Jñeyam* (Intelligible) no *pramāṇa*, no worldly source of valid knowledge, can provide adequate information. They may provide correct pointers but these remain apophatic, God's Absolute remains the complete Mystery and man's most radical and co-essential desire seems destined to be ever frustrated.

Is this the ultimate answer? Is there no other possibility? There is, says St Thomas, the possibility of receiving gratuitously what we cannot conquer. Since the potentiality of the intellect for the intelligible is unlimited, it is thinkable that the Absolute itself, which is all intelligibility, may through a free and magnanimous self-surrender inform directly our intellect about Itself. In such an event, he says, God's very Infinite Essence would be communicated to our finite intellect not only as the Known of a blissful intuition but as that by which it is known. We would know the Absolute through its own Essence of Consciousness. And since "the intellect in act and the intelligible in act are one," we would truly become, not ontologically but epistemically, namely, through this perfect actuation of our intellect, God the Absolute itself.

As a Christian believer, St Thomas held that this God-dependent possibility was the supreme promise warranted by Christ. It supported his whole life as a scholar, a mystic and a saint and, we may believe, he at last reached its fulfilment.

5. Conclusion

This paper is only a bird's eye view of the method devised by Aristotle for investigating the *psychê*-phenomenon and of some important features of his conception of man as completed by St Thomas. His method is phenomeno-philosophical. Its problematics is not artificial but arises from an extensive observation and analysis of the phenomenon. This analysis does not result in mere units of description, classifications and valuational hierarchisation: it never loses sight of the field-unitariness of the phenomenon. Consequently, it is followed by a philosophical re-synthetization of the analysed data around an arthāpattic discovery of their immanent necessary conditions. The formulation of the theory of Act and Potency (*Energeia* and *Dynamis*) does not precede but emanates from this endeavour. It yields the important result that the *psychê* is to be viewed as the first entelechy in any life-manifesting body. Thus it cancels the myth of the soul imagined as an eternal, free substance mysteriously incarcerated in a body and alienated by the vicissitudes of the world of space and time.

Through his further special study of the human *psychê*, Aristotle arrived at a holistic understanding of man. It bridged over the gap between the intellect with its space-and-time transcending activities and the senses bound to time and space. Yet he remained uncertain about the capacity of the intellect to reach the fully transcendent Absolute. This uncertainty was overcome by Thomas Aquinas. Adopting and expanding both the method and the holistic psychology of Aristotle, he went on to explore more deeply the *nous*-phenomenon and discovered as pertaining to the very essence of the noetic dynamism a desire for intuiting the very Absolute of Godhead. He showed this desire to be constitutive of the intellect and, therefore, preconscious but at work at every point of the noetic activity. By itself alone this desire can only tend towards an achievement which it cannot conquer due to the very transcendence of the Absolute. Yet where conquering is impossible, receiving may achieve its goal. The One supremely free may surrender freely to man's desire.[3]

Notes

[1] [First published in the *Indian Philosophical Quarterly* 2/4 (July 1975) 307-318. It was reprinted, together with "The Discovery of the Person," "The Loss of the Person," and "The Rediscovery of the Person" (cf. above, chapters 3-5), as an abstract under the title *A Short History of the Person*. Permission to publish has been obtained from the *Indian Philosophical Quarterly* and is gratefully acknowledged.]

[2] [Substituting 'individuality' for 'individually.']

[3] I am very conscious that this paper has omitted so much that the picture it gives is quite incomplete and somewhat lopsided. It has stressed certain features at the expense of others. But this was intended to suggest that a holistic understanding of man is possible and that psychology need not be alienated from philosophy.

12

THE CHRISTIAN CONCEPTION OF MAN[1]

Hermeneutics, the search for meaning, which originally referred mainly to the interpretation of texts, extends today to the more problematic field of man's search for his own meaning. Though it is true that man was always a meaning-seeking animal, and that through his cultures and religions he gained a rich variety of understandings of himself, it seems undeniable that today he has become thoroughly problematic to himself in the very midst of that variety. His mental anguish is caused by the fear of his own meaninglessness not only as an individual but as a species.

Now religions, whatever else we find them to be, have everywhere been the providers of self-meaning for man as individual and as community. Through their teachings, rules and hopes, by way of their myths, symbols and rites, they have proposed and preserved patterns of meaning on the level of man's ultimate concerns. Christianity in particular, while being essentially focused on faith in the absolute God, stands by its very foundation, the "Logos made flesh and become as truly man as he is eternally God," for a definite conception of man, the universality and fruitfulness of which offer vistas ever contemplated anew and ever inspiring new experiments of man's life in community. This Christian conception of man has a unity which it is my task to present. At the same time I shall show, at least through some examples, the variety of approaches to its inspiring complexity.

1. The Biblical Conception of Man in the Old Testament

The books of the Bible are no systematic treatises of philosophy. Yet we can find in them fundamental themes which are subjacent to their narratives. Such themes are: man's wholeness as a person; his relationship with God in the covenant-community, his creatureliness; his responsibility; his hope for salvation despite his sinfulness.

(a) Man is a *living personal whole*. His being is not analyzed into heterogeneous components; he is not an aggregate of parts. Yet he presents various aspects, principally 'flesh,' 'soul' and 'spirit.' 'Flesh' (*basar*) is not something that he has but he is flesh (or flesh and blood) in the fragility of his living being. 'Soul' (*nefesh*) is not his vital principle but man is soul in the concrete manifestations of his vitality, especially those which emanate from his face, eyes, lips, hands and from his heart, the seat of knowledge and will. Again 'spirit' (*ruah*) is what he is insofar as the divine influence becomes specially manifest when inrushes of insight, wisdom, power, religious enthusiasm or poetic inspiration happen to him beyond the expected norm.

The significance of this integral view of man's being is shown by the fact that well-being or calamity affect the entire man as an indivisible whole. As 'whole person' in this sense, with 'will' as his definitive aspect, man does not 'have' a soul and body, he 'is' soul and body. Thus in the later period of the Old Testament the hope of salvation is expressed in terms of hope of the resurrection, i.e., of the divine redintegration of the whole man and the substitution of immortality for his mortality. The quite different idea of the immortality of the soul which appears briefly in the Book of *Wisdom* (2, 22; 3, 4) is of Greek provenance and is not developed in the rest of the Bible.

(b) Man as a being of flesh and blood is *socially involved* in family, tribal and national relationships. As *Adam*, the generic concrete term for the human being, he is *male and female*, complementary to each other but equal in creaturely dignity and called to share love and responsibility in monogamic union. Further it is from within his fellowship in society that he lives his relationship with God, the Lord of history, and feels committed to his fellow man in virtue of this relationship. The responsibility of man for man is especially inculcated by the prophets.

(c) The pattern of man's relationship with God is dominated by an awareness of his *creaturehood*, As a creature, he is not simply a product from dust but he owes his very existence and life to a creative command of God who made him in his own image and similitude by insufflating into him the 'spirit' thanks to which he stands out among all animals as gifted with speech and intelligence. Thus he is dominant among all creatures, worthy of respect even on the part of God, and his vice-gerent in the conduct of history. Marked with the dignity of a true person, he is addressed by God as 'thou' and in turn can address him as 'Thou.'

(d) As person, however deficient and dependent, man acts in his own right and has an inalienable *responsibility for his own acts*. Involved in partnership with God, he is not responsible *in vacuo* but before his Lord. Confronted with decisions to be taken individually or collectively, he is a responsible agent of historical change in the struggle against injustice, oppression and all kinds of evil. For he is *free*, not only *from* gross determinism, but *for* the triumph of values which are the marks of God's reign on earth. Man's single lifetime is not mere *chronos* but *kairos*, opportunity, the urgency of which is heightened by the certainty of inexorable death.

(e) Against this background of freedom and responsibility, man's refusals, betrayals, disobedience and pride project out in sharp relief. *Sin* is not a mere failing to conform, but an offense against God, a betrayal (often assimilated to adultery) of the loyalty expected to undergird man's relationship with God.

(f) In spite of man's sinfulness, he is carried onwards by *hope*. This hope of man is originally oriented towards a joyful, replete life on earth for the afterlife beyond death is too shadowy to attract. But with the increase of political calamities the later Biblical man deepens his consciousness of guilt and looks for a renewal of heart only from God; gradually there develops in him a hope for Salvation, for resurrection and new life, and this hope begins to acquire concretion in the slowly emerging image of a future *Messiah*, i.e., a God-anointed and thus appointed saviour.

2. The Biblical Conception of Man in the New Testament

In the New Testament, man stands in focus in the person of Jesus acknowledged as saving Messiah. Jesus as truly God-man integrates the whole mankind he saves into a mystical body of which he is the head. Let us consider, first, Jesus' vision of man and then its interpretation by Paul and John.

(a) *Jesus'* vision of man prolongs the views and hopes of the prophets but goes beyond them. He regards all men as called to a radical conversion through which they will be born again into divine sonship. He does not describe the nature of man in abstract terms but brings man to the crisis of decision and thereby to his authentic existence. True to the tenor of Old Testament, though, he situates man within the true sense of history which he divulges. It is with man as he exists in concrete history that he is concerned and it is this man that he addresses and endeavours to save. This emphasis on man in concrete history is clearly exemplified in Jesus' radical reinterpretation of the command to love one's neighbour. His parable of the good Samaritan who took care of his enemy, the Jew beaten half-dead by robbers, redefines 'neighbour' as any man in need, even one's enemy. Thus God's summons to the critical decision reaches man through the concrete demand presented to him by the continuous presence of all types of neighbours, friendly or inimical. By serving them in love he fulfils the duty of loving and serving God. And through this he attains the complete salvation exemplified by the resurrection of Jesus.

(b) *Paul*, in the perspective of this resurrection, makes more explicit the anthropology latent in the teachings of Jesus. He contrasts dialectically the man of flesh with the man of spirit. The first is what he calls the 'old' man, i.e., man as bound by self-seeking and sinful passions; the second is the 'new' man, namely, man as changed by his faith in Christ and transformed internally by the power of his saving grace. As 'new,' man enjoys the freedom of a child of God. In this freedom, all individual, social and national or sex distinctions lose their ultimate significance.

Although Paul takes over concepts from his Greek milieu, he adheres to the Biblical line of thought in refraining from speculative analysis of the components and properties of man.

He particularly resists Greek dualism through his emphasis on the hope for resurrection of the whole man. Among the Greek concepts he uses (*sôma*, body; *psychê*, soul; *pneuma*; spirit; *zoe*, life; *nous*, intellect; *syneidesis*, consciousness or conscience; *kardia*, heart; *sarx*, flesh; etc.), *sôma*, the most complex, and *sarx*, the most difficult, deserve attention.

Sôma, body, is not a part of man but describes the human person as a whole in his objective manifestation and in his relations with men, world and God. Man is *sôma*, but he is also *sarx*, flesh, when, a prey to his self-sufficiency and self-seeking, he alienates his self sinfully to the world in rebellion against God. Then he stands in a state of radical division which prevents him from achieving a free and integral existence. But 'flesh' can be 'put off' through conversion of heart, and 'body,' man as a physical whole, can be transformed at resurrection,

(c) For *John*, man belongs to the 'world' which is characterized as 'darkness,' the breeding-ground of lie and evil. But through the incarnation of the Logos this darkness is pierced and rent asunder by 'light' from above. Darkness resists and tries vainly to smother this light. Every man who avails himself of this invasion of light is mercifully drawn away from darkness and becomes 'reborn from above.' In his new existence he lives as a child of God, estranges himself from the world of lie and hatred, and finds a new home in the community of his love for all, a love no longer hampered by selfishness, hypocrisy or resentment.

3. The Development of the Christian Conception of Man

During the next centuries, these data of the Biblical revelation are assimilated as life-transforming and pondered upon in a common effort of 'faith seeking understanding.' This reflection develops within a community very much in contact with the dominating trends of the Greco-Roman world. In this reflective effort we may single out its adoption of the term 'person' and of the concept of immortal soul.

(a) The Roman courts of law have then begun to use the term 'person' to designate the subject of legal rights, i.e. the citizen as opposed to the slave who is still a non-person. The term, therefore, characterizes the kind of dignity which the law sanctions. The Christians get hold of this term to express the ontological dignity of the spiritual beings: the Father, Logos and Pneuma which are consubstantially One God, namely, the undifferenced spiritual Absolute whose perfect Godhead makes him worthy of unrestricted worship: and all human beings, whether male or female, citizens or slaves, because they are all created in his image and likeness, reverenced and loved by him, and called to share by grace in his very divinity. In adopting the term 'person,' Christians wish to convey all that our term spirit implies: transcendence over merely biological existence, intelligence reaching to the depths of mysticism, freedom, eternal validity, dignity, inviolability. But they inject into it the idea of wholeness. Personality is the property of the whole man, not only of the spiritual soul in him.

(b) Some later statements of the Bible have actually prepared them to adopt the Greek and especially the Platonic conception of the soul as a distinct spiritual principle in man. Many of them, like Origen, welcome it as the special bearer of spiritual life and immortality in man. But many others resist infeodation to it[2] because it threatens their holistic conception of man as totally loved and saved by Christ. It threatens also their conviction that the condemnation of the innocent Christ to death on a cross was a terrible crime and in general that death is for every man a physical evil since it deprives him, at least until resurrection, of his ontological wholeness. This would not be the case if whatever were worthy of dignity and eternal life in him would be a soul actually heterogeneous to the rest of his being. They, therefore, grope towards a different conception of the soul, that of a spiritual principle intimately connected with matter. Aristotle would be able to provide such a conception of the soul as substantial form of matter. But his writings will not become fully known, at least to Western Christianity, before the thirteenth century.

Although it is true, for instance, that St Augustine knows Aristotle's (and Porphyry's) writings on Logic and Ethics and relies on them in his treatise *On the Trinity*, they do not deeply help him to elaborate his conception of man which remains continuous with the Biblical one.

Rather, in his understanding of the latter, Augustine is influenced by the Neoplatonic insistence on the importance of the 'inner man.' Did not Plotinus say: "It is in the *nous* that we are mostly ourselves: that which comes before is ours [not we].... We are up there directing the animal from the top" (*Enneades* 1, 7, 7)? Augustine conjoins this view with the notion of wholeness:

> ...a man is not just a body, or just a soul, but a being made up of both body and soul.... The soul is not the whole man, but the better part of man; the body is not the whole, but the inferior part of man. *When both are joined together they have the name 'man' which, however, they do not either one lose when we speak of them singly.* Does holy Scripture follow no such usage? On the contrary it so thoroughly adopts it that even when a man is alive, and his body and soul are joined together, it calls each of them singly by the name 'man' speaking of the soul as the 'inner man' and of the body as the 'outer man' as if there were two men, although both together are one man.[3]

4. The Thomistic Elaboration of the Christian Conception

St Thomas Aquinas' access to the full Aristotelian Corpus allows him to strike a balance between Aristotelianism and Christian Platonism and to make good use of both in his teaching concerning man. Some main features of his doctrine may be presented here.

(a) First of all, St Thomas improves the notion of 'person' as follows. *'Person' means an integral, unitary, intelligent subsistent.* For instance, man taken in his wholeness of body and soul (= integral), as an individual subject (= unitary) existing in his own right by his own (however received) energy of being (= subsistent) and whose nature displays itself as source of rational and even highly intellectual, besides biological and animal, life is a person. God also verifies this definition which implies no limitation of perfection. Obviously man compared with God is a very inferior type of person: his very existence is his own but as received from the Creator; his wholeness is that of a compound liable to die; his unitariness is not that of a self-sufficient monad but of a limited individual very much in need of the society of his fellows; his intelligence is much like the sight of the owl, more adapted to the night of the material world than to the dazzling light of the spiritual realm and of the divine Absolute.

(b) From the definition of person St Thomas derives the properties which it implies in the case of man. Man's subsistence being a caused one, he is in his totality dependent on the source of all caused subsistence, i.e., he is a creature. He has his being in himself and for himself but not from himself. As intellectual creature he can develop his self-awareness down to the depth of his grounding and acknowledge that the Absolute is his uppermost and innermost source, support and end. To acknowledge this with admiration, gratitude and worshipful surrender is the essential act which makes man religious. Religion is thus inviscerated in the ontological core of man. Again because the metaphysical dimension belongs to authentic intellectuality, man can know beings as beings and the Godhead as absolute Being. And because intellectuality implies free-will and the capacity for love-surrender to persons, man is capable of universal love. Thus man can initiate, besides innumerable actions concerned with non-personal realities, acts of knowledge and love which found interpersonal relationships. Such acts and relations are valuable for their own sake and are thus ends in themselves. Man, their agent is therefore a being which, as agent and being, is an end in itself. If this is true, he never ought to be treated as a sheer means. Although as a member of a community of similar persons he is to subserve the common good, he cannot be reduced to being a mere cog in the machinery of society. And this society, instead of being an extensive organization for the exclusive production of material goods, requires to be an interpersonal community of justice, peace and love by which each member is helped to attain his self-fulfilment. For this he must be able to exercise his human rights, many of which are already defined by St Thomas. The mutual preservation of these rights commands a whole ethics which the latter develops extensively.

(c) What St Thomas calls the 'nature' of man is not a static datum as sometimes misunderstood. Rather, it is like a projecting bush of innate dynamisms which drive man towards fulfilment in the many directions of hierarchised needs: material welfare and biological security; sexual love, family affection and friendly fellowship; group security, social justice and peace; educational and cultural development; self-assertion and role-playing in society; share in responsibility and progress, spiritual values: truth, beauty, selfless love, holiness and ultimate salvation. The mutually competing urges of these dynamisms are bound to engender inner conflicts. But man's intellectual dynamism is sufficiently high to lead him to a recognition of their hierarchy, especially in the added light of Christian revelation, and through the exercise of his will helped by divine grace he can discipline himself. As a Christian teacher, St Thomas often urges man to attain that recognition and to discipline himself. He is vividly aware, of course, that man's harmonious development is constantly threatened by his pride, self-seeking, anger and sinful passions. But he also believes that divine grace is at work in the heart of every man to heal, absolve, direct and strengthen him. Christ's promise of salvation has established for every man a solid foundation of hope. It transforms man from a creature of anarchic desires into an assured pursuer of hope concerning his final fulfilment. Moreover, because this promise is not private but addressed to the community of man, it dynamises this whole community in its pursuit of the highest level of happiness.

Thus the Thomistic doctrine of man is radically optimistic. Better than the teaching of St Augustine it keeps the balance between earth and heaven, matter and spirit, individual and society, terrestrial sinfulness and call to divinization.

(d) At the centre of its holistic conception of the human person is the idea (inherited from Aristotle) of the substantial union between soul and body or, more correctly, soul and prime matter. The human soul is not a complete spiritual substance pre-existing to the body but a spiritual substantial form informing prime matter and thus constituting the essential unitary substance of man with all its powers and 'natural desires' as dynamically ready to act in the diverse ways characteristic of man. The union between human soul and individuating matter is neither illusory, nor accidental, nor merely instrumental, but substantial. It is not the extrinsic union of two substances but the intrinsic union of two complementary co-principles uniting as 'act' and 'potency' (Aristotle's *energeia* and *dynamis*). The one substance they compose exists in itself, i.e., by an energy of existence which is its own though it belongs primarily to the soul by right of dignity. This is why the human soul, even though deprived of its body by death, continues to subsist in immortality (since, being spiritual, it is simple and, hence, incorruptible.)

(e) Man as a creature, being totally caused by God in whatever is positive in him, depends also primarily on God in his knowing. God is the transcendent illuminer of his intellect. Yet, man's knowing is his own since as self-subsistent he is active in his own right. How does he know himself? Not as a mere object but as the total subject of his diverse activities. His conscious activities reveal to him not only their own happening and their objects but himself as their active subject. He has no demonstrable privileged access to the mystery of his own reality by which he would intuit it directly but he is self-aware through immediate reflectivity in and through his conscious activities. Thus he knows that he exists and at least confusedly what he is so that further reflection can enlighten him more and more about the rich complexity of his being. It is thus, indeed, that man's conception was elaborated by St Thomas though in the added light of the Christian revelation.

5. M. Scheler's Conception of the Human Person

By way of concluding I shall put forth a twentieth century conception, that of Max Scheler (1874-1928). In his *Formalism in Ethics and Non-Formal Ethics of Value*, translated by M.S. Frings and R.L. Funk (Evanston: Northwestern University Press, 1973), he writes: "The person is the immediately coexperienced *unity* of *experiencing*; the person is not a merely thought thing behind and outside what is immediately experienced." (371) "In opposition to Kant's attempt to deny the ego of individual experience and to degrade the meaning of this term by calling it a mere interconnection of experience in time attached to the idea of a merely logical subject, we must affirm the intuitive datum of an *ego of individual experience* as an incontestable *phenomenon*." (377) However, as all forms of 'transcendentalism' claim, the *individual* ego does not coincide with the '*empirical* ego,' if by the term *empirical* we mean the domain of observation and induction. Every individual ego possesses its 'essence' [as understood in phenomenology] and this essence is co-given *in all its empirical experience*, insofar as they are given fully and adequately. But this 'individual essence' is never accessible to any form of observation, nor is its cognition accessible to any kind of induction. Nevertheless, the intuition of its essence is the presupposition of all applications of laws of empirical psychology." (379) Hence, we must speak "of a *transcendental individual ego*, which is at the same time 'transempirical' but nevertheless a non-formal content of intuition. It is therefore by no means an unknowable thing, like Kant's *homo noumenon*, or a hypothetical one, like the soul-substance." (380)

"We can now enunciate the essential definition in the above sense: *the person is the concrete and essential unity of being of acts of different* [phenomenological] *essences* which in itself [...] precedes all essential act-differences (especially the difference between inner and outer perception, inner and outer feeling, loving and hating, etc.) *The being of the person* is therefore the 'foundation' of all essentially different acts." (33) "If an act-essence is to be concrete, its full intuitible givenness *presupposes* a reference to the essence of the *person*, who is the executor of acts." (383-384)

"Surely the person *is* and experiences himself only as a being that *executes acts*, and is in no sense 'behind' or 'above' acts [...] like a point at rest. For all of this is a picture taken from the spatiotemporal sphere and it [...] always leads to a substantialization of the person [as a static X 'behind' the acts]. But the *whole person* is contained in *every* fully concrete act, and the whole person '*varies*' in and through every act—without being exhausted in his being in any of these acts and without changing, like a thing in time. [....] For this very reason there is no necessity for an *enduring being* that subsists [statically...] in order to safeguard the 'identity of the individual person.' Identity lies solely in the qualitative direction of this pure becoming different. [....] By way of images we can say that the person lives *into* time and executes his acts into time in becoming different. But the person does not live within phenomenal time [...] nor in the objective time of physics. [....] Because the person lives his existence precisely in the *experiencing* of his possible *experience*, it makes no sense to try to grasp the person in past lived experiences. As long as we look only at the so-called experiences and not at their *being* experienced, the person remains completely transcendent [...]. But, on the other hand, a glance at the person himself and his essence yields a peculiarity for every act that we know him to execute." (385-386)

"An *act* is never an object. No matter how much knowledge we have of an act, our reflecting on its naive execution (in the moment of such execution or in reflective, immediate memory) contains nothing like the objectification which marks, e.g., all inner [...] observation. If an act can therefore never be an object, then the *person* who lives in the execution of acts can *a fortiori* never be an object. The only and exclusive kind of givenness of the person is his *execution of acts* (including the execution of acts reflecting on acts). It is through this execution of acts that the person experiences himself at the same time." (386-387)

"If one understands *psychology* [...] as a science of objective happening [...] in inner perception, everything that deserves the name *act* as well as everything that deserves the name *person*, must, for this reason, remain transcendent to psychology." (387) "Our claim that acts (and especially the person) do not belong to the psychic sphere does not imply that they are physical. We maintain only that both act and person are psychophysically *indifferent*. We are not at all troubled by the old Cartesian alternative, which requires that every thing be either psychic or physical. [....] Still we use the term *mind* / *Geist* for the entire sphere of acts (following our procedure of many years). With this term we designate all things that possess the nature of act intentionality, and fulfilment of meaning, wherever we may find them. This of course implies at once that all mind is by essential necessity '*personal*,' and that the idea of a '*non-personal mind*' is contradictory. But no 'ego' at all belongs to the essence of mind, and hence no division between '*ego and outer world*.' It is, rather, the person that is the single and necessary existential form of mind insofar as we are concerned with concrete mind." (389)

"The use of the word *person* in *language* already reveals that the form of unity meant by this term has nothing to do with the form of unity of the 'consciousness'-object of inner perception or consequently the 'ego' [as opposed to a 'thou' or to the 'outer world']. For *person*, unlike these terms, is an absolute, not feelably *relative*, name. [....] The 'I' does not speak. The man does. All of this clearly shows that *person* means something that is completely indifferent to the oppositions 'I-thou,' 'psychic-physical,' and 'ego-outer world.' [....] It *belongs to the essence of the person* to exist and to live solely in the execution of intentional acts. The person is therefore essentially never an 'object.'" (389-390)

This precis in Scheler's own words may suffice to show the homogeneity of the achievement of this Christian phenomenologist with the earlier Christian elaborations of the notion of 'person.' His phenomenological method differs from that of St Thomas but like him he holds that the person can only be self-grasped in and through the execution of its acts, that it is not an object but the total, self-subsistent and dynamic concrete subject co-experienced in the experience of the exercise of its intentionalities, that as origin and foundation of experience it is an absolute, that it is spiritual or intellectual (*geistig*), that it is thus trans-temporal, trans-historical and irreducible to spatiotemporal categories. I have no room here to show the incidences of his central conception with regard to 'lived body,' community, history, world, ethics and values but there also his views confirm in a modern and welcome fashion the soundness and consistency of the Christian tradition regarding the conception of man.

Notes

[1] [First published in *Southern Chronicle* **8**/1 (1982) 21-27; subsequently reprinted in two parts under the titles "The Biblical Concept of a Human Person," *Ignis* **19** (1990) 59-64, and "The Christian Concept of a Human Person," *Ignis* **19** (1990) 127-130, with the omission of the last part, '5. M. Scheler's Conception of Human Person.' Permission to publish has been obtained from the Editors of both *Southern Chronicle* and *Ignis*, and is gratefully acknowledged.]

[2] [The 1990 text drops "infeodation to it".]

[3] Augustine, *The City of God* 13, 24, 2. [Italics added by De Smet.]

13

THE CONCEPT OF MAN IN THOMISM AND NEO-THOMISM[1]

1. The Teaching of St Thomas Aquinas

The initial question with which St Thomas Aquinas starts his *Summa Theologiae* is, "what kind of discipline is Christian theology and what does it treat about?" His answer is that Christian theology is the rational investigation of God's revelation culminating in Jesus Christ. The purpose of this revelation being the fulfilling salvation of all men, its contents comprise whatsoever truth this end requires. That is to say, not only those divine truths which cannot be known otherwise than through testimony and thus stand beyond the grasp of philosophizing reason, but even many religious matters which the human reason is able to investigate but only with great difficulty, for instance, the very existence and essence of God, the immortality of the human soul, etc. Such truths, indeed, while directly relevant to the salvation of all men, could be attained philosophically "only by few, and even so after a long time and mixed with many mistakes."[2]

The distinction between philosophy and Christian theology is stated unambiguously: "philosophy is founded on the natural light of reason" whereas "Christian theology is founded on the light of faith" (*Commentary on Boethius'* De Trinitate 2, 3). Nevertheless, as a theologian St Thomas defends his right of using philosophy ancillarily ('as a handmaid') in his proper task of 'faith seeking understanding' and of including a whole world of philosophical truths under the perspective of revelation without their being adulterated thereby. In particular, his teaching concerning man is part and parcel of his theological works and is yet chiefly philosophical.

1.1 Man includes both matter and spirit in his substantial unity

> *Man exists on the brink of two worlds, the spiritual and the corporeal, combining the qualities of both; he is their horizon, their common frontier.* (*In III Sententiae*, prologue)

The consideration that man is a frontier being has a respectable pedigree. It appears first in Plato's *Timaeus* 35a, where the soul is described as the centre point between the variable and the invariable, the divisible and the indivisible. Again Philo of Alexandria views man as the frontier being (*methorion*) situated on the confines of both mortality and immortality. For Plotinus, the soul is located on the extreme edge of the intelligible world bordering on the sensible. Existing thus in the middle place (*mesēn taxin*), it is 'amphibious' (*amphibios*), i.e., it leads a double life that belongs to both spheres, the intelligible and the sensible. And, according to its behaviour, it either spiritualizes or temporalizes itself more and more. Simplicius too compares it to those animals which can live both on land and in water, because it is in the centre of reality. He even calls it the link which joins the two parts of reality. This illustrates the wide range of meaning of the term 'frontier' (*methorion*): its meaning is both metaphysical and ethical. Other Neo-Platonists, Damascius, Priscian, Hierocles, and the *Corpus Hermeticum* too, support this doctrine. But it is important to note that for both Plato and the Neo-Platonists it is not man himself but the soul which is the 'in-between' of reality and ensures its unity.

On the contrary, for the Christian writers of the fourth century who adopt this theme, man is the intermediary bond. It is so in four important passages of Gregory of Nyssa (PG 44, 181 B-C; 45, 25 B-26 B; 45, 52 D; and *Contra Eunomium* 3, 121) and it is discussed in detail by Nemesius of Emesa in his *De Natura Hominis* ch. 1. For the latter it is thanks to man that the universe is a coherent entity. "Man," he writes, "is that living being which unites in itself the mortal and the immortal, the rational and the irrational creatures, collating and bearing in its own nature the image of the whole creation and on that account being called the microcosm." These ideas are found repeated in many other writings up to St Thomas and are one of the favourite topics discussed after him by the authors of the Renaissance whose chief concern is to establish the privileged position of man in the hierarchy of creation and to exalt his dignity.

Again, after the upheavals of the turn of the eighteenth century, the theme of man the microcosm reappears. The young minds of the *Sturm und Drang* period yearn for a philosophy which should embrace the whole creation as a unity and at the same time open a way to infinity. "Through the ego leads the vast stairway, from the lichens on the rocks to the seraphs." This yearning leads many to a rediscovery of Thomism as a philosophy that should prove more satisfactory than its modern rivals in answering even modern questions. And so, about a century ago, Neo-Thomism like a reborn phoenix shakes its wings and soars up to the heights of the philosophical sky.

But, if the theme of man as the horizon in which the meeting of the spiritual and the material realms takes place and as the microcosm that links into one the macrocosmic totality of creation is as old as Platonism and Neo-Platonism, what is it that is original in its handling by St Thomas?

In order to perceive this, we have to see how he developed it under the perspective of Christian revelation. And to see this, we have for a moment "to live with the great debates of the early Church, when the 'Word became flesh' was translated into 'God's Logos became a man' or the axiom that nothing was healed by Christ that was not assumed by him. To maintain this position against Marcion and the Manichees had meant accepting man's vegetable life as an essential part of him. Against Arius and Apollinaris, it had meant understanding man as at once body, soul and spirit, a *natural* unity of the spiritual and the psychical and the physical. Against the Monophysites it had meant making it clear that Christ, like man, has one existence but not, like man, one nature only. The technical terms, the linguistic precision tools, with which the early Councils lifted the Christian system clear of confusions are the terms that govern the Thomistic analysis of man: substance, nature, person, subsistence, reason, will."[3] The Council's proclamation was that Jesus Christ is one divine Person subsisting in two integral natures, the divine and the human, without any adulteration of either or commixture of both, and, against differing opinions, they had made it clear that as man he not only has a genuine human soul but all the powers too of such a soul: intellect, will, senses, affectivity and the life-powers by which it animates matter into an individual human body which is integral to his human nature. Thus like every man he is a microcosm and a frontier being but, as the incarnated Son of God the Father, he is the horizon and the bridge between the created macrocosm and the uncreated Divinity.

It is in the light of this Christology that St Thomas upholds the holistic unity of man as soul and body and refuses any Platonic dualism in his anthropology. But it is with the help of Aristotle's key-conception of actuality (*energeia* or *entelecheia*) and potency or potentiality (*dynamis*)[4] that he establishes this non-dualism philosophically. However, whereas Aristotle had not in practice extended the range of these notions beyond the domain of essence, St Thomas analyses with their help the whole ontological realm of essence and existence. Since actuality means perfection or entelechy of any sort, it must designate not only the enhancing results of actions and, in every essence, the determining components which Aristotle named forms, whether substantial or accidental, but also in every being the immanent cause of its being or existing, that energy or *energeia* in it by which its essence obtains the rank of actual reality. This is referred to in every existential judgment by the verb 'to be' (in Latin, *esse*), i.e., by 'is' not as mere copula but in its strong sense as 'exists' or 'subsists.' 'To subsist,' says St Thomas, means not simply 'to be there' but 'to exist by one's own *esse*, by one's own energy of being.' This must be thought of not as an abstract 'is-ness' (*astitā*) but as the energy proper to every existent as such and of which its several partial energies or powers are but specifications. It does not pertain to the category of nouns but of verbs. It is not logical but ontological, not static but energetic.

The existential unity of man is the internal unity of two co-principles, his energizing *esse* or 'is' by which he subsists and his *human essence* by which he is man as to his species and this individual man according to his becoming. These two unite as actuality and potency. Neither pre-existing entities nor existence in their own right, they are internal co-causes (not of the efficient or the final types but of the Aristotelian formal and material types) whose common effect is the concrete human person. As potency, the essence is receptive of the *esse* but limits it to its own specific rank, whereas the *esse* as actuality causes it to be real.

Now the human essence is not a pure form but a particular corporeal substance. As particular, it does not exhaust all the possibilities of its specific degree: it is not humanity but only *a* human essence distinct from other similar ones. This particularity or individuality is the sign and the effect of another internal composition, that of *substantial form* and *prime matter*. Since this kind of individuality means imperfect specific realization, it must be resulting from two co-principles again of the actuality and potency types. The first must be an internal cause of specific determination, i.e., a substantial form; and the second the internal cause of indetermination which Aristotle named prime matter. Prime matter while receiving that form 'indetermines' it. The common result of their synthesis is therefore a substance that is human but only somehow, so that as subsistent by its own *esse* it is this or that particular man, an individual among others of the same species.

It should already be clear that this metaphysical explanation of man in terms of *esse* and essence, substantial form and prime matter, accounts for his internal dynamism. Man is a being of tension on two levels; first, owing to the mutual complementarity and contrariety of the co-principles of his essence, he endeavours unceasingly to become more and more perfectly human (though humanity as such remains the unattainable limit of this endeavour); second, due to the contrariety-in-complementarity of his *esse* and his essence, the co-principles of his being, he strives towards the universality of being (and of its equivalents, the actual, the true, the good, etc.); in this case, the limit of his striving is God, the subsistent *Esse* or Fullness of being.

Man exercises this twofold teleology through his operations which actuate his dynamism on several levels from the physical and the organic to the sensible and the spiritual. This variety of activities constitutes his actual existence. As their agent, he is called *person*. As the radical principle of determination of these activities, his essence is called his *nature*. Their proximate principles of determination are called his *powers* or *faculties*: physical, vital, sensible and intellectual or spiritual. The substantial form in his essence/nature, when here considered as the inner mover of these powers, is called *soul* (the inner principle of life of whatever degree) and, more precisely, the *human soul* or the *spiritual soul*. The diagram given at the next page sums up man's ontological composition.

Thus man is complex but internally one. Of all the types of unity in complexity, none is stronger than that which obtains between a potency and the actuality that actuates it. The human person's inner unity of his *esse* and essence is sometimes called hypostatic (= personal) union. The inner unity of his essence as a substance composed of spiritual soul and prime matter is called *substantial union.*

Below the level of man, what results from the union of a substantial form and prime matter is either (1) a unit of concrete matter, a physical substance or body, or (2) a unit of living matter, a vegetable substance or organic body, in which case the substantial form is called a vegetative soul, or (3) an animal substance or body endowed with some sense knowledge and affectivity owing to its animal soul, or (4) a rational animal, a man, i.e., a superior animal substance or body endowed with properly intellectual knowledge and free will owing to its being animated by a spiritual soul. In each case the substantial form is one and is responsible for the lower as well as for its own specific activities of concrete existence. "To be," says St Thomas, "does not mean simply to be there but, in the case of living beings, to live, in the case of animals, to have a sense life, and, in the case of human beings, to have a life of intellectual activities, etc." (*In* De Anima 2, 7; *S.Th.* I, 18, 2; etc.) "We should assert that the mind (the soul as intellectual: cf. *De Veritate* 19, 1, ad 14), the principle of intellectual activity, is the form of the human body.... Indeed, that which is the first principle of vital activities in the various grades of living beings is the soul. For by soul primarily we take nourishment, feel, move about, and also understand. Call it mind or intellective soul, this principle is the form of our body. If anyone wishes to deny this, let him explain how otherwise he can attribute the activity of understanding to the individual man. Everybody experiences in himself that it is veritably himself who understands." (*S.Th.* I, 76, 1, c)

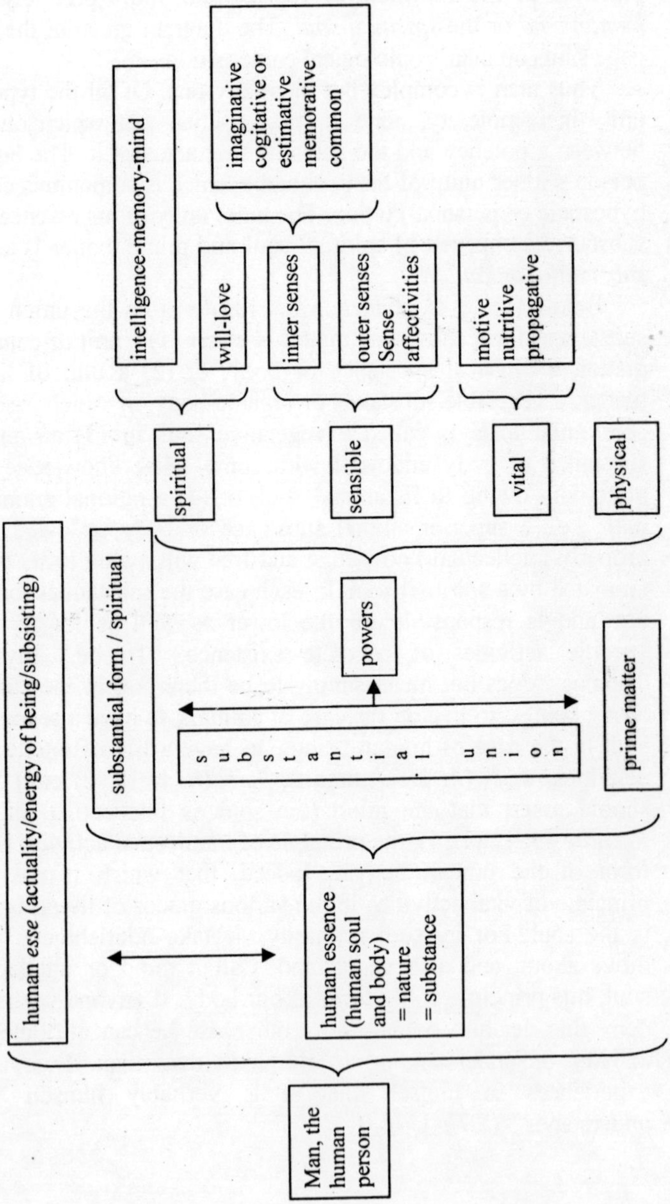
Man, the human person
human *esse* (actuality/energy of being/subsisting)
human essence (human soul and body) = nature = substance
substantial form / spiritual
substantial union
powers
prime matter
spiritual
sensible
vital
physical
intelligence-memory-mind
will-love
inner senses
outer senses Sense affectivities
motive nutritive propagative
imaginative cogitative or estimative memorative common

This call to self-experience will be the *leit-motiv* of my second section. For the unity of man's integral being and the all-pervading role of his intellective soul, which so far have simply been exposed, must now be established on the ground of his self-knowledge.

1.2 Man knows himself and his soul in knowing other things

> *When I know a material object, say a stone, I at the same time know that I know it, and the nature of my act of knowing it, and myself as knowing it. And when I want it, I know that I want it, and the nature of my act of wanting it, and myself as wanting it.* (*S.Th.* I, 87 passim)

It is a well considered opinion of Aristotle and St Thomas that we know nothing through simple intuition (in the strict sense of immediate knowledge of essence). We know things only insofar as they impinge on us through their activities, for instance, by reflecting light upon our retinas. They do not thereby make our knowledge but we make it on the occasion of their impact. The latter is not cognitional but chemico-physical and as such causes a modification of the same chemico-physical order in the organs of our outer senses, not in the senses themselves. This modification begins to be interpreted by our five outer and four inner senses, namely, the first which is called common because it is immediate to all the outer senses, then the imaginative, the cogitative (called estimative on the level of mere animals) and the memory-sense (cf. *S.Th.* I, 78, 3, c). These are, therefore, not to be likened to passive mirrors for they are actively receptive. The interpretation they have initiated is perfected by the active intellect, that power of our spiritual soul which immediately pervades them. This interpretation may be understood as a kind of reading:

> To understand, *intelligere*, is as it were to read within, *intus legere*. Indeed, 'understanding' implies a certain intimate knowing.... Intellective knowledge penetrates as far as the essence of a thing, its goal being, according to Aristotle's *De Anima* III, 6, 430b27, what a thing really is. Now this essence or 'within' which a man's knowledge should penetrate can be of many types. For under the accidents of a thing lies its substantial nature; under words lies what they signify: under likenesses and figures lies the truth which they represent; in some way also intelligible realities lie within outwardly experienced objects of sense; and so do effects in

causes, and conversely. Accordingly we can speak of 'understanding' (*intellectus*) in all such cases. (*S.Th.* II-II, 8, 1, c)

One of those "intelligible realities which lie within outwardly experienced objects of sense" is our own inner self and, in particular, our soul. Of this also we have no simple intuition; otherwise there would be no dispute about its existence and its essence. Yet we have a certain habitual knowledge of it. How is it obtained? Here too we must say, through its activities or, more precisely, its operations. The two terms are often used as equivalents by St Thomas but at times he distinguishes them carefully: "Action properly speaking designates that kind of activity by which an agent modifies an external object, for instance, by shedding light on it; whereas operation is that kind of activity which does not pass outward but is immanent to an agent as its own endowment, for instance, shining." (*De Veritate* 8, 6, c) Accordingly, he says, the activities of the senses and of the understanding (*intellectus*) being thus immanent are, in the propriety of terms, operations. The human soul, therefore, is known by its operations:

> Our intellective soul knows itself, not by its own essence, but by way of its operations. (*S.Th.* I, 87, 1, c).
>
> Because in its present life our intellect is connaturally occupied with material, sensible things, it follows that it knows itself through its actuation by representations abstracted from such things by the light of the agent intellect. (Ibid.)

In the same act in which I know a material object, say a stone, I know the act by which I know it and my intellect that knows it but there is a logical order of those cognitions:

> What is first known by the human intellect is this object; then, in the second place the act by which the object is known is itself known; and, finally, by way of the act, the intellect, of which the act of understanding is the perfection, is itself known. (*S.Th.* I, 87, 3, c)

We have here a duplicate of Prabhākara's *triputi-pratyakṣa-vāda*, itself probably a Brahmanic adaptation of the Buddhistic law of simultaneous apprehension (*sahopalambha niyama*). For St Thomas also, the intellective soul is not a self-luminous essence since it is not always actually self-known, but as soon as it perceives an object it comes to know itself by way of that very perception. Is this indeed not attested by our own experience?

Self-knowledge is, first of all, a particular event, "as when a man perceives himself to have an intellectual soul from the fact that he perceives himself to be actually acting. Then, there is the abstract and universal knowledge of the intellectual soul which is obtained when we consider philosophically the nature of the human intellect from the nature of this intellect's operations." (*S.Th.* I, 87, 1, c)

> There is a difference between these two kinds of knowledge. For, in order to have the first kind of knowledge of the intellect the very presence of this intellect is sufficient, since it is the principle of the operation by means of which the intellect perceives itself. Thus it is said to know itself by being present to itself. To have the second kind of knowledge of the intellect, however, mere presence is not sufficient, and a diligent, subtle inquiry is needed. Many, for this reason, are simply ignorant of the soul's nature and many are positively mistaken about it. This is why St Augustine traces the way of this inquiry when he says, *Let the mind not strive merely to see itself as if it were an absent object, but strive to discern itself as present subject*, i.e., to know how it differs from other realities, which is to know its whatness and nature. (*S.Th.* I, 87, 1, c)

This inquiry is a philosophical introspection in the form of a complete reflection of the mind upon itself. But this reflective turning back to oneself would be impossible were there not an immediate complete reflection of the mind in any of its intellective operations. The philosophy of mind does not discover it as an object previously absent to the philosopher but discriminates it as the subject already present to itself. It does not infer it as Kumārīla Bhaṭṭa's *jñātatāvāda* or even as in Descartes' pseudo-inference '*Cogito ergo sum.*' No, St Thomas says that the philosophical enquiry is preceded by the philosopher's perception of his own soul present as knowing subject in any one of its intellectual perceptions of an object. This self-perception, however, is enveloped in the object-perception; attention to the object leaves it in the margin of its field; but it can attend to it if we decide to introspect it. Thus the *immediate complete reflection* which puts us in possession of the two poles, knowable and knower, of our knowing makes possible the philosophical and *mediate complete reflection*.

> It is by the soul itself that we know that it exists because we are conscious of it by perceiving its activity; then we go on to explore its nature by a scientific study of its operations and objects. Similarly, as regards its powers endowments and habits, we know that they exist because we perceive their activities; but to know their characteristics we must ascertain them by the properties of these activities. (*SCG* 3, 46).

The valid sources of knowledge or *pramāṇas* accepted by St Thomas are perception, inference of diverse kinds, and testimony. Beyond this classification, there is the more radical one of the acts or operations of the intellective soul: judgment, simple apprehension and reasoning, not to speak of doubting, questioning, etc. The first even in time and the most important is judgment because it is directly concerned with reality about which it makes an assertion (either affirmative or negative) which is either true or untrue. Simple apprehension is often considered as first because it is simpler but, at least in time, it is really second. It is the apprehension of an idea or concept in isolation from the judgment in which at least our first ideas originate. In its perfect degree it is definition which in its expression resembles the judgment; however, definition is not either true or untrue but only either correct or incorrect. Logical truth is defined as conformity of the intellect with reality and, therefore, can only be found in the judgment which alone is the act in which I make a pronouncement about a reality and thus commit myself intellectually in regard to it.

Judgment, not as a piece of language but as an intellective operation and, more precisely, perceptual judgment, is the real and sufficient starting point of metaphysics. Why? Because in its very structure we find at work the first principles of identity, contradiction, etc. and the primordial ideas of being, true, existence, essence, etc. which are subjacent to any metaphysics worthy of the name. It is particularly basic to the metaphysics of the human self and of its soul since, as we have already seen, their very perception is obtained as *at work* in it.

If I explore any of my perceptual judgments, I shall realize that it is very complex in its making. The complexity which Kant investigated in his *Critique of Pure Reason* through a transcendental analysis is similarly analyzed by St Thomas. There is, first, the fact that the judging intellect is actively receptive, hence, that we must distinguish the receptive or passive or possible intellect, which is ultimately actuated by truth and the factive or active or *agent intellect*, which processes the data for the assertion of truth. This assertion, however, has an intelligibility, a universality and a necessity which transcend material particularity. Hence, judging implies the collaboration of outer senses immediately receptive of the particular datum and of inner senses that elaborate it into a sensible representation or image. It is this image which the agent intellect reads, as it were, thus producing an intellectual interpretation of it. This is called concept or idea and is said to result from an abstraction of the first, second or third degree, since it abstracts more or less completely from the materiality of the image. The power of the agent intellect which forms it is called light. By its light the agent intellect is said to illumine the sensible representation or to read its within (*intus-legere*), which actually means to interpret it according to the categories of being which are constitutive of the intellective power. Finally, this interpretation-concept as related to the sense-representation from which it has originated is, as it were, presented to the receptive intellect which pronounces the judgment. All this and the de-materialization it comprises would be impossible if the intellect did not pervade the sense-powers and were not immaterial.

Now the best explanation of this pervasion and of the continuity of the intellective power with the sense-powers is that they equally belong to the same soul and that this is the substantial form of the sensing body.

This body could not be sensing if it were not living but of the vital powers we have hardly any immediate perception and know them through an observation which is quasi-external as is also our observation of our body as a physical reality. Yet, we are aware that we are the same man who understands, who senses, who lives, who moves, etc. As St Thomas says, "everybody experiences in himself that it is veritably himself who understands, etc." (*S.Th.* I, 76, 1, c)

The substantial unity of man is a unity-in-complexity since materiality cannot be reduced to spirituality. Hence, the idea common to Aristotle and St Thomas that this one substance is compounded of two co-principles, prime matter and its substantial form, the spiritual soul. The soul is spiritual because it is intellectual and, therefore, simple. This simplicity is directly inferred from the soul's capacity of complete reflection which has been explained above. But this ontological simplicity does not prevent the soul from having a diversity of powers, intellectual, sensitive, appetitive, etc. It is by investigating them that we come to know the high perfection of the soul and, hence, of man. Let us now turn to the powers of appetition which St Thomas enumerates as: appetite in general, emotion, will and choice. (*S.Th.* I, 80 prologue)

1.3 Man adheres to the good by desire, free-choice and interpersonal love

> *Man has free choice, otherwise counsels, exhortations, precepts, prohibitions, rewards, and punishments would all be pointless.* (*S.Th.* I, 83, 1, c)

> Appetition or propensity follows form. Things without knowledge possess only one form limiting them to one condition of natural being. The resulting propensity is called natural appetite. But, in things that can know, forms exist more perfectly for they can receive the forms of other things; this is why above the natural propensity they evince another one, termed the animal appetite, resulting from perception and tending to an object, not merely because it is congruous to this or that power, as colour to sight or music to the ear, but also because it is wanted by the whole organism. (*S.Th.* I, 80, 1, c and ad 3)

> This *animal* or *sensitive appetite* is one generic power but is divided into two kinds, namely, the concupiscible and the irascible. By the former the soul works according to the pain-pleasure principle; by the latter it deals with emergency reactions. The irascible is as it were, the champion of the concupiscible, attacking what hinders pleasure or inflicts harm. Anger starts from desire and leads to it. (*S.Th.* I, 81, 2, c)

> Reason governs the emotional life not despotically but by manner of civil life, because like a free citizen the sensitive appetite has something of its own and thereby can resist the commands of the reason. For of its nature it is swayed, not only by the particular reason guided by the universal reason, but also by the imagination and the senses. We experience a resistance when we imagine something pleasant forbidden by the reason or something unpleasant commanded by the reason. (*S.Th.* I, 81, 3, ad 2)

The *rational appetite* is called *will*. "An activity from within and with some knowledge of purpose—that is the mark of voluntary action. But there is a twofold knowledge of an end, imperfect and perfect. Imperfect knowledge is merely perceiving a goal without understanding of purpose as such or of the adaptation of means to ends; animals enjoy that kind of knowledge through their senses. Perfect knowledge requires more namely, understanding of the meaning of purpose and of the relation of means to ends; it is proper to an intelligence. Hence, the complete character of voluntary activity, endowed with deliberation and freedom, is found in rational natures alone." (*S.Th.* II-I, 6, 2, c)

St Thomas frequently notes the difference between knowledge and appetition. They are the only two possible forms of the active relation of a subject to an object. In knowledge, the subject 'becomes intentionally' the object by getting hold of its meaning and thus actuating himself by its truth; in appetition, the subject goes out to the object itself after apprehending it as somehow good and thus tries to actuate himself by its goodness or value. Even in volition proper, which works through intellectual knowledge, the attraction is for a reality more than for a meaning and a truth. Of course, the intellect is dynamised by its own 'natural appetite' for the truth, which thus is its good and goal, but this good is precisely truth, i.e., not the object simply in its actuality but the intellect's conformity to it. On the contrary, what dynamises the will is its natural appetite for the good as such, i.e., for the object simply in its actuality or positivity of being for it is in virtue of this positivity that it is desirable.

But, if the will itself is driven by a 'natural appetite,' is it not moved to choice from necessity? Simply speaking, no, because by its natural dynamism it is only inclined towards good in general so that any thing revealed as good by the intellect is presented to its possible choice. Yet, it is also polarized towards man's supreme happiness which consists in man's apprehension of the supreme good, God. This is man's last end. And, obviously, he will of necessity cleave to this perfect happiness once he can apprehend the very essence of God, the absolute Good, intuitively and without any veil or indirection. But, precisely because only that can necessitate his will, the latter remains free with regard to any particular and imperfect good. And, says St Thomas, "before God's connexion with our perfect happiness strikes us in the certitude of vision, our will does not cleave to God of necessity." (*S.Th.* I, 82, 2, c)

"If the object proposed by knowledge is not universally and in every respect good, then the will is not moved of necessity.... Particular goods which fall short of some goodness... can be adopted or rejected by the will." (*S.Th.* II-I, 10, 2, c) Let us still note that "wishing and choosing are from the same faculty of will. The will and the freewill are not two powers, but one." (*S.Th.* I, 83, 4, c)

Just as the intellect is intimate to the senses and depends on them, so the will pervades the sensitive appetite or sensuality and is affected by its passions. It is, indeed, this lowest form of desire which is the seat of passions. They are its intensest movements; and it is through them that man experiences most strongly, sometimes most tragically, that he is not a pure Intelligence but the union of a soul and a body. If we consider the whole of the human appetite when it is confronted with some desirable object, we observe that it is modified by it in such a way that it takes pleasure in it. This is an immediate experience of affinity and complementarity. This pleasure or complacency (*complacentia*) is what constitutes love as a passion. Scarcely is it produced that it arouses a movement of the appetite towards possessing, not merely a representation, but the real object itself. This is the desire born of love. If it reaches its end, it reposes in the possession of the object loved. Such repose is joy, the satisfying of desire. (Cf. *S.Th.* II-II, 26, 2, c)

The passion of love, in the proper sense of the term, is encountered on the level of vital and organic desire. It is only by extension that the term 'love' is generalized to include the higher appetition of the will. The complacency of a will in its object is called *intellectual love*. Man's love is both sensual and intellectual and, as such, it is a matter of freewill having to control the wild spontaneousness of a passion. Love as a free choice is called *dilection*. If its object is esteemed of great worth, it is called '*charity*' (*caritas*, in Greek *agape*), i.e., cherishing, which is from person to person. (Ibid. 3, c) If this love has become a lasting disposition of the soul, a 'habit', it is called *friendship*. Often mixed with coveting (*concupiscentia*) it is, however, distinct from it. Friendship is towards persons apprehended as ends-in-themselves, i.e., beings whose intrinsic goodness and worth is not reducible to another. Coveting is towards things viewed as means that can subserve the coveter's desire.

> Not every love has the quality of friendship. In the first place it is reserved to that love for another which wills his well-being. When what we will is not the other's good for his sake, but the desire of it as it affects us, that is not friendship, but self-regarding love and some sort of concupiscence. Neither does benevolence suffice for friendship; in addition a mutual loving is required, for friend is friend to friend. This interplay of well-wishing is founded on companionship. (*S.Th.* II-II, 23, 1, c)

The effect of friendship is affective union, spiritual intimacy, treating the friend as another self. A curious transference of personalities accompanies this love. The beloved is, as it were, in the lover and the lover in the beloved by knowledge and by desire. The lover seeks to penetrate by thought to the heart of his beloved and finds joy in his presence. Whatever good or evil befalls one of the two friends, befalls the other as well. Perfect love allows but one life to subsist for two beings. Each can speak of his 'self' and his 'other self'. (Cf. *S.Th.* II-I, 28, 2, c)

Another way to put it is to say that love is ecstatic. It transports the lover out of himself. This is an ecstasis of the will more than of thought. The friend wills nothing but the good of his friend, takes care of nothing but the needs of his friend and rejects whatever would harm him. (Cf. ibid. 3, c)

On this analysis of the love of friendship, St Thomas bases his analysis of the virtue of charity which inclines us to cherish God above all, and other persons, even enemies, as creatures made in his very image.

1.4 Man has rights and duties as a social being

> *To be a social and political animal living in partnership with others is even more natural to man than to the other animals.* (*De Regimine Principum* 1)

St Thomas treats extensively of man's social life and morality and of the various forms of man's right which determine the various forms of justice. His ethics is essentially a rational naturalism. An adequate idea of it cannot be presented in the compass of this writing, but we can at least sketch out his position in the fundamental debate of his time between those who upheld that the life of a person knows no bounds and those who wanted it regulated by the needs of his group.

On one side, St Thomas departs from the traditional doctrine that political subordination is an arrangement forced on men because of their sinfulness; together with the naturalism of Aristotle, he recovered the political temper of loyalty to the present city: the State is no mere conventional makeshift, but a natural fulfilment, the object, not just the occasion, of virtue.

On the other side, he insists on the rights of conscience and on the relationship of men as persons to God, the universal Good transcending the collectivity, without intervention from anything less, however large.

To the question of the claims of the common good as against any private good, two lines of approach may be sketched though nothing like a programme is offered. Corresponding to the conception of the universe after the fashion of an organic whole, the political community is taken as a collective group demanding at need the sacrifice of parts. Corresponding to the conception of an association after the fashion of partnership, the political society is taken in the suppler and more distributive terms of a union of friendship, based on possession by knowledge rather than by physical appropriation. The former calls for the surrender of private inclination and is swayed by might and coercive law. The latter is already passing beyond the laws and precepts to their purpose and enjoying an intercourse where gain is unaccompanied by loss.

Social and civilized groups are mixtures of these two types. Law is reason controlling force in order to reach even beyond justice, and the political group should combine respect for the non-rational conditions of community with an attempt to enlarge the field of freedom and agreement.[5]

By nature all men are equal in liberty, but not in other endowments. One man is not subordinated to another as though he were a utility. (*In II Sententiae* 44, 1, 3, ad 1)

Security is banished and everything is uncertain when people are cut off from law and depend on the will, not to say the greed, of another. A tyrant oppresses the bodies of his subjects, but, what is more damnable, he threatens their spiritual growth, for he is set on his own power, not their progress. He is suspicious of any dignity they may possess that will prejudice his own iniquitous domination. And he is more fearful of good men than of bad men, for he dreads their strange virtue.... When men are brought up under such a regime of fear, they inevitably degenerate. They become mean-spirited and averse from many and strenuous feats. (*De Regimine Principum* 3)

> In human affairs there is the common good, the well-being of the state or nation; there is also a human good which does not lie in the community but is personal to each man in himself.... Human persons come under divine providence in their own right, for the activities of rational creatures alone are divinely directed for the sake of the individual as well as of the species. (*SCG* 3, 80 and 113)[6]

1.5 Man, created by God in His own image, is a person

> *Person signifies what is noblest in the whole of nature.* (*S.Th.* I, 29, 2. c)

Man, like the other beings of the universe, is a creature of God. When the term 'creation' is used most properly, it means the "emanation or flowing out of the whole of (finite) being from the universal cause" (*S.Th.* I, 14, 1, c). It, therefore, presupposes nothing apart from God. St Thomas professes unequivocally a form of *satkāryavāda*: whatever is positive being in the universe has God alone as its supreme and total cause. The term 'emanation' in the above definition must be understood in its etymological meaning as 'flowing out' or' 'effusion':

> Multiplicity can proceed from unity in three ways.... The third one is by effusion, as when many rivers rise from one source, and water from one spring spills into many streams. In this last comparison there is some likeness to the going out and distribution of distinct goods [i.e., beings, for 'every being *qua* being is a good': *S.Th.* I, 5, 3] from the divine goodness, though here no lessening of the original or archetype is involved in the multiplication, for the divine goodness remains undivided in its essence, unspent and simple. (In *De Divinis Nominibus* of Pseudo-Dionysius 2, 6)

We can produce things by transformation of some material on which we impose a form either by art or biologically as in sexual reproduction, but God alone can produce the entirety of a being without recourse to any pre-existing matter or form and without gain or loss in his essence. In other terms, he alone is omnipotent because he alone is absolute Energy of being (*subsistens Esse*) and hence can freely cause any conceivable participation of being.

> God is totally actual, both in himself, for he is pure actuality unmixed with potentiality, and with reference to actual beings, for he is their origin. The whole of subsisting [finite] being is produced by his action; to this

> action nothing is presupposed. He is the principle of being entire according to his entire simplicity; for which reason he can produce something 'out of nothing' [i.e., out of no pre-existing components]. (*De Potentia* 3, 1).

No agent can cause except in the measure of its own actuality and in the manner of its being. Because God is Fullness of Being, he and he alone produces beings as such. They are really beings ("to hold creatures cheap is to slight divine power": SCG 3, 69) but they are only beings by participation of his Fullness, beings ever dependent on him as to their entire reality (which comprises their origination, conservation, government, operations and destiny), beings necessarily indwelled by him:

> Since it is God's nature to exist, he it must be who properly causes existence in creatures... and he does this not just when they begin to exist but all the time they are maintained in existence.... Hence, as long as a creature exists, God indwells it according to the manner in which it possesses existence. Now existence is more intimately and profoundly interior to things than anything else (for everything else is potential when compared to existence). So God must exist in all things most intimately, not however as part of their substance or as a quality, but as a total agent which acts without intermediaries and thus is most immediate to his effects. (*S.Th.* I, 8, 1, c)

Thus God is everywhere because he is actively in all things, giving them their energy of being, their substance, their powers and their operations. Consequently, we can also say that they are in him:

> In two senses creatures are said to be in God. First, insofar as they are contained and preserved by the divine power, even as we say that things within our power are in us. So by their own very reality are creatures in God. This is the meaning of the words of St Paul, '*in him we live and move and have our being.*'
>
> Secondly they are said to be in God as in the one who knows them. And thus, as known by him, they are none other than the divine nature itself, [since in God there is no distinction between knower, knowing. and knowable]. (*S.Th.* I, 18, 4, ad 1).

According to all the above quotations, it is obvious that St Thomas professes no gross dualism of God and creatures but rather a type of non-dualism which agrees to a large extent with Śaṅkara's doctrine of *advaita*, as I have elsewhere demonstrated at length.[7] For him, as for St Augustine, "God is more interior to me than my innermost, and superior to my uppermost." Indeed, God is my creative Cause wherefrom I constantly receive my being, my inner unmoved Mover in all my activities, my inner Governor, the Illuminer and supreme Agent Intellect of my intellect, and the inner Polarizer of my freewill towards the absolute Goodness that he is. I simply cannot be, live, know, love, apart from him who is my Source. If St Thomas had known Śaṅkara's usage of *ātman* in its *pāramārthika* (most elevated) senses, he would have had no hesitation to say, "God, who is absolute *Esse*, is my supreme *Ātman*."

However, he says something more because for him the effects of an operative cause cannot but be similar (which implies also non-identical, dissimilar) to it since such a cause can act only in virtue and in the measure of its own actuality (cf. *S.Th.* I, 75, 2, c). He says, therefore, that God, who is Being (fullness of the actuality of beings) causes effects which are truly and properly beings, though derived beings. They are genuinely similar to him, although this similarity with the Perfect Being can never be so great that their dissimilarity from him be not greater due to his superexcellence (cf. *S.Th.* I, 8, 1, ad 3).

In the universe, there are essentially two degrees of likeness of God namely, trace and image. "A *trace* portrays without achieving a likeness *in kind* to its cause; for example, footprints are called traces, ashes are the traces of fire, and a ravaged countryside the trace of a hostile army. But an image portrays by being a likeness in *kind*.... While all creatures bear some resemblance to God, only in a rational creature do you find a resemblance to God in the manner of an image; other things resemble him in the manner of a trace.' (*S.Th.* I, 93, 6, c)

In *Genesis* 1, 26, God says, *Let us make man after our own image and likeness*; commenting on this, St Augustine says, *Herein lies man's eminence, that God made man after his own image in so far as he gave him an intelligent mind, which is where he surpasses the animals*. "So whatever lacks intelligence is not after God's image," concludes St Thomas and he explains further: "things are likened to God, first and most generally in so far as they are; secondly in so far as they are alive; thirdly and lastly in so far as they have discernment and intelligence. It is these latter, as Augustine says, which are *so close in likeness to*

God that there is nothing closer in all creation. Thus it is clear that only intelligent creatures are properly speaking 'after God's image.'" (*S.Th.* I, 93, 2, c).

This is why intelligent beings, such as man, are called persons, for "person signifies what is noblest in the whole of nature." (*S.Th.* I, 29, 1, c) The noblest creatures are the rational individuals "who, unlike other substances, are masters of their own activity and act of themselves; these receive the special name of *persons*." (*S.Th.* I, 29, 1, c).

Starting from the classical but insufficient definition of person which he inherits from Boethius (AD 470-525), St Thomas retouches it again and again so that he arrives at the following: We agree with Boethius when he says that 'person' signifies 'an individual substance of rational nature' but we must add that such a substance must also be (1) *subsistent*, i.e. existing by its own *esse* (actuality or energy of being), whether *esse* be its very essence, as in the case of God, or received from God; (2) taken in its *completeness*, i.e., with all its powers (for instance, in the case of man, corporeal, vital, sensitive as well as spiritual), habitual dispositions (such as virtues and vices) and passions, operations and qualities, in short in its totality as an agent; (3) it is better to say, '*of intelligent nature*' rather than 'of rational nature' which seems to limit unduly the manner of knowing to be found in a person. We should not, for instance ignore that man is capable of insight as well as reasoning or that God is Intelligence and thus knows by essence and without any reasoning or other process.

We must also understand the properties which follow from the right definition of 'person.' A person is at least virtually omniscient, because no reality stands outside the field of intelligence. It is endowed with freewill, because this is implied by intelligence. It, therefore, determines itself at least on the level of its spiritual activities. It can establish interpersonal relations, especially through acts of justice, of mutual acquaintance and friendship and charity (*caritas*) up to the highest forms of religious and mystical love. It can, in its society of persons, obey the law for the sake of the common good, vindicate its own rights and the rights of other persons, exercise authority, pursue values especially those that are ends-in-themselves, develop with others a genuine culture, be an agent of progress in history, seek and practise true religion, etc. All this explains why we should say that a person is in its very being an end-in-itself and thus inviolable: this is the ontological 'dignity of the person.'[8]

Since this dignity is ontological, i.e., implied by what a person such as man is, it follows that every human being has it, as well as the rights it implies, in every phase of his existence. This view commands the ethics of St Thomas which is based on the reverence due to every human being and by which we imitate God who himself says the Bible, 'deals with us with great reverence.'

1.6 Man's last end is to intuit God and find in him his lasting repose

> *The virtue of religion is a bond which attaches us to God as to the unceasing source of our being and the satiating object of our highest desire.* (Cf. *S.Th.* II-II, 1)

In spite of man's high dignity, he is mortal because he is composed of prime matter and soul. Prime matter as pure potency is ever liable to get informed by any substantial form and thus makes all material substances substantially mutable. The substantial change of the living ones among them is death. "Man is mortal like the other animals." (*S.Th.* I, 66, 3, ad 2)

Although man is mortal, it can nevertheless be established philosophically that his soul is immortal in spite of being the substantial form of the living body that he is and not an independent spiritual substance imprisoned or residing in his body. Among all animal souls the human soul alone is immortal because it alone is intelligent in the proper sense of the term. Intellectual knowledge, indeed, is possible only because its principle, the intellective soul, is capable of complete reflection in the sense explained earlier. And complete reflection over its own operation would be impossible were not this soul immune of materiality and simple, hence, not liable to decomposition. Besides, that whose operation is an end-in-itself in the class of activities is itself an end-in-itself in the class of agents; now the intellective operation, whose fruit is truth, is an end-in-itself among activities; hence, its agent, the intellective soul, is an end-in-itself among agents. But such an end-in-itself exists in its own right, which means that it exists by an energy of being which is its own. This *esse* is of the whole man but primarily of his soul. Hence, though man the composite perishes through dissolution, his soul which is simple and exists by its own *esse* escapes dissolution and continues to subsist. (Cf. *SCG* 2, 50 and 79; *S.Th.* II-I, 4, 5, ad 2 and 85, 6, c; etc.)

"It is by reason of its intrinsic incorruptibility that man's substantial form, the rational soul, is consonant with the end of man, everlasting happiness." (*S.Th.* II-I, 85, 6, c) It is by its activities that a being perfects himself and, thus, if there is a supreme end of man in which his deepest desire attains to fulfilment it must consist in the highest type of his activities. There are the operations of intellectual knowing and loving which are proper to his soul precisely as self-subsistent and simple and, therefore, immortal.

> The best activity is of the best power about the best object. The best power is the intelligent mind, its best object the divine perfection and goodness, its best activity contemplation. (*S.Th.* II-I, 3, 5, c)
>
> At the sight of God the mind cannot but delight. (*Compendium Theologiae* 165)

Thus it appears that intuiting God's very essence is our possible supreme end because it would satiate our highest-reaching desire for complete truth and love. For, as St Gregory the Great (quoted by St Thomas) says, "*What is there that they would not see who see the Seer of all things?*" This exclamation, which seems to echo the Upaniṣad, marks well the completeness of fulfilment achievable if God can become immediate to our soul's sight and love. But is this possible?

The difficulty resides in this that we can know only that about which we get information. But all the information we can get through our agent intellect derives from sensation to whose field God's absolute essence does not belong. Hence, it seems impossible that we ever get to know God's very essence.

> Our mind is in natural potentiality to those objects which can be presented by the agent intellect.... Such presentation cannot comprehend our last end, for it is limited to those things whose acquaintance we make through

> the senses.... There are many objects which are scarcely hinted at by sense-knowledge; we may be aware of their existence but not of their nature, because spiritual realities are in a different class from bodily realities and surpass them exceedingly. Even among sensible objects there are many... about which we are blankly ignorant. This natural ignorance is the spring of our restlessness and natural desire for more perfect knowledge. Yet it is impossible for a natural desire to be pointless. Our last end can be achieved only if that natural desire for perfect knowledge is actualized and stilled by an active principle nobler than anything that is part of us or of our sort of world. This desire is such that, when an effect is perceived, we crave to know its cause.... It will therefore not be quieted until we know the first cause, not from reflections, but by its very essence. The first cause is God. Therefore, the ultimate end of rational creatures is the vision of the essence of God. (*Compendium Theologiae* 104)

This ultimate end is within the reach and scope of our mind's natural desire but it is not within the active grasp of our mind. We can only hope for it and expect it from God's love for us, because it can only be achieved by a self-gift of God directly to our mind. Indeed, "in such a vision the divine essence itself must be both medium of information and object." (*SCG* 3, 51) Nothing short of God himself can inform us by such an immediate and thorough information that we simply see him as he is and in the same act unite with him in perfect love and joy. The divine self-gift which this actuation implies can only be a gratuitous self-gift of person to person. It depends on God's freewill and infinite goodness. Christianity asserts in the name of Christ that we may expect it with firm hope because, indeed, God calls all men to it and "wills all men to be saved."

Whether or not men are aware of all this, the natural desire for God's realization is at work in all of them. It appears especially at work in the development of a religious sense and of religion as a human virtue. Religion binds us, as it were, to God as to the very source of the totality of our being and life and as to our ultimate goal.

The chief act of religion is the worship called *latria* which consists in acknowledging with praising delight and admiration that God exists as the Absolute, the infinitely perfect Being, the Source and Providence of the universe and our ultimate Goal. This is an act of faith imbued with love and hope. It should structure prayer and rituals and it demands to blossom, as it were, into trust, holy desires, obedience to God's will, repentance for our sins, imitation of God's impartial kindness and love for all persons even despicable or inimical, disinterested service of humanity, personal devotion to God, religious self-developing up to even mysticism, etc.

> Besides worship addressed directly and solely to God, which is the proper and immediate act of religion, there is another kind of religious act. They proceed from other virtues commanded by religion and directed to the reverence of God. Thus to visit orphans and widows in their tribulation, which is an act of mercy, and to keep oneself unspotted from the world, which is an act of the virtue of self-control, but may be dictated by religion. (*S.Th.* II-II, 81, 1, ad 1).

Finally, let us note that St Thomas warns us against the excesses of the religious sense, such as superstition and bigotry "which is religion observed beyond measure." (*In III Sententiae*, 9, 1, 1, 3, ad 3).

> Every moral virtue lies in a mean between extremes, and two classes of vice correspond to each of them, one by excess, the other by defect.... Thus superstition is a vice against religion by excess... because superstitious worship is offered to the wrong objects or in the wrong manner. (*S.Th.* I-II, 92, 1, c)

> When in worship there is anything unbefitting the glory of God, when it neither helps man to God nor disciplines inordinate desire, or when it is against proper manners, then it must be dismissed as so much waste and superstition. (*S.Th.* I-II, 93, 2, c)

2. The Contributions of Neo-Thomists

Among modern Thomists, we may single out the contributions of four outstanding scholars, J. Maritain, J. Maréchal, E. Gilson and K. Wojtyła, better known as the present Pope, John Paul II.[9]

2.1 The Contribution of Jacques Maritain

With Maritain, the Thomist revival invaded the world of universities. His creativity lay in his untiring application of principles established by St Thomas to new areas of modern concern. Thus to epistemology in his classic *Degrees of Knowledge*,[10] to aesthetics in *Creative Intuition in Art and*

Poetry,[11] and especially fruitfully to social and political philosophy as can be gathered from *The Social and Political Philosophy of Jacques Maritain: Selected Readings*.[12]

His teaching on the human person warrants attention even in our limited space. He distinguishes *person* from *individual* in order to mark a tension, a polarity in every man. 'Individual' means a corporeal unit of form and matter, 'person' an individual subsisting in a rational nature. They co-exist as two levels in man.

> They mean that the human being is held between two poles: a material pole, which in reality does not concern authentic personality, but rather the material condition and the shadow, as it were, of personality; and a spiritual pole, which concerns personality itself.[13]

> I am wholly an individual, by reason of what I receive from matter, and I am wholly a person, by reason of what I receive from spirit.[14]

As *individual*, man is narrow, closed in upon himself, needy and grasping, subject to physical determinisms, dependent upon others for satisfying his material needs, subject to disease and death, etc. But, as *person*, man is spirit, open to all goodness and truth, free and responsible master of his acts, subordinate only to God, and he must be seen as:

> a whole which subsists and exists in virtue of the very subsistence and existence of its spiritual soul, and acts by setting itself its own ends; a universe in itself; a microcosm which, though its existence at the heart of the material universe is ceaselessly threatened, nevertheless possesses a higher ontological density than the whole universe. Only the person is free; only the person possesses in the full sense of these words, inwardness and subjectivity—because it contains itself and moves about within itself.[15]

Because man is both person and individual, he lives in society both as a free and generous master of himself reaching out to others in understanding and love, and as a dependent and needy member seeking the help of the group. If the goal of society, the common good, is to be achieved, man's needs as an individual must be provided for and man's rights as a person must be respected. From these principles, Maritain developed a comprehensive and coherent account of the relation of man to man in society.

2.2 The Contribution of J. Maréchal

Fr J. Maréchal, SJ, whom I came to know when I read philosophy in Louvain, became the leader within Thomism of a progressive movement which is focused on man's 'intellectual dynamism.' After his *Studies in the Psychology of the Mystics*[16] which put him on the way to his method, he published a series of '*Cahiers*'[17] (not yet translated from the French) on the starting point of metaphysics. *Cahiers* III, IV and V are the fruit of his sympathetic, lifelong dialogue with Kantian philosophy. He was outstanding in those virtues which Socrates (in Plato's *Gorgias* 487 2-3) defines as proper to a genuine partner in dialogue: learning (*epistêmê*), friendly feelings (*eunoia*) and frankness of speech (*parrhêsia*).

All that Kant's *Critique of Pure Reason* leaves to the speculative reason is a world of phenomena whose necessity derives from the *a priori* forms of sensibility and categories of understanding in man's mind. The central insight in Maréchal's thought is found in his reply to Kant: The necessity, and thus the noumenal character, of the essences of finite beings is revealed in the dynamism of the act by which the intellect affirms them. What we have here has been aptly termed 'a reversal of the terms of the problem.' Where Kant rejected metaphysics conceived as a grasping of the Absolute by the intellect, Maréchal defends it as a grasping of the intellect by the Absolute. The act of judgment by which the intellect affirms reality is an act marked with a 'finality' or purposiveness of its own. It reveals the natural orientation of man's intellect toward the Absolute Being and, hence, on its way towards it, in all beings-by-participation.

In every judgment, the essence abstracted by the mind from the sensible image is caught up into, and measured by, a dynamism directed toward Absolute Being, which is present to the mind not as an object of intuition but as goal of its natural tendency. The thing represented by the abstracted form is recognized as an object distinct from the knower, as a particular end of the mind's dynamism, only insofar as it is somewhat similar to the ultimate goal of that dynamism—which is the self-subsisting *Esse*.

A relating of the finite to Absolute Being is thus at work, though only implicit, in every affirmation. This is how each one of us, from infancy onward, comes to apply to the manifold phenomena the principles which determine being as being. The metaphysician's task is to reflect upon the very exercise of the judgments which we all spontaneously make, and in it to trace out the relation of contingent and necessary, of particular and universal.

Virtually the whole Thomistic structure of finite being can be traced out in this dynamic relation and also a convincing demonstration of God's existence and essence,[18] and of the innateness of our quest for him as our ultimate goal.

> In virtue of the principle of the infinite virtuality of what Aristotle and St Thomas call 'actuality,' the gap between the limitation of the form and the absolute fullness of *Esse*, between the degree and the maximum, must measure, in the finite form or essence, the range of an inward impulse or aspiration to unlimited self-transcendence.[19]

The dynamism lived out in the judgment thus corresponds to the natural appetite by which finite man seeks his last end. Its goal, the intuitive realization of the Absolute Being, is not merely parallel but identical with that of the will.

Maréchal's original contribution to the study of man consists in bringing to light, while following the footsteps of St Thomas, the latter's deep insights regarding the dynamic working of the human mind and the whole metaphysics implied in this working.

2.3 The Contribution of É. Gilson

The vocation of Étienne Gilson as historian of medieval philosophy was revealed to him when in his research for his doctoral dissertation on Descartes he reached the startling conclusion that the thought of Descartes was in many respects less cogent and rigorous than that found in his medieval sources. From that time on, Gilson became engaged in defining and exploring the realms of medieval thought. He grew to be the most outstanding of its historians.

His most important insight concerns the centrality and the originality of St Thomas conception of *esse* as actuality and of God as the absolute actuality-of-being. What St Thomas offers is at once the deepest meaning of the name of God as 'He-who-Is' (*Yahwe*) and a new insight into the reality of creatures. God is the being whose whole nature is to be the existential actuality designated by the verb 'to be.' To say that God is *ipsum esse subsistens* (self-subsisting *Esse* itself) is to say that in Him essence or quiddity is identified with the absolute and unqualified actuality-of-being. He *is* absolutely; whatever else may be said of him must be an unfolding of this highest metaphysical insight. It is just this which makes clear the ineffability of God. "Since, in God, there is no something to which existence could be attributed, his own *esse* is precisely that which God is. To us, such a Being is strictly beyond all possible representation."[20]

At the same time, this insight sheds considerable light upon the created world and man, taking off from the exploration of "concrete being itself, the original, unique, and, in the case of man, unpredictable and free actualization of an inexhaustible essence by its own actuality-of-being."[21] At the heart of each creature lies a real distinction (as between actuality and potency) between *that which it is*, its essence, and the actuality by which it is, its *esse*. It expresses the fact that a being whose essence is not its actuality of being has not of itself the wherewithal to exist. This opens up the question of the cause of finite existences and it also serves to establish the distinction of the creatures from God.

Aristotelian substances seem to exist in their own right; the created substances of St Thomas are radically contingent. Gilson is fond of repeating the comparison which St Thomas makes between the presence of *esse* in the creatures and the presence of light in air. This explains St Thomas' indifference to the concern of his contemporaries about the origin of the world in time; the world as he conceives it is so radically contingent in its being that even were it thought to be eternal, its "actual existence still would remain an eternal gratuity."[22]

2.4 The Contribution of Karol Wojtyła (John Paul II)

It is not because Karol Wojtyła became pope that his book, *Osoba i czyn* (Person and Act), published in Kraków in 1969,[23] was translated into English with the title, *The Acting Person.*[24] The translation was begun by A. Potocki years before, prompted by the book's success in Poland.

It is a book inspired by the Thomistic tradition viewed under the light of Max Scheler's personalistic phenomenology. Its basic argument is that the essence of being human can best be illumined through an extensive analysis of voluntary action. Action is the distinguishing feature of spirit. Passivity, or all that happens either in or to human beings, pertains to their psychosomatic centres—the realm of nature. Although little place is devoted to purely intellectual activity Wojtyła begins with an analysis of consciousness. More traditional, cosmological approaches, he thinks, often neglect the personalization of action that occurs through consciousness. For the most part, he focuses on freedom, whose primary act is self-determination and whose principal object is the subject's self-fulfilment. Moral decisions, which in later essays he calls the 'drama of the will,' are creative encounters with the truth of values presented through emotions. This aspect of truthfulness saves the basic argument from what might otherwise appear to be a heavy voluntarism.

The central dialectic of human existence involves the dynamisms of self-transcendence and integration. The human spirit moves beyond all determinisms, and at the same time it must integrate into itself the semi-independent dynamisms of the *sôma* and the *psychê*.

In his last chapter the author argues that everyone has a right to self-direction and to effective dissent. He rejects ranking any limited community ahead of the entire human community. He opposes individualism and totalitarianism as well as conformism and non-involvement, because each of these denies the complementary truth that the individual person is primary and that it can achieve self-fulfilment only through a participatory being-and-acting-with-others.

Notes

[1] [Paper delivered at the Symposium on 'The Concept of Man' held at the S. Radhakrishnan Institute for Advanced Study in Philosophy, University of Madras, and published in the *Indian Philosophical Annual* (University of Madras) **15** (1982-83) 1-32. Reprinted in *Indian Theological Studies* **26**/4 (1989) 336-372. Permission to reprint has been obtained from *Indian Theological Studies* and is gratefully acknowledged.]

[2] *S.Th.* I, 1, 1, c which means *Summa Theologica*, part I, question 1, article 1, corpus, i. e., *siddhānta*. This work comprises 3 parts; part II is divided into 2, referred to as II-I and II-II; each part is divided into main questions and each question into articles. The structure of an article comprises (1) the particular question or topic it treats, (2) several prima facie solutions (*pūrvapakṣa*), (3) the countersolution (*uttarapakṣa*), (4) the corpus or body or magisterial reply (*siddhānta*) in which the author discusses the topic thoroughly and arrives at a well-established solution, (5) his particular replies to each of the *pūrvapakṣas*; these replies are referred to as: ad 1, ad 2, etc. Another important work, the *Summa Contra Gentiles*, will be quoted as *SCG*. Other works will be indicated specifically.

[3] T. Suttor, "Introduction," St Thomas Aquinas, *Summa Theologiae*, vol. 11: Man: I, 75-83 (Blackfriars in conjunction with London: Eyre & Spottiswoode / New York: McGraw-Hill, 1970) xv.

[4] Cf. my article, "The Aristotelian-Thomist Conception of Man," *Indian Philosophical Quarterly* **2**/4 (July 1975) 307-318 [chapter 11 above].

[5] Thomas Gilby, *St Thomas Aquinas: Philosophical Texts* (London: OUP, 1951) 367-368.

[6] To complement this section, see my "Natural Law," *Indian Law Review* **1**/11 (May 1980) 53-63, or an enlarged version of it in *Indian Theological Studies* **17**/3 (Sept. 1980) 247-265.

[7] See my article, "Śaṅkara and Aquinas on Creation," *Indian Philosophical Annual* **6** (1970) 112-118; or "Origin: Creation and Emanation," *Indian Theological Studies* **15**/3 (1978) 266-279.

[8] Cf. also my triple article, "The Discovery of the Person," "The Loss of the Person," and "The Rediscovery of the Person," *Indian Philosophical Quarterly* IV/1 (1976) 1-23 and IV/2 (1977) 413-426 [cf. chapters 3-5 above], or "The Open Person and the Closed Individual," *Journal of the Philosophy Association* **15**/47 (1974) [cf. chapter 6 above].

[9] [Karol Wojtyła, Pope John Paul II, d. 2005.]

[10] [J. Maritain, *Distinguish to Unite: or, The Degrees of Knowledge*, tr. under the supervision of G.B. Phelan (New York: Charles Scribner's Sons, 1959).]

[11] [J. Maritain, *Creative Intuition in Art and Poetry* (New York: Pantheon Books, 1953).]

[12] J. Maritain, *The Social and Political Philosophy of Jacques Maritain: Selected Readings*, ed. J.W. Evans and L.R. Ward (New York: Ch. Scribners Sons, 1955).

[13] J. Maritain, *Scholasticism and Politics*, ed. M.J. Adler (New York: The Macmillan Company, 1940) 58.

[14] Ibid. 65.
[15] J. Maritain, *Existence and the Existent*, tr. L. Galantiere and G. B. Phelan (New York: Pantheon Books, 1948) 68.
[16] J. Maréchal, *Studies in the Psychology of the Mystics*, tr. A. Thorold (New York: Benziger, 1928)
[17] [J. Maréchal, *Le point de départ de la Métaphysique*, Cahiers 1-5 (Bruges-Louvain, 1922-47).]
[18] This is developed in my "The Problematics of the Knowledge of God," *Indian Philosophical Annual* 7 (1971) 121-125.
[19] [J. Maréchal, *Mélanges Joseph Maréchal* (Bruxelles: Éd. Universelle, 1950) 1:87.]
[20] É. Gilson, *History of Christian Philosophy in the Middle Ages* (London: Sheed & Ward, 1955) 368-369.
[21] É. Gilson, *The Philosophy of St Thomas Aquinas* (New York: Random House, 1956) 370.
[22] É. Gilson, *Being and Some Philosophers* (Toronto: Pontifical Institute of Medieval Studies, 1949) 161.
[23] K. Wojtyła, *Osoba i czyn* (Kraków, 1969).
[24] K. Wojtyła, *The Acting Person*, tr. A. Potocki (Boston: Reidel, 1979). [Wojtyła became pope in 1978.]

14

MATERIALS TOWARD AN INDO-WESTERN UNDERSTANDING OF THE DIGNITY OF THE HUMAN PERSON[1]

Person signifies what is noblest in the whole of nature. (St Thomas Aquinas, *Summa Theologiae* I, 29, 2)

It is usually through a reference to Kant that the notion of dignity of the human person is defined. In *Groundwork of the Metaphysics of Morals* (p. 429 of the critical edition) he writes:

> Rational nature exists as an end in itself.... The practical imperative will thus be as follows: So act as to treat humanity, whether in your own person or in that of any other, always at the same time as an end and never merely as means.[2]

The dignity of man is thus to be an end in himself owing to his rational nature. It is for the same reason that all human beings are declared to be equal in dignity and rights in the very first article of the *Universal Declaration of Human Rights*:

> All human beings are born free and equal in dignity and rights. They are *endowed with reason and conscience* and should act towards one another in a spirit of brotherhood.

Let us examine how this notion of human dignity originated in the diverse cultures of India and the West.

1. In Vedic India

In the Vedas, we find several hymns to Speech or to Thought. For instance, the following verses on Thought:

> That which is foresight, consciousness and persistence,
> Which is the immortal light within beings,
> Apart from which no act can be performed, my Thought,
> That immortal through which all things are apprehended,
> The past, the present, the future [...],
> That which masterfully drives the humans,
> Like a good charioteer drives his steeds with his reins,
> The swift, the quickest of all, which is based in the heart,
> My Thought—may it conceive happy things!
>
> (*Vajaseniya Saṃhita* 34, 3-6)

Thought or the Mind (*manas*) is viewed here as the dynamic principle which is the sovereign characteristic of man. It is not simply a psychological but a cosmic principle, as already in *Ṛgveda* 129, 4 and in numerous passages of the Upaniṣads, for instance, *Kena Up.*: "moved, propelled by whom will Thought fly?" It makes the greatness of man:

> He knows tomorrow, he knows the world and what is not the world. By the mortal he desires the immortal, being thus endowed.... Man is the sea. He is above all the world. Whatever he reaches, he desires to go beyond it.
>
> (*Aitareya Āraṇyaka* 2, 1, 3)

2. In Ancient Greece

In Greece, we have first the famous text of Sophocles in his *Antigone:*

> There are in the world many marvels but none greater than man.... Speech, though swift like the wind, aspiration whence are born cities; all that he taught to himself as well he could, while making shelters for himself.

Here, the thought which makes man's greatness is identified as the technical and political thought which (like the architectonic *māyā* of the Vedas) raises buildings and creates organized republics.

The same sort of thinking is continued in the *Protagoras* of Plato and its famous myth of Epimetheus and Prometheus. Epimetheus provided qualities so lavishly on the animals devoid of reason that he had none left to endow man with. Prometheus, his brother, then stole from the workshop of Hephaistos and Athene the technical arts and the fire they required and endowed man with them. Thus provided, man could build shelters but he could not organize his society. Then Zeus, worried lest man become extinct, sent Hermes to men "*bearing reverence and justice* (*aida te kai dikên*) *to be the ordering principle of republics and the bonds of friendship and conciliation*...." Hermes asked Zeus how he should impart justice and reverence among men: Should he distribute them as the arts are distributed: that is to say, to a favoured few only, or should he give them to all?—To all, said Zeus, for states cannot exist if a few only share in the virtues as in the arts. (*Protagoras* 320-323)

But it is in *The Republic* that Plato manifests his position in its full complexity. Human excellence is not only an education to the political values but a comprehension of the *ideals* to which the state itself is to subject itself. The excellence and thus the 'dignity' of men cannot be maintained by a bare political art but only by a political art axed upon the absolute Good which is the object of philosophical contemplation.... The human dignity is thus fed on the divine Excellence.

For Aristotle also the dignity of political excellence attaches to the fact that one is a citizen entitled to share in the democratic government at the city. This excludes foreigners and slaves. In India similarly, human excellence belongs to the man belonging to one of the *varṇas*, especially the upper three; a *varṇa* being a class of people entitled to share in some way or other in sacrifices. This excludes the aliens and the outcastes

It is with the Stoics that a truly universal notion appears. For the Stoic, that is estimable (*axios*) which conforms to nature. Conformity to the nature of humanity and thus to the great whole makes the dignity (*axia*) of a human person. It is on account of this sense of the universal that early Christians felt an affinity with the Stoics and made use of their philosophy rather than of another during the first two or even three centuries AD.

But Christianity introduces a bigger change in the notion of that dignity. It is now because every human, whether free or slave, is a creature "in the image and resemblance" of the absolute God and is assured of salvation through Jesus Christ that all are equally worthy of a fundamental worthiness which the world cannot give.

3. In India

In India, it is with the apparition of the conception of *mokṣa* and its accompaniment *saṁnyāsa* that a similar change begins. *Mokṣa* is a new value, antinomic to the first three goals of man, and which demands renunciation of them. *Saṁnyāsa* is this renunciation which sets a man in the margin of society and excludes him from all his rights and duties to it. But paradoxically they raise him to a new status of excellence, this time in connection with the eternal realities, the *Brahman* (or negatively *nirvāṇa*), immortality, perfect knowledge, transcendence of all that is finite. The *saṁnyāsin* is not only venerated but he is the true individual, completely on its own, detached from *varṇa* and caste, indifferent to all differences of status; he has secured his personality through a free option made with reference to a transcending aim. This is what we find in the Upaniṣads or, in reverse, in Therāvāda Buddhism.

Yet, the chasm is too deep that separates him from the caste people. An important advance is made by King Aśoka through the new *dharma,* best designated as *Law of Piety*, which he proclaims in his rock- or pillar-edicts. It is a civil version of the Buddhist *dharma* adapted to ordinary citizens. What it conveys chiefly throughout is *Respect*; no wonder that his concept of *dharma* is rendered in Greek as *eusebeia* (respectful piety) in the bilingual (Greek-Aramaic) inscription discovered in 1957 at Kandahar, Afghanistan. He describes what it prescribes as follows:

> This is excellent, this should be done.... right treatment of slaves and servants, obedience to mother and father, liberality to friends, acquaintances and kinsmen, gifts to *śramaṇas* and *brāhmaṇas*, and abstention from slaughter of living beings (*Rock Edict XI*). *Pillar Edict VII* adds helpful sympathy towards the wretched and miserable. Concludes *Rock Edict IX*: These and other similar acts constitute, what may be called *dharma-mangala*, the ceremonial of the Law of Piety, which ought to replace the worthless ceremonials so far used for birth, marriage, illness, departure on a journey, etc.

This is no longer a purely ethnic *dharma* but one imbued with a sense of universality. "The welfare of all people (*sarva-loka-hitam*) is my highest duty," says the king in *Rock Edict VI.*

To the special "great ministers of the Law of Piety" (*dharma-mahāmātras)* who supervise the observance of this new Law, he says:

> You are set over thousands of living beings that you may surely secure the affection of all men, for all men are my children. (*First Separate Rock Edict of Kalinga*)

This is why he extends the proclamation of his *dharma* to the Greek and other kingdoms beyond the limits of his empire. To the officers in charge of faraway border districts or forest tracts, he says to excite their zeal:

> All men should be consoled (by you) so that they think, 'the king is to us as a father; he sympathises with us as he sympathises with himself; we are to the king as his children'.... You are capable of consoling them, and ensuring their welfare and happiness pertaining to both this world and the next. (*Second Separate Rock Edict*)

> They have been appointed... for the welfare and happiness of both hired servants and masters, *brāhmaṇas* and wealth-owners, old people and helpless ones, and to free citizens from hardship. They are employed to see to the reversal of judicial sentences, the freedom from hardship and the release of prisoners who are responsible for children, or engulfed by misery, or too old. (*Rock Edict V*)

His deeds prove his deep sense of the dignity of all and, so it seems, preferentially of those whose life is most harsh:

> He has procured medical attendance for men and beasts even beyond his dominion (Rock *Edict III*), planted medicinal herbs, roots, fruit trees, banyan trees along the roads, and mango orchards; he has dug wells at every half a *krosa*, provided sale stalls and watering places for travelling men and beasts (*Rock Edict II*): he and his queens have distributed charities; he has taken pleasure in forgiving and procured amnesties to prisoners 25 times during the first 26 years after his consecration. (*Pillar Edict V*)

Asoka's *Dharma* did not endure because it displeased the tenants of the Brahmanic *Dharma.* Within fifty years of his death, his dynasty comes to an end (BC 185) and the strongly reactionary Sunga takes up its succession (BC 176).[3]

However, a more durable advance, probably favoured by this Brahmanical revival, is set in motion by the *Bhagavad Gītā* and its raising of *bhakti* to the religious level. Through *bhakti*, the goal of the Upaniṣadic *saṁnyāsin* is obtainable by everyone; and everyone means, as in Buddhism, every male or female whether of caste or non-caste. Like Stoicism in the West, Buddhism had here played a universalizing role; but, due to its teaching of no substance and no person, it cannot be said to have rooted in an idea of the universality of the dignity of person. This is rather done by the *Gītā* in the name of the *Brahman* manifested as Kṛṣṇa. And it is done in such a way that the individual person is not cut away from his associations with his fellows but linked with them "for the fight" of secular life.

Henceforth there will be frequent assertions that a human birth is preferable to others because it ushers in the possibility of salvation (*mokṣa*). But the belief in the possibility of the same soul being reborn in all sorts of bodies prevents the choice of a special term, like in the West the term 'person,' to designate the status of the human being.

4. In Christianity

On the contrary in the West, the Christian thinkers get hold of the term 'person' which has begun to be used in law courts and define it in such a way that it will designate precisely this privileged status. Writes St Thomas Aquinas:

> Among particular individuals, some have a more perfect existence than others. They are those that are masters of their own activity and act of themselves. Therefore, those singular rational substances receive the special name of *person.* (*S.Th.* I, 29, 1) *Person* signifies what is noblest in the whole of nature. (Ibid. I, 29, 2) Intelligent creatures excel all others in the perfection of their nature and the dignity of their end: they are masters of their activity and act freely. They reach their destiny by their own proper activity that is, by knowing and loving God. Rational creatures are governed by him, no doubt, but for their own benefit. Men are principals, not mere instruments. They are not made for anyone's utility. Their actions have a personal value and are not simply from and for human nature. (*SCG* 3, 111 sq.)

From St Thomas onwards, attention is directed increasingly to intellectual consciousness and the various acts of the intellect and will. This had already begun with St Augustine and is henceforth continued by the Augustinian thinkers.

5. In both Śaṅkara and St. Thomas

In India, the question is: Who am I? And the conviction grows that it cannot be answered in final depth apart from a recourse to the *Śruti* with the help of Vedānta exegetes. The answer of Śaṅkara and in their own way Rāmānuja and Vallabha is that the ground of the self, the supreme *Ātman*, is the *Brahman* itself. This tends to decrease the importance and dignity of the finite self. But Madhva vindicates it by exalting the inner witness, the *sākṣin* which is man's own consciousness.

But there is something more important that we find in Śaṅkara as well as in St Thomas Aquinas: a clear notion of the intellectual dynamism of man and of its range and goal. The desire of knowing, he says, which is innate (*naisargika*) extends up to the *Brahman* and its goal is an intellectual penetration (*avagati*) into the divine Essence itself.

> The direct object of the desire of knowing *Brahman* (*brahmajijñāsā*) is a knowledge culminating in an intellectual penetration (*avagati paryantam jñānam*), desires having reference to fruits. Knowledge, indeed, constitutes the means (*pramāṇa*) through which the *Brahman* is desired to be intellectually penetrated into (*avagatum iṣṭam*). For this penetration of the *Brahman* is the end of man (*brahmāvagati hi puruṣārthaḥ*) since it extirpates completely that which is bad, namely, nescience, etc. which are the seeds of the entire *saṃsāra* (*B.S.Bh.* 1, 1, 1). The knowledge that discerns the *Brahman* and discards nescience terminates in experience (*anubhava* + *avasānum*). (Ibid. 2, 1, 4) Nothing finite can set the intellect's desire at rest. This is proved by the fact that the intellect, given any finite thing, strives to go beyond it. Now the excellence and power of any created substance is finite; hence the knowledge of any of them is unable to satisfy our natural desire which tends to grasp that substance which is of an infinite excellence.

> Moreover, just as there is a natural desire for knowledge in all intellectual natures, so there is in men a natural desire to rid themselves of ignorance or nescience.... Now they know that God's essence is above them and above everything that they understand; hence, they know that the divine essence is unknown to them. Therefore their natural desire tends to know the divine essence.
> Besides: the nearer a thing is to its end, the greater the desire with which it tends to that end. Now, however much we know that God exists and other

> things that this includes, we still go on desiring and seeking to know Him in his essence.
> Hence, we conclude that man's ultimate happiness does not consist in the knowledge whereby we know God through our own unaided power, but our desire still leads us on to the very essence of God. (*SCG* 3, 50) If, therefore, the divine essence is to be seen at all, it must be that the intellect sees it through the divine essence itself; *so that in that vision the divine essence is both the object and the medium of vision* (*SCG* 3, 51).

It is obvious that the existence in man of such a dynamism gives him an excellence and a dignity which surpasses all others. The consequences of this are abundantly developed by St Thomas but there is no need of expatiating here over them.

Because the term 'person' does not exist in Sanskrit, it is often thought that India had in the past no awareness of the dignity of the human person. But, in conclusion, we may say that the parallel lines of development sketched out above show that India has known the reality of that dignity in a manner not unlike that of the West.

Notes

[1] [First published in *Journal of Dharma* **21** (1996) 39-46. Permission to publish has been obtained from *Journal of Dharma* and is gratefully acknowledged.

[2] I. Kant, *The Moral Law: Kant's Groundwork of the Metaphysic of Morals*, tr. Herbert James Paton (New York, Barnes & Noble, 1967) 429.

[3] For an integral presentation of Asoka's Law of Piety, see my "Indian Roots for the Lord-Vassal Relationship in the Spiritual Exercises of Saint Ignatius," in E. de Meulder, ed., *When Two Great Hearts Meet* (Allahabad: St Paul, 1978) 192-220. Reprinted in *Ignis Studies* 6-7 (1984) 5-39. Also in *Indian Journal of Spirituality* **6** (1993) 191-206; 294-321.

RICHARD V. DE SMET, SJ
A BIBLIOGRAPHY

The bibliography of primary sources is arranged chronologically. It makes use of various bibliographies compiled by De Smet himself, as well as those of Kozhamthadam and Malkovsky, making corrections where necessary. In addition, it includes unpublished material found in the libraries of Jnana Deepa Vidyapeeth (JDV), Pune, and De Nobili College (DNC), Pune (cf. especially Collected Papers A, B, C, D reserved in the JDV library), and notes taken by students. Offprints of articles have also been included, both because their pagination is often different from the original article, and because De Smet circulated a number of these among his students, friends and acquaintances. I have tried to be as complete as possible, but I am conscious that there is probably still a certain amount of material that has escaped me, especially by way of notes taken by students.

The bibliography of secondary sources is arranged alphabetically; it is very much still a work in progress.

I. Primary Sources

1929

1. "La croix au bord de la route." *Trait d'union* (Charleroi) (December 1929).

1933

2. "Deviens un chef." *Trait d'union* (Charleroi) (May 1933).

1935

3. "Approximations Mariologiques." (1935).
4. "Spiritualité (Ascetique et Mystique)." (1935).

1937

5. "Les Trois Thébains du 'Phedon'." (1937).
6. "Germanicus." (1937).

1938

7. "Nada ou les chemins de négation vers Dieu." *Dialogue* (1938).
8. "Témoignages sur nous: 'François' de Valensin." (1938).
9. "De la durée comme transcendental." (1938).
10. "Poèmes." (1938).
11. "La mediation mariale." *Congrégations Mariales* (June 1938).
12. "La philosophie du Patriotisme." (1938).

1939

13. "Petite histoire du Japon." *Collection Xaveriana* (Louvain) **16**/188 (August 1939). 32 pp.
14. "Pologne en Croix." *Revue du Collège St Servais*. (November 1939).

1940

15. "Humanité de nos saints." *Revue du Collège St Servais* (March 1940).

1941

16. "Stalag XVII B." *Revue des Routiers* (1941).

1942

17. "Dialogues Transeuropéens: I. Le possible et ses implications. II. L'obéissance religieuse et le probabilisme. III. De l'immortalité et de la peine du dam. IV. De la prière et de la liberté." (1942-43).
18. "Souffles sur la Braise." (1942-43).
19. "Correspondance sur le sujet du devenir humain." (1942).

1943

20. "Connaissance de la personne." (1943).
21. "L'épistemologie de Bergson." (1943).

1944

22. "'Le Cimetière Marin' de Paul Valéry: Essai de Commentaire." *Nova et Vetera* (July 1944) 38-74.

1945

23. "1001 questions sur la loi scoute." (1945).

1948

24. "Soeren Kierkegaard's Existentialism." *The New Review* **28**/8-9 (Aug.-Sept. 1948) 85-97, 185-199.

25. "A Note on Sankara's Doctrine of Creation." 1 June 1948. Typescript, Collected Papers D, 7-25.
26. "Notes for a Sermon." 1 June 1948. 2 pp. Typescript, Collected Papers D, 96-97.

1949

27. "Upadhyay's Interpretation of Śaṅkara." Kurseong, Ascension Day, 1949. 6 pp. Typescript, Collected Papers D, 1-6.
28. "Upadhyay's Interpretation of Śaṅkara." (1949).
29. "Introductory Lectures to Metaphysics." Lectures II-VI. N.d. Typescript, Collected Papers D, 27-31; p. 28 missing.
30. "The Personal God of the Bhagavad-Gita." N.d. 2 pp. Typescript, Collected Papers D, 73.
31. "A Note Concerning Śaṅkara's Doctrine of Creation." (1949.)

1950

32. "Team-Spirit and Team-Work according to the Constitutions of the Society of Jesus." (1950.)

1952

33. "The Theory of Knowledge of Kanada." Rome, 15 March 1952. 23 pp. Typescript, Collected Papers B, 305-327 = DNC 73/DES/COL 305-327. (Published as no. 200 below.)
34. "Jesus's Message and Indian Thought." Poona: De Nobili College, n.d. 5 pp. Typescript, Collected Papers C, 543-547. (Cf. no. 112 below.)
35. "The Doctrines of Hinduism." N.d. 2 pp. Typescript, Collected Papers C, 550-551.

1953

36. *The Theological Method of Śaṃkara*. Doctoral dissertation. Director: R. Arnou, SJ. Limited roneotyped edition. Rome: Pontifical Gregorian University, 1953. Xi+370 pp. (Cf. no. 37 below.)

1954

37. "Langage et connaissance de l'Absolu chez Çaṃkara." *Revue Philosophique de Louvain* (3e série 52/33) (February 1954) 31-74. (Cf. no. 36.)
38. *The Theological Method of Śaṅkara*. Excerpta. Louvain, 1954. Containing no. 37 + Table of Contents + Bibliography of no. 36. 56 pp. (Cf. no. 36.)
39. *Notes on the Sāṃkhya-Kārikā*. Ad mentem M. Ledrus, S.J. Cyclostyled notes for students. 64 pp. 1954. (Incorporated into no. 283 as ch. 6.)
40. "The Correct Interpretation of the Definitions of the Absolute according to Śrī Śaṃkarācārya and Saint Thomas Aquinas. Paper to be read in December 1954 Philosophical Congress, Colombo." 8 pp. Typescript,

Collected Papers A, 5-12 = DNC 73/DES/COL. (Published as no. 41 below.)

41. "The Correct Interpretation of the Definitions of the Absolute according to Śaṃkarācārya and Saint Thomas Aquinas." *Proceedings of the Indian Philosophical Congress* (1954) 1-10. (Cf. no. 40 above. Reprinted as no. 50 below.)
42. "The Fundamental Antinomy of Śr[ī] Śaṃkarācārya's Methodology." Lecture given at Philosophical Association, 24 August 1954. 1 p. + 1 p. summary + 7 pp. Typescript, Collected Papers A, 23-31 = DNC 73/DES/COL. (Published as no. 56 below.)
43. "From Existence to Being." Review [1954]. 4 pp. Typescript, Collected Papers A, 1-4. (Published as no. 44 below.)
44. "From Existence to Being." Review of Roger Troisfontaines, *De l'existence à l'être: La philosophie de Gabriel Marcel. The Clergy Monthly* **18** (April 1954) 106-109. (Cf. no. 43 above.)
45. Introductio in Philosophiam + Logica Minor. Latin cyclostyled notes for students. Pune: Jnana Deepa Vidyapeeth, n.d. (Mentioned in no. 726, 12b.)
46. Metaphysica Generalis. Latin cyclostyled notes for students. Pune: Jnana Deepa Vidyapeeth, n.d. (Mentioned in no. 726, 12b.)
47. Quaestiones Speciales de Metaphysica. Latin cyclostyled notes for students. Pune: Jnana Deepa Vidyapeeth, n.d. (Mentioned in no. 726, 12b.)
48. Theologia Rationalis. Latin cyclostyled notes for students. Pune: Jnana Deepa Vidyapeeth, n.d. (Mentioned in no. 726, 12b.)
49. Quaestiones Speciales de Theologia Naturali. Latin cyclostyled notes for students. Pune: Jnana Deepa Vidyapeeth, n.d. (Mentioned in no. 726, 12b.)

1955

50. "The Correct Interpretation of the Definitions of the Absolute, according to Śaṃkarācārya and Saint Thomas Aquinas." *The Philosophical Quarterly* **27**/4 (January 1955) 187-194. (Reprint of no. 41 above.)
51. "Some Characteristics of the Doctrine of Saint Thomas Aquinas." Poona: De Nobili College, 10 September 1955. 2 pp. Typescript, Collected Papers B, 340-341.
52. "The Value of Astrology." N.d. 6 pp. Typescript, Collected Papers B, 414-419.
53. "The Point of Departure of Metaphysics." Poona: De Nobili College, [1955]. 10 pp. Typescript, Collected Papers A, 13-22 = DNC 73/DES/COL. (Published as no. 54 below.)
54. "The Point of Departure of Metaphysics." *Proceedings of the Indian Philosophical Congress* (1955) 211-219. (Cf. no. 53 above. Reprinted as no. 55 below.)
55. "The Point of Departure of Metaphysics." *The Philosophical Quarterly* **28**/4 (1956) 265-271. (Reprint of no. 54 above.)

1956

56. "The Fundamental Antinomy of Śrī Śaṅkarācārya's Methodology." *Oriental Thought* (Nashik) **2**/4 (Oct. 1956) 1-9. (Cf. no. 42 above.)

57. "Towards Re-Orienting Indian Philosophy: Hints from a Thomist." Poona: De Nobili College, [1956]. 8 pp. Typescript, Collected Papers A, 32-39 = DNC 73/DES/COL. (Published as no. 58 below.)
58. "Towards Re-Orienting Indian Philosophy: Hints from a Thomist." *Proceedings of the All-India Philosophical Congress* (1956) 191-197. (Cf. no. 57 above. Reprinted as no. 63 below.)
59. "Christian Religion. Scholasticism." [Post-1956: cf. mention of Gilson 1956 on p. 333.] 6 pp. Typescript, Collected Papers B, 328-333.
60. "The Sāṃkhya System." In Latin. [Probably 1956: p. 119 is in English, with title, "2. Elements of Permanent Value in Sāṃkhya," and dated 11 July 1956.] 9 pp. Typescript, Collected Papers A, 113-119 = DNC 73/DES/COL 113-119.

1957

61. "Saint Thomas Aquinas." [Post-1957: cf. mention of Gilson 1957 on p. 339.] 6 pp. Typescript, Collected Papers B, 334-339.
62. "Remarks to Fr Panikkar Concerning His Bhāṣya on Vedānta Sūtra 1.1.2." Letter of De Smet to Panikkar, dated 11 October 1957. 3 pp. Typescript, Collected Papers C, 552-554.
63. "Towards Re-Orienting Indian Philosophy: Hints from a Thomist." *The Philosophical Quarterly* **29**/4 (1957) 237-243. (Reprint of no. 58 above.)
64. "Elements of Permanent Value in Sāṃkhya." Poona: De Nobili College, [1957]. 1-13. Typescript, Collected Papers A, 120-132 = DNC 73/DES/COL 119-131. (Published as no. 65 below.)
65. "Elements of Permanent Value in Sāṃkhya." *Oriental Thought* (Nashik) **3**/2-4 (1957) 135-156. (Cf. no. 64 above.)
66. "Persona, Anima, Ātman." [1957.] 9 pp. Typescript, Collected Papers A, 42-50, and DNC 73/DES/COL. (Published as nos. 67 and 73.)
67. "*Persona, Anima, Ātman.*" *Proceedings of the Indian Philosophical Congress,* part II (1957). (Cf. no. 66 above. Reprinted as no. 73.)
68. "Nouvelles de Poona, 1957, 3." 18 November 1957. To relatives and friends, in French. 2 pp. Referred to as "Lettres de Poona" in the Table of Contents. Typescript, Collected Papers C, 696-697.
69. "Gioacchino Patti, S.J. *Der Samavāya im Nyāya-Vaiśeṣika System.*" Review [1957]. 2 pp. Typescript, Collected Papers A, 40-41. (Published as no. 70 below.)
70. Review of G. Patti, *Der Samavāya im Nyāya-Vaiśeṣika-System. The Clergy Monthly Supplement* **3**/7 (Oct. 1957) 297-298. (Cf. no. 69 above.)
71. [Translator.] G. Patti. "Transmigration of Souls in Hinduism." An abridged translation of the article entitled "La trasmigrazione delle anime nell'Induismo," *La Civiltà Cattolica,* Anno **108**/quaderno 2569 (1957) III:49-59. Typescript, Collected Papers B, 527-536.
72. "Teaching Philosophy in India: A Report on the Work of the Philosophy Section." [1957-58.] 6 pp. Typescript, Collected Papers A, 51-56 = DNC 73/DES/COL. (Published as no. 75 below.)

1958

73. "*Persona, Anima, Ātman.*" *The Philosophical Quarterly* **30**/4 (1958) 251-260. (Reprint of no. 67 above. Cf. no. 74.)
74. "Persona, Anima, Ātman." 6 pp. Typescript, Collected Papers D, 56-58. (This seems to have been copied from no. 73, as indicated in note 1 on p. 56.)
75. "Philosophical Topics: A Report on the Work of the Philosophy Section." Bangalore Conference on Seminary Training in India, 28 December 1957 – 2 January 1958. *The Clergy Monthly Supplement* **4**/2 (1958) 85-90. (Cf. no. 72.)
76. "Missionary Tasks Ahead." [1958.] 11 pp. Typescript, Collected Papers A, 60-70. (Published as nos. 77 and 78 below.)
77. "Missionary Tasks Ahead." *The Clergy Monthly Supplement* **4**/1 (1958) 3-14. (Cf. no. 76 above. Reprinted as no. 78 below.)
78. "Missionary Mind and Missionary Tasks Ahead." *Lumen Vitae* (Brussels) **13**/4 (1958) 727-742. (Cf. no. 76. Reprint of no. 77 above.)
79. "The Christian Meaning of Work." Poona: De Nobili College, [1958]. 4 pp. Typescript, Collected Papers A, 71-74. (Published as no. 80 below.)
80. "The Christian Meaning of Work." *The King's Rally* **35**/5-6 (May-July 1958) 127-142. (Cf. no. 79 above.)
81. "The Meaning of Sacrifice." Poona: De Nobili College, [1958]. 9 pp. Typescript, Collected Papers A, 75-84 = DNC 73/DES/COL. (Published as no. 82 below.)
82. "The Meaning of Sacrifice." *The Voice of Ahiṁsā* **8**/9-10 (Sept.-Oct. 1958) 296-303, 308. (Cf. no. 81 above.)
83. "The Great Hindu Theologies: 1. Shankara's Advaita or Non-Dualism." Hinduism: A Course by Letter. Lesson XVIII. 1 October 1958. 12 pp. Typescript, Collected Papers A, 85-96 (p. 97 missing) = DNC 73/DES/COL 85-97. (Published as no. 84 below.)
84. "The Great Hindu Theologies: 1. Shankara's Ādvaita or Non-Dualism." *Hinduism, A Course by Letter*. Lesson XVIII (October 1958) 1-15. (Cf. no. 83 above. German tr. in no. 129 below. French tr. in no. 258. Rev. versions in nos. 190, 191, 270, 748.)
85. "The Great Hindu Theologies: 2. Rāmānuja's Vishiṣṭādvaita or Non-Dualism of the Qualified Brahman." Hinduism: A Course by Letter. Lesson XIX. November 1958. 11 pp. Typescript, Collected Papers A, 98-109 = DNC 73/DES/COL 98-109. Includes "3. Madhva's Savisheṣādvaita or Simply Dvaita (Dualism)," 105-109. (Published as no. 86 below.)
86. "The Great Hindu Theologies: 2. Rāmānuja's Vishiṣṭādvaita or Non-Dualism of the Qualified Brahma. 1. [sic] Madhva's Savisheṣādvaita or simply Dvaita (Dualism)." *Hinduism, A Course by Letter*. Lesson XIX (November 1958) 1-14. (Cf. no. 85 above. German translation in no. 130 below. French tr. in no. 258. Rev. versions in nos. 192, 271, 749.)
87. "Omniscience in Christian Thought." N.d. 3 pp. Typescript, Collected Papers C, 650-652.
88. "Notes sur les problèmes essentials de l'âme indienne d'aujourd'hui." Poona: Pontifical Athanaeum, n.d. In French. 4 pp. Typescript, Collected Papers C, 653-656.

89. "Training in Spiritual Life." [1958.] 7 pp. Typescript, Collected Papers A, 133-139 = DNC 73/DES/COL 133-139. (Published as no. 90 below.)
90. "Training in Spiritual Life." *Silver Jubilee Commemoration Volume, Nowrosjee Wadia College*. Poona, 1958. 1-11. (Cf. no. 89 above.)
91. "Gordon Leff. Medieval Thought from Saint Augustine to Ockham." Review [1958]. 2 pp. Typescript, Collected Papers A, 140-141 = DNC 73/DES/COL 140-141. (Published as no. 92 below.)
92. Review of Gordon Leff, *Medieval Thought from St Augustin to Okham* (Pelican, 1958). *Notes on Islam* **11**/4 (Dec. 1958) 153-154. (Cf. no. 91 above.)

1959

93. "The Secret of Christianity." [1959.] 6 pp. Typescript, Collected Papers C, 537-542. (Published as no. 94 below.)
94. "The Secret of Christianity." In Marathi. *Rāma-taraṅg* (1959). (Cf. no. 93 above. Mentioned in no. 232 below.)
95. "Some Problems of Scholastic and Vedanta Philosophy." Abstract of lecture given on 8 February 1959 at a meeting of Darshana Cakra, Shanti Bhavan, Calcutta. 1 p. Typescript, Collected Papers A, 142 = DNC 73/DES/COL 142.
96. "Shaivism and Shaiva-Siddhanta." Hinduism: A Course by Letter. Lesson XX. 1959. 8 pp. Typescript, Collected Papers A, 110/1-8 = Collected Papers C, 558-565. (Published as no. 97 below.)
97. "Shaivism and Shaiva-Siddhānta." *Hinduism, A Course by Letter* XX (January 1959) 1-14. (Cf. no. 96 above. German translation no. 131 below.)
98. "Method and Doctrine of Saint Thomas Aquinas." [1959.] 10 pp. Typescript, Collected Papers D, 32-41. (Published as no. 99 below.)
99. "Method and Doctrine of Saint Thomas Aquinas." *Bulletin of the Ramakrishna Mission Institute of Culture* (Calcutta) **10**/10 (1959) 217-224. (Cf. no. 98 above.)
100. "Parapsychology and Catholicism." [1959.] 14 pp. Typescript, Collected Papers A, 152-165 = DNC 73/DES/COL 152-165. (Published as no. 101 below.)
101. "Parapsychology and Catholicism." *The Indian Journal of Parapsychology* **1**/4 (1959) 164-177. (Cf. no. 100 above.)
102. "Aux Sources de l'Existentialisme Chrétien: Kierkegaard. Par Régis Jolivet." Review [1959]. 2pp. Typescript, Collected Papers A, 111-112 = DNC 73/DES/COL 111-112. (Published as no. 103 below.)
103. Review of R. Jolivet, *Aux Sources de l'Existentialisme Chrétien: Kierkegaard. The Clergy Monthly* **23**/2 (1959) 77-78. (Cf. no. 102 above.)

1960

104. "Theological Method and Vedānta." Poona: De Nobili College, [1960]. 13 pp. Typescript, Collected Papers A, 167-179 = DNC 73/DES/COL 167-179. (Published as no. 105 below.)

105."Theological Method and Vedānta." *Oriental Thought* (Nashik) **4**/12 (1960) 20-35. (Cf. no. 104 above.)
106."Philosophy and Science as Integral Parts of Wisdom." Pune: De Nobili College. 5 pp. Typescript, Collected Papers D, 51-55. To be dated post 1958, cf. citation of Ladrière 1958 on p. 54. (Published as no. 107 below.)
107."Philosophy and Science as Integral Parts of Wisdom." *The Philosophical Quarterly* **33**/1 (1960) 31-39. (Cf. no. 106 above.)
108."L'activité philosophique au Pakistan." 60 pp. Typescript, Collected Papers A, 181-240 = DNC 73/DES/COL 181-240. (Published as nos. 109, 115 and 136 below.)
109."L'activité philosophique au Pakistan." *Archives de Philosophie* **23**/3 (1960) 402- 453. (Cf. no. 108 above. Published in English as nos. 115 and 136 below.)
110."Indian Catholicism." Letter to the Editor. 3 pp. Typescript, Collected Papers B, 241-243 = DNC 73/DES/COL 241-243. (Published as no. 111 below.)
111."Indian Catholicism." *The Examiner* (Bombay) **111**/39 (1960) 490-491. (Cf. no. 110 above.)
112. "Jesus's Message and Indian Thought." In Hindi. 1960. (Cf. no. 34 above. Mentioned in no. 232 below.)
113. "The Logical Structure of 'Tattvamasi' according to Sureśvara's Naiṣkarmya-Siddhi." Poona: De Nobili College.12 pp. Typescript, Collected Papers B, 244-256 = DNC 73/DES/COL 244-256. (Published as nos. 114 and 118 below.)
114. "The Logical Structure of 'Tattvamasi' according to Sureśvara's Naiṣkarmya-Siddhi." *Proceedings of the Indian Philosophical Congress* (1960) 51-61. (Cf. no. 113 above. Reprinted as no. 118 below.)

1961

115. *Philosophical Activity in Pakistan.* Pakistan Philosophical Congress Series. Lahore, 1961. (Enlarged English translation of no. 109 above. Reprinted as no. 136 below.)
116.[With J. de Marneffe.] "The Philosophy of Christianity." Poona: De Nobili College, n.d. 6 pp. Typescript, Collected Papers C, 681-686. To be dated post-1961: cf. mention of Tresmontant 1961 on p. 686. (= no. 117 below.)
117."Philosophy of Christianity." Article no. 65. 8 pp. Typescript, Collected Papers D, 42-50. (= no. 116 above, but de Marneffe's name is omitted. Handwritten note on title page: "finalized copy for Dr De Smet for own record.")
118."The Logical Structure of 'Tattvamasi' according to Sureśvara's Naiṣkarmya-Siddhi." The *Philosophical Quarterly* **33**/4 (1961) 255-265. (Reprint of no. 114 above.)
119."God and the World: An Historical Enquiry into Various Patterns and Theories of Causality." *The Journal of Viśvabhārati Study Circle* (Śāntiniketan) **2** (1961) 21-38.
120."Language and Philosophy in India." 1 p. summary, 6 pp. text. Typescript, Collected Papers B, 276-282 = DNC 73/DES/COL 276-282. (Published as no. 121 below.)

121."Language and Philosophy in India." *Proceedings of the International Congress of Philosophy* (1961) 47-54. DNC 73/DES/PUB 44,752 (2) and (3). (Cf. no. 120 above.)

122."Christian Charity." [1961]. 6 pp. Typescript, Collected Papers B, 297-302 = DNC 73/DES/COL 297-302. (Published as no. 123 below.)

123."Christian Charity." *The Voice of Ahiṅsā* **11** (1961) 296-299, 302. (Cf. no. 122 above.)

124."Indian Contribution to General Metaphysics." [1961]. 16 pp + 3 pp where the article starts again + 1 p. in Latin. Typescript, Collected Papers B, 342-360 = DNC 73/DES/COL 342-360. (Cf. no. 125 below.)

125."Indian Contribution to General Metaphysics." Poona: De Nobili College, [1961]. 23 pp. Typescript, Collected Papers D, 59-70. (Cf. no. 124 above. Published as no. 127 below.)

126."Corrections and Additions." [1961]. 4 pp. Typescript, Collected Papers B, 361-364. In the Table of Contents of Collected Papers B, the title of this item is given as "Indological Notes to German Translation of Preceding" (cf. no. 125 above).

127."Indiens Beitrag zur allgemeine Metaphysik." [Indian Contribution to General Metaphysics.] *Kairos* (Salzburg) **3**/4 (1961) 161-182. (Cf. nos. 124, 125, 126 above.)

128."Lettres de Poona." Poona 6: De Nobili College, December 1961. To relatives and friends, in French. 2 pp. Typescript, Collected Papers C, 698-699. The title has been taken from the Table of Contents of Collected Papers C. The letter itself has no title.

1962

129."Die grossen Hindu Theologen – I. Śaṅkaras Advaita oder Nichtdualismus." *Hinduismus und Christentum: Eine Einführung*. Ed. J. Neuner. (De Smet is not listed as co-editor.) Vienna: Herder, 1962. 170-181. (German translation of no. 84 above.)

130."Die grossen Hindu Theologen – II. Rāmānujas Viśiṣṭādvaita oder Nichtdualismus des Qualifizierten Brahma." *Hinduismus und Christentum: Eine Einführung*. Ed. J. Neuner.Vienna: Herder, 1962. 182-191. (German translation of no. 86 above.)

131."Śivaismus und Śaiva-Siddhānta." *Hinduismus und Christentum: Eine Einführung*. Ed. J. Neuner.Vienna: Herder, 1962. 192-201. (German translation of no. 97 above)

132."God and the World: An Historical Enquiry into Various Patterns and Theories of Causality." 1 p. = 257. Alternative start on next page: "Patterns and Theories of Causality." 18 pp. = 258-275. Typescript, Collected Papers B, 257-275 = DNC 73/DES/COL 257-275. (Published as nos. 133, 162 and 228 below.)

133."Patterns and Theories of Causality." *Essays in Philosophy presented to Dr. T. M. P. Mahadevan on his 50th Birthday*. Madras: Ganesh, 1962. 347-367. DNC 73/DES/PUB 44,752 (2) and (3). (Cf. no. 132 above. Reprinted as nos. 162 and 228 below.)

134."The Jesuits and the Jains." 3 pp. Typescript, Collected Papers B, 463-465. (Published as no. 135 below.)

135."The Jesuits and the Jains." *The Voice of Ahiṁsā* **12** (1962) 81-82. (Cf. no. 134 above.)

136."Philosophical Activity in Pakistan: 1947-1961." *International Philosophical Quarterly* **2**/1 (1962) 110-184. (Enlarged version of no. 109 above. Reprint of no. 115 above.)

137."Stumbling-Blocks or Stepping-Stones?" Poona: De Nobili College. 9 pp. Typescript, Collected Papers B, 379-387. (Published as no. 138 below.)

138."Stumbling-Blocks or Stepping Stones?" *Western and Eastern Spiritual Values of Life*. Ed. Swami B. H. Bon Mahārāj. Vrindāban: Institute of Oriental Philosophy, 1962. 68-75. (Cf. no. 137 above.)

139."All-India Symposium on Western and Eastern Values of Life. (Vrindaban, Jan. 6-8, 1962). A Report by Dr R.V. De Smet, S.J. (Nobili College, Poona - 6)." 7 pp. Typescript, Collected Papers B, 398-404. (Published as no. 140 below.)

140."Western and Eastern Values of Life: An All-India Symposium (Vrindāban, Jan. 6-8, 1962)." *The Clergy Monthly Supplement* **6**/2 (1962) 49-56. (Cf. no. 139 above. Summarized in no. 141 below.)

141."All-India Symposium on Western and Eastern Values of Life (Vrindaban, Jan. 6-8, 1962." *France-Asie* (Tokyo) **18**/173 (May-June 1962) 303-306. (Summary of no. 140 above.)

142."Un Dialogue Orient-Occident." Poona: De Nobili College. 10 pp. Typescript, Collected Papers B, 388-397. (Published as no. 143 below.)

143."Un Dialogue Orient-Occident." *Archives de Philosophie* **25** (1962) 280-287. (Cf. no. 142 above.)

144."'The Spiritual Dialogue of East and West' by J.A. Cuttat, summarized by Dr. R.V. De Smet, S.J." Poona: De Nobili College. 9 pp. Typescript, Collected Papers B, 405-413. (Published as no. 145 below.)

145."The Spiritual Dialogue of East and West." A Summary by De Smet of J.A. Cuttat's lecture delivered in April 1961 and published as a booklet by Max Müller Bhavan, German Cultural Institute, New Delhi. *The Clergy Monthly Supplement* **6**/2 (1962) 57-65. (Cf. no. 144 above.)

1963

146."Values and the Art of Taking Decisions." Chapter 20. 12 pp. Typescript, Collected Papers B, 283-296 = DNC 73/DES/COL 283-296. (Published as no. 147 below.)

147."Values and the Art of Making Decisions." *The Art of Living*. Jullundur City: University Publishers, 1963. 91-106. (Cf. no. 146 above.)

148."Some Governing Principles in Indian Philosophy." 10 pp. Typescript, Collected Papers B, 427-436. (Published as nos. 149 and 229 below.)

149."Some Governing Principles in Indian Philosophy." *The Philosophical Quarterly* (Amalner, India) **35**/4 (1963) 249-258. DNC 73/DES/PUB 44,752 (2) and (3). (Cf. no. 148 above. Reprinted as no. 229 below.)

150."A Herald of Social Reform in India, Swami Vivekānanda." 7 pp. Typescript, Collected Papers B, 420-426. (Published as no. 151 below.)

151."A Herald of Social Reform in India, Swāmi Vivekānanda." *Social Action* **13** (1963) 181-189. (Cf. no. 150 above.)

152."Remarks on Samāj-Dharma and Sādhana-Dharma." 4 pp. Typescript, Collected Papers B, 459-462. (Published as no. 153 below.)

153."Comments on Samāj-Dharma and Sādhana-Dharma." *The Clergy Monthly Supplement* **6**/4 (1963) 335-337. (Cf. no. 152 above.)

154."The Council and the Poor." *The Examiner* (Bombay) **114**/8 (Feb. 23, 1963) 114. (Reprinted as no. 155 below.)

155."The Council and the Poor: Will the Council Create a Secretariate to Watch Present-Day Needs?" *The Herald* (March 15, 1963). (Reprint of no. 154 above.)

156."The Love of Wisdom." 3 pp. Typescript, Collected Papers B, 466-468. (Published as no. 157 below.)

157."The Love of Wisdom." *The Voice of Ahinsā* **13**/9 (1963) 240-245, 207. (Cf. no. 156 above.)

158."Categories of Indian Philosophy and Communication of the Gospel." Preparatory Reading Material no. 6, Conference on Philosophy and Religion, Bangalore 6-9 May 1963. 4 pp. Typescript, Collected Papers D, 71-72. (Cf. nos. 159 and 160 below.)

159."Categories of Indian Philosophy and Communication of the Gospel." 10 pp. Typescript, Collected Papers B, 449-458. (Cf. no. 158 above. Published as no. 160 below.)

160."Categories of Indian Philosophy and Communication of the Gospel." *Religion and Society* **10**/3 (1963) 20-26. (Cf. nos. 158 and 159 above.)

161."Lettres de Poona." Poona 6: De Nobili College. December 1963. Addressed to relatives and friends, in French. 2 pp. Typescript, Collected Papers C, 700-701. (The title has been taken from the Table of Contents to Collected Papers C; the original letter has no title.)

162."Patterns and Theories of Causality." *Indian Ecclesiastical Studies* **2** (1963) 169-190. (Reprint of no. 133 above; cf. no. 228 below.)

163.[Translator, with others.] J. Maréchal. "The Intellectual Dynamism in Objective Knowledge." [Original in *Revue néoscolastique de Philosophie* **28** (1927) 137-165 = *Mélanges Joseph Maréchal* (Brussels / Paris, 1950) **1**:75-101.] Poona: De Nobili College, 1963-65. 1-37. Unpublished. JDV N13/M332. (J. de Marneffe, in *General Metaphysics: Study Guidelines*. Poona: Pontifical Athenaeum, 1966 [cyclostyled notes for students] 23, notes that De Smet translated this text in collaboration with others.)

164.[Translator, with others.] J. Maréchal. "At the Threshold of Metaphysics: Abstraction or Intuition?" [Original in *Revue néoscolastique de Philosophie* **31**(1929) 27-52, 121-147, 309-342.] Poona: De Nobili College, 1963-65. 38-149. Unpublished. JDV N13/M332. (J. de Marneffe, in *General Metaphysics: Study Guidelines*. Poona: Pontifical Athenaeum, 1966 [cyclostyled notes for students] 23, notes that De Smet translated this text in collaboration with others.)

165.[Translator, with others.] J. Maréchal. "The Natural Desire for Perfect Happiness." [Original in *Mélanges Joseph Maréchal* (Brussels / Paris, 1950) **2**:323-337.] Poona: De Nobili College, 1963-65. 150-170. Unpublished. JDV N13/M332. (J. de Marneffe, in *General Metaphysics: Study Guidelines*. Poona: Pontifical Athenaeum, 1966 [cyclostyled notes for students] 23, notes that De Smet translated this text in collaboration with others.)

166."Amesha Spentas." Typescript, Collected Papers C, 566. (Published as nos. 167, 516, 640 below.)

167."Amesha Spentas." *Verbo: Enciclopedia Luso-Brasileira de Cultura.* Lisboa: Editorial Verbo, 1963. 1:1817-1818. (Cf. no. 166. Reprinted as nos. 516, 640.)[1]

168."Amida." Typescript, Collected Papers C, 567. (Published as nos. 169, 517, 641.)

169."Amida." *Verbo: Enciclopedia Luso-Brasileira de Cultura.* Lisboa: Editorial Verbo, 1963. 1:1823-1824. (Cf. no. 167. Reprinted as nos. 517, 641.)

170. "Anāhitā." Typescript, Collected Papers C, 567. (Published as nos. 208, 518, 642.)

171."Ārya." Typescript, Collected Papers C, 568.

172."Ārya-Samāj." Typescript, Collected Papers C, 568. (Published as nos. 209, 519, 643.)

173."Āshrama." Typescript, Collected Papers C, 568. (Published as nos. 210, 520, 644.)

174."Asura." Typescript, Collected Papers C, 568. (Published as nos. 211, 521, 645.)

175."Avatāra." Typescript, Collected Papers C, 570. (Published as nos. 233, 523, 647.)

176."Avesta." Typescript, Collected Papers C, 570-571. (Published as nos. 234, 524, 648.)

177."Bhagavadgītā." Typescript, Collected Papers C, 571. (Published as nos. 235, 525, 649.)

178."Bhakti." Typescript, Collected Papers C, 572. (Published as nos. 236, 526, 650.)

179."Bhil." Typescript, Collected Papers C, 572. (Published as nos. 237, 527, 651.)

180."Brahmā." Typescript, Collected Papers C, 573. (Published as nos. 238, 528, 652.)

181."Brahman." Typescript, Collected Papers C, 573. (Published as nos. 239, 529, 653.)

182."Brāhmaṇa." Typescript, Collected Papers C, 574. (Published as nos. 240, 530, 654.)

183."Brahmanism." Typescript, Collected Papers C, 574-575. (Published as nos. 241, 531, 655.)

184."Brahmo-Samāj." Typescript, Collected Papers C, 575. (Published as no. 242, 532, 656.)

1964

185.[Editor, with J. Neuner.] *Religious Hinduism: A Presentation and Appraisal.* 2nd rev. ed. (of *Hinduism: A Course by Letter*, 1957-59). Allahabad: St. Paul Publications, 1964. (Reprinted as nos. 266 and 745. Cf. the German tr. in nos. 129, 130, 131; French tr. in no. 258.)

186."F. Śruti and Divine Inspiration." 3 pp. Typescript, Collected Papers C, 635-638. (Published as no. 187 below.)

187.“F. Śruti and Divine Inspiration.” Chapter 2: Sacred Books and Religious Literature. *Religious Hinduism: A Presentation and Appraisal*. Ed. R. De Smet and J. Neuner. 2nd rev. ed. Allahabad: St. Paul Publications, 1964. 38-40. (Cf. no. 186 above. Reprinted as no. 268 below.)

188.“Ancient Religious Speculation.” Chapter 3. 12 pp. Typescript, Collected Papers C, 620-631. (Published as no. 189 below.)

189.“Ancient Religious Speculation.” Chapter 3. *Religious Hinduism: A Presentation and Appraisal*. Ed. R. De Smet and J. Neuner. 2nd rev. ed. Allahabad: St. Paul Publications, 1964. 41-51. (Cf. no. 188 above. Reprinted as nos. 203, 204 and 269 below.)

190.“Śaṅkara's Non-Dualism (Advaita-Vāda). Chapter 4. 3 pp. Typescript, Collected Papers A, 1-3, without the running pagination of the rest of the volume, inserted just before no. 76 (Collected Papers A, 85-96) = Collected Papers C, 632-634. (Probably a partial revision of no. 84 above. Cf. last line, p. 3: “Continued in the printed text, p. 5.” Published as no. 191 below.)

191.“Śaṅkara's Non-Dualism (Advaita-Vāda). *Religious Hinduism: A Presentation and Appraisal*. Ed. R. De Smet and J. Neuner. 2nd rev. ed. Allahabad: St. Paul Publications, 1964. 52-62. (Cf. nos. 83, 84, 129, 190, 191 and 258. Reprinted as nos. 270 and 748 below.)

192.“Rāmānuja and Madhva.” *Religious Hinduism: A Presentation and Appraisal*. Ed. R. De Smet and J. Neuner. 2nd rev. ed. Allahabad: St Paul Publications, 1964. 63-72. (Cf. nos. 85, 86, 130. Reprinted as nos. 271 below and 749 below.)

193.“Sin and Its Removal.” 11 pp. Typescript, Collected Papers C, 639-649. (Published as no. 194 below.)

194.“Sin and Its Removal.” *Religious Hinduism: A Presentation and Appraisal*. Ed. R. De Smet and J. Neuner. 2nd rev. ed. Allahabad: St. Paul Publications, 1964. 122-131. (Cf. no. 193. Reprinted as nos. 230, 272 and 750 below.)

195.“D. Appraisal.” Chapter 12: Hindu Calendar and Festivals. *Religious Hinduism: A Presentation and Appraisal*. Ed. R. De Smet and J. Neuner. 2nd rev. ed. Allahabad: St. Paul Publications, 1964. 139-140. (Reprinted as no. 273 below.)

196.“Bhopal Institute of Oriental and Social Studies.” 3 pp. Typescript, Collected Papers C, 555-557. (Published as no. 197 below.)

197.“Bhopal Institute of Oriental and Social Studies.” *The Clergy Monthly Supplement* 7 (1964) 154-156. (Cf. no. 196 above.)

198.“The Eucharist and the Sacramental-Sacrificial Aspirations of India.” 10 pp. Typescript, Collected Papers B, 469-478. (Published as no. 199 below.)

199.“The Eucharist and the Sacramental Aspirations of India.” *India and the Eucharist*. Ed. S. Rayan and S. Kappen. Ernakulam: Lumen Institute, 1964. 19-28. (Cf. no. 198 above.)

200.“Kanāda's Teaching on Knowledge.” *Indian Antiquary* (3rd series) **1** (1964) 13-30. DNC 73/DES/PUB 44,752 (2) and (3). (Cf. no. 33 above.)

201.“Saint Thomas Aquinas.” *The Telugu Encyclopedia*. Madras, 1964.

202.“Scholasticism.” *The Telugu Encyclopedia*. Madras, 1964.

203.“Ancient Religious Speculation in India.” *The Divine Life* **26** (1964) 208-215. (Reprint of no. 189 above. Reprinted as no. 269.)

204."Ancient Religious Speculation in India." N.d. 1-8. (Probably an offprint of no. 203 above.)
205."Śruti and Biblical Inspiration." *The Divine Life* **26** (1964) 314-315. (Reprint of no. 187 above.)
206."M.D. Paradkar. *Similes in Manusmṛti.*" Review. 2 pp. Typescript, Collected Papers B, 303-304 = DNC 73/DES/COL 303-304. (Published as no. 207 below.)
207.Review of M.D. Paradkar, *Similes in Maṇusmṛti. Indian Antiquary* (3rd series) **1** (1964) 64-65. (Cf. no. 206 above.)
208."Anāhitā." *Verbo: Enciclopedia Luso-Brasileira de Cultura.* Lisboa: Editorial Verbo, 1964. **2**:61. (Cf. no. 169. Reprinted as nos. 518, 642.)
209."Aryo-Samaj." *Verbo: Enciclopedia Luso-Brasileira de Cultura.* Lisboa: Editorial Verbo, 1964. **2**:1467-1468. (Cf. no. 172. Reprinted as nos. 519, 643.)
210."Āshrama." *Verbo: Enciclopedia Luso-Brasileira de Cultura.* Lisboa: Editorial Verbo, 1964. **2**:1506-1507. (Cf. no. 173. Reprinted as nos. 520, 644.)
211."Asura." *Verbo: Enciclopedia Luso-Brasileira de Cultura.* Lisboa: Editorial Verbo, 1964. **2**:1697. (Cf. no. 174. Reprinted as nos. 521, 645.)
212."Ātman." *Verbo: Enciclopedia Luso-Brasileira de Cultura.* Lisboa: Editorial Verbo, 1964. **2**:1754-1755. (Cf. nos. 522, 646.)
213.The Hindu Samskāras. Cyclostyled notes for students. Pune: [Jnana Deepa Vidyapeeth], 1964. 34 pp. (Mentioned in no. 726, 5a.)

1965

214."Parallel Arguments for the Existence of God in Aquinas and Sankara." Poona Philosophy Union, lecture by Dr R.V. De Smet, S.J. 26 August 1965. 2 pp. Typescript, Collected Papers D, 74.
215."An Academic Centre for Ecclesiastical Studies. Philosophy: (Suggested) General Syllabus: I." 4 pp. Typescript, Collected Papers D, 75-76. To be dated pre-1962: cf. allusion to the imminent affiliation of St Peter's Seminary, Bangalore (p. 75); St Peter's was affiliated to the Pontifical Urban University, Rome, in 1962.
216."The Lag between Sanātana Dharma and Darshanic Wisdom." Poona: De Nobili College, n.d. 4 pp. Typescript, Collected Papers C, 659-662. (Published as no. 217 below.)
217."The Lag between Sanātana Dharma and Darsanic Wisdom." *Transactions of the Indian Institute of Advanced Study* **1** (1965) 105-108. (Cf. no. 216 above.)
218."Is There an Order of the Supernatural?" Poona: De Nobili College, n.d. 4 pp. Typescript, Collected Papers C, 663-666. (Published as no. 219 below.)
219."Is There an Order of the Supernatural?" *Transactions of the Indian Institute of Advanced Study* **1** (1965) 119-122. (Cf. no. 218 above.)
220."The Adaptive Development of Christian Monasticism." Poona: De Nobili College, n.d. 14 pp. Typescript, Collected Papers C, 667-680. (Published as no. 221 below.)

221.“The Adaptive Development of Christian Monasticism.” *Transactions of the Indian Institute of Advanced Study* **1** (1965) 191-202. (Cf. no. 220 above.)
222.“The Doctrine of Sacrifice in Hinduism.” *The Divine Life* **27** (1965) 54-58. (Reprinted as no. 316 below).
223.“Traditional Values to be Promoted in Modern India.” N.d. 4 pp. Typescript, Collected Papers B, 506-509. (Published as no. 224 below.)
224.“Traditional Values to be Promoted in Modern India.” *Seminar on Education*. Poona, May 1965. Vol. 1, paper 7. (Cf. no. 223 above. Reprinted as no. 306 below.)
225.“Materials for an Indian Christology.” N.d. 9 pp. Appendix. 3 pp. Typescript, Collected Papers B, 510-518 + 518b-c. (Published as nos. 226, 227.)
226.“Towards an Indian Christology.” *The Clergy Monthly Supplement* **7/6** (1965) 254-260. A note on p. 254 describes this paper as a shortened and slightly improved version of a paper read at the Nagpur session of the Indian Christian Theological Association, 22-24 March 1965. (Cf. no. 225. Reprinted in no. 227.)
227. “Materials for an Indian Christology.” *Religion and Society* **12** (1965) 6-15. (Cf. no. 225 above; reprint of 226 + appendix.)
228. “Patterns and Theories of Causality.” *Philosophy Today* **9/2-4** (1965) 134-146. (Reprint of nos. 133 and 162 above.)
229.“Some Governing Principles in Indian Philosophy.” *Philosophy Today* **9/3-4** (1965) 192-199. (Reprint of no. 149 above.)
230.“Sin and Its Removal in India.” *Indian Antiquary*, third series, **1/3** (1965) 163-173. DNC 73/DES/PUB 44,752 (2) and (3). (Reprint of no. 194 above.)
231.“Lettre de Noël 1965.” Poona: De Nobili College. 1 December 1965. To relatives and friends, in French. 4 pp. Typescript, Collected Papers C, 702-705.
232.“Publications of Dr Richard V. De Smet, S.J.” [Post-1964]. 8 pp. Unpublished. DNC 73/DES/PUB 44,752 (2) and (3).
233.“Avatāra.” *Verbo: Enciclopedia Luso-Brasileira de Cultura.* Lisboa: Editorial Verbo, 1965. **3**:98. (Cf. no. 175. Reprinted as nos. 523, 647.)
234.“Avesta.” *Verbo: Enciclopedia Luso-Brasileira de Cultura.* Lisboa: Editorial Verbo, 1965. **3**:132, 135. (Cf. no. 176. Reprinted as nos. 524, 648.)
235.“Bhagavadgītā.” *Verbo: Enciclopedia Luso-Brasileira de Cultura.* Lisboa: Editorial Verbo, 1965. **3**:1226-1227. (Cf. no. 177. Reprinted as nos. 525, 649.)
236.“Bhakti.” *Verbo: Enciclopedia Luso-Brasileira de Cultura.* Lisboa: Editorial Verbo, 1965. **3**:1227. (Cf. no. 178. Reprinted as no. 526, 650.)
237.“Bhil.” *Verbo: Enciclopedia Luso-Brasileira de Cultura.* Lisboa: Editorial Verbo, 1965. **3**:1229. (Cf. no. 179. Reprinted as nos. 527, 651.)
238.“Brama.” *Verbo: Enciclopedia Luso-Brasileira de Cultura.* Lisboa: Editorial Verbo, 1965. **3**:1775. (Cf. no. 180. Reprinted as nos. 528, 652.)
239.“Braman.” *Verbo: Enciclopedia Luso-Brasileira de Cultura.* Lisboa: Editorial Verbo, 1965. **3**:1775-1776. (Cf. no. 181. Reprinted as nos. 529, 653.)

240."Bramana." *Verbo: Enciclopedia Luso-Brasileira de Cultura*. Lisboa: Editorial Verbo, 1965. **3**:1776. (Cf. no. 182. Reprinted as nos. 530, 654.)

241."Bramanismo." *Verbo: Enciclopedia Luso-Brasileira de Cultura*. Lisboa: Editorial Verbo, 1965. **3**:1778-1779. (Cf. no. 183. Reprinted as nos. 531, 655.)

242."Bramo-Samaj." *Verbo: Enciclopedia Luso-Brasileira de Cultura*. Lisboa: Editorial Verbo, 1965. **3**:1782-1783. (Cf. no. 184. Reprinted as nos. 532, 656.)

243."More about Karma." *Prem Mārg* **1**/6 (1965) 3-5. (Mentioned in no. 726, 5c.)

1966

244."Devotion to the Sacred Heart in Ancient Times." *The Messenger of the Sacred Heart* (Bombay) **59**/10 (Oct. 1966) 4.

245."The Law of Karma: A Critical Examination." N.d. 8 pp. Typescript, Collected Papers B, 519-526. (Published as no. 246 below.)

246."The Law of Karma: A Critical Examination." *Indian Philosophical Annual* **2** (1966) 328-335. (Cf. no. 245 above. Reprinted as no. 293 below.)

247."Māyā or Ajñāna?" *Indian Philosophical Annual* **2** (1966) 220-225. (Reprinted as no. 308 below).

248."Zum indischen Menschenbild." [Concerning the Indian View of Man.] *Kairos* (Salzburg) **8**/3-4 (1966) 197-202.

249."Salvation of Non-Christians according to Xavier's Companions." N.d. 2 pp. Typescript, Collected Papers C, 657-658. Post-1964: cf. citation of Schurhammer, *Xaveriana*, 1964, on p. 658. (Published as no. 250 below.)

250."Salvation of Non-Christians according to Xavier's Companions." *The Clergy Monthly Supplement* **8**/2 (1966) 86-87. (Cf. no. 249 above.)

251."Pastoral Counselling." (Review of A. Godin, *The Pastor as Counselor*, New York, 1965.) N.d. 5 pp. Typescript, Collected Papers C, 691-695. (Published as no. 252 below.)

252."Pastoral Counselling." (Review of A. Godin, *The Pastor as Counselor*, New York, 1965.) *The Clergy Monthly Supplement* **6**/3 (1966) 126-129. (Cf. no. 251 above.)

253."Short Replies to Four Questions Concerning Existentialism." *Aumol* **13** (1966).

254."M. K. Venkatarana [sic] Iyer. *Advaita Vedānta*." (Review.) Poona: De Nobili College, n.d. 2 pp. Typescript, Collected Papers C, 689-690. (Published as nos. 255 and 256 below.)

255.Review of M. K. Venkatarana [sic] Iyer, *Advaita Vedānta. Boletin de la Asociaciòn Española de Orientalistas* **2** (1966) 223-224. (Cf. nos. 254 above and 256 below.)

256.Review of M. K. Venkatarama Iyer, *Advaita Vedānta. Indian Ecclesiastical Studies* **5**/1-2 (1966) 144-145. (Cf. nos. 254 and 255.)

257.Review of A. Pezzali, *La cultura del India ieri e oggi. Indian Ecclesiastical Studies* **5**/1-2 (1966) 145.

1967

258.[Editor, with J. Neuner.] *La Quête de l'Éternel: Approches Chrétiennes de l'Hindouisme*. Museum Lessianum, Section missiologique, no. 48. Paris: Desclée de Brouwer, 1967. (French translation by R. Dumortier of no. 185, revised and enlarged.)

259."The Present State of Traditional Hinduism." *The Clergy Monthly Supplement* **8**/5 (1967) 182-187.

260."Le dialogue vivifié par les textes." *Rythmes du Monde* **15**/3-4 (1967) 197-205.

261.Review of *Symbolon: Jahrbuch für Symbolforschung*, Bd. 5 (1966). *Kairos* **9**/1 (1967) 61-64.

262."Dharma." *Verbo: Enciclopedia Luso-Brasileira de Cultura*. Lisboa: Editorial Verbo, 1967. **6**:1213. (Reprinted as nos. 533, 657.)

263."Dharma-Sastra." *Verbo: Enciclopedia Luso-Brasileira de Cultura*. Lisboa: Editorial Verbo, 1967. **6**:1213. (Reprinted as nos. 534, 658.)

264."Dhyana." *Verbo: Enciclopedia Luso-Brasileira de Cultura*. Lisboa: Editorial Verbo, 1967. **6**:1214-1215. (Reprinted as nos. 535, 659.)

265."Digha-Nikaya." *Verbo: Enciclopedia Luso-Brasileira de Cultura*. Lisboa: Editorial Verbo, 1967. **6**:1360. (Reprinted as nos. 536, 660.)

1968

266.[Editor and contributor, with J. Neuner.] *Religious Hinduism*. 3rd rev. ed. Allahabad: St Paul Publications, 1968. (Reprint of no. 185; reprinted as no. 745.)

267."Foreword." *Religious Hinduism: A Presentation and Appraisal*. Ed. R. De Smet and J. Neuner. 3rd rev. ed. Allahabad: St Paul Publications, 1968. (Cf. revised version in no. 746.)

268."F. Śruti and Divine Inspiration." *Religious Hinduism: A Presentation and Appraisal*. Ed. R. De Smet and J. Neuner. 3rd rev. ed. Allahabad: St Paul Publications, 1968. 38-40. (Reprint of no. 187.)

269."Ancient Religious Speculation." Chapter 3. *Religious Hinduism: A Presentation and Appraisal*. Ed. R. De Smet and J. Neuner. 3rd rev. ed. Allahabad: St Paul Publications, 1968. 41-51. (Reprint of no. 189. Cf. nos. 203, 204.)

270."Śaṅkara's Non-Dualism (Advaita-Vāda)." Chapter 4. *Religious Hinduism: A Presentation and Appraisal*. Ed. R. De Smet and J. Neuner. 3rd rev. ed. Allahabad: St Paul Publications, 1968. 52-62. (Reprint of no. 191. Cf. revised version in no. 748.)

271."Rāmānuja and Madhva." Chapter 5. *Religious Hinduism: A Presentation and Appraisal*. Ed. R. De Smet and J. Neuner. 3rd rev. ed. Allahabad: St Paul Publications, 1968. 63-72. (Reprint of no. 192. Reprinted in no. 749.)

272."Sin and Its Removal." Chapter 11. *Religious Hinduism: A Presentation and Appraisal*. Ed. R. De Smet and J. Neuner. 3rd rev. ed. Allahabad: St Paul Publications, 1968. 126-135. (Reprint of no. 194. Revised version in no. 750.)

273."D. Appraisal." Chapter 12: Hindu Calendar and Festivals. *Religious Hinduism: A Presentation and Appraisal*. Ed. R. De Smet and J. Neuner.

3rd rev. ed. Allahabad: St Paul Publications, 1968. 143-144. (Reprint of no. 195.)

274."The Nature of Christian Philosophy." Contribution to Dr. D.M. Datta Commemoration Volume. N.d. 6 pp. Typescript, Collected Papers B, 437-442. (Published as no. 275.)

275."The Nature of Christian Philosophy." *World Perspectives in Philosophy, Religion and Culture: Essays presented to Prof. Dhirendra Mohan Datta.* Patna: Bihar Darshan Parishad, 1968. 362-368. (Cf. no. 274.)

276."Vyāsa and the Indian Epic." 4 pp. Typescript, Collected Papers B, 443-446.

277."Church and Intellectuals in India. Responsa additiva." In Latin. N.d. 2 pp. Typescript, Collected Papers B, 447-448. The title is taken from the Table of Contents of Collected Papers B.

278."Un Missionaire en Inde." *Contacts* (Charleroi, Collège du Sacré-Coeur) (March 1968). 3 pp.

279."The Indian Renaissance: Hindu Philosophy in English." *International Philosophical Quarterly* **8**/1 (1968) 5-37. (Tr. of no. 445.)

280."Concerning Atheism." Poona: De Nobili College, n.d. 2 pp. Typescript, Collected Papers C, 687-688. (Published as no. 281.)

281."Concerning Atheism: What to Do." *Asian S.J. Interprovincial News* **10** (April 1968) 6-17. (Cf. no. 280.)

282.Review of Mohan Singh Uberoi Diwana, *My Spiritual Experiences. Indian Ecclesiastical Studies* 7/2 (1968) 129-131. (Reprinted as no. 294.)

283.Guidelines in Indian Philosophy. Cyclostyled notes for students. Poona: De Nobili College, 1968. 314 pp.

284.A Selection of Texts from Śaṅkarācārya. Cyclostyled notes for students. Pune: Jnana Deepa Vidyapeeth, n.d. 30 pp. (Mentioned in no. 726, 3.)

1969

285."Śaṅkara and Aquinas on Liberation (Mukti)." *Indian Philosophical Annual* **5** (University of Madras) (1969) 239-247. (Reprinted as no. 314.)

286."Mutation of Values in Present-Day Europe." *Quest* **60** (Jan.-Mar. 1969) 21-27.

287."Theology of Hope and the Meaning of Mission." *Reflection* (Rajpur, Dehradun) **3** (1969) 3-10.

288."Die Theologie in Indien." *Bilans der Theologie im 20° Jahrhundert.* Ed. H. Vorgrimler and R. Vander Gucht. Freiburg: Herder, 1969. 405-421. (Cf. no. 298.)

289."The Contemporary Crisis in the Indian Mind." *Dialogue* (IRFED, Paris) **2** (March 1969) 34-37, 49-51.

290."Affinities between Guru Nanak and Jesus Christ." *Indian Ecclesiastical Studies* **8**/4 (1969) 260-268. (Reprinted as nos. 328 and 488.)

291."The Marxist-Protestant-Catholic Rediscovery of Hope." *Bethany Golden Jubilee Souvenir*. Trivandrum: Bethany Ashram, 1969. 121-126.

292."En Inde: Colloque oecuménique au sujet de la mission." *Rythmes du Monde* **17**/1 (1969).

293."The Law of Karma: A Critical Examination." *Indian Ecclesiastical Studies* **8**/3 (1969) 181-187. (Reprint of no. 246.)

294.Review of Mohan Sing [sic] Uberoi Diwana, *My Spiritual Experiences. Boletin de la Asociaciòn Española de Orientalistas* **5** (1969) 227-229. (Reprint of no. 282.)
295.Review of Ramakant Sinari, *Reason in Existentialism* (Bombay: Popular Prakashan, 1966). *Journal of the Philosophical Association* **12**/41-42 (1969) 151-153. (Reprinted as no. 312.)
296."Gandhi." *Verbo: Enciclopedia Luso-Brasileira de Cultura*. Lisboa: Editorial Verbo, 1969. **9**:151-152. (Reprinted as nos. 537, 661.)

1970

297."Śaṅkara and Aquinas on Creation." *Indian Philosophical Annual* **6** (1970) 112-118. (Reprinted as no. 348.)
298."La théologie en Inde." *Bilan de la Theologie du XXe siecle*. Vol. 1: Le monde contemporain. Les grands courants théologiques. Ed. R. Vander Gucht et H. Vorgrimler. Paris: Casterman, 1970. 360-374. (Cf. no. 288.)[2]
299."The Most Important Verse in the Gītā, XVIII, 65." Typescript, Collected Papers B, 501-505. (Published as no. 300.)
300."The Most Important Verse in the Gītā." *Studies in the Gītā*. Ed. M.D. Paradkar. Bombay: Popular Prakashan, 1970. 174-178. (Cf. no. 299.)
301."The Catholic Church and the Modern World." *Islam and the Modern Age* **1**/2 (1970) 59-67.
302."The Atheists' Meeting at Vijayawada." *The Clergy Monthly* **34**/5 (1970) 213-214.
303."Introduction." *In Diverse Ways*. Poona: Marga Prakashan, De Nobili College, 1970. 3-6.
304."The Open Person vs. the Closed Individual." *Indian Ecclesiastical Studies* **9**/3 (1970) 161-171. (Reprinted as no. 390.)
305."The Indian Understanding of Man." Presidential Address, History of Philosophy Section, 44th Session, Indian Philosophical Congress, under the auspices of the University of Poona, 5-8 November 1970. 12 pp. Published by author and printed at St Paul Press Training School, Bandra, Bombay – 50. (Reprinted as nos. 329, 326, 330, 331 and 343.)
306."Traditional Values to be Promoted in India." *The School Teacher* **2**/3 (March 1970) 108-111. (Reprint of no. 224.)
307."Gandhi, the Pursuit of Truth." *Journal of the University of Poona* (Humanities Section) **33** (1970) 135-137. (Reprinted as no. 339.)
308."Māyā or Ajñāna? A Textual Analysis." *Indian Ecclesiastical Studies* **9**/2 (1970) 80-84. (Reprint of no. 247.)
309."Et l'Ange me dit." *La Vie Spirituelle* (January 1970) 26-28.
310."A Note on Atheism in India." *Asian Interprovincial News* **1**/4 (1970).
311."Présince di M'Moman." *Les Cahiers Wallons* (March 1970) 49-50.
312.Review of Ramakant Sinari, *Reason in Existentialism. Indian Ecclesiastical Studies* **9**/2 (1970) 124-126. (Reprint of no. 295.)
313.Review of Pritibhushan Chatterji, *The Philosophy of Josiah Royce. Indian Ecclesiastical Studies* **9**/3 (1970) 195-196. (Reprinted as no. 334.)

1971

314.“A Twofold Approach: Śaṅkara – Aquinas: Śaṅkara and Aquinas on Liberation (Mukti).” *Indian Ecclesiastical Studies* **10**/1 (1971) 10-17. (Reprint of no. 285.)
315.“The Problematics of the Knowledge of God.” *Indian Ecclesiastical Studies* **10**/2 (1971) 92-96. (Reprinted as nos. 325, 499.)
316.“The Doctrine of Sacrifice in Hinduism.” *Indian Ecclesiastical Studies* **10**/2 (1971) 99-103. (Reprint of no. 222 above.)
317.Review of Secretariatus pro Non-Christianis, *Towards a Dialogue with Buddhism*, 2 vols. *Indian Ecclesiastical Studies* **10**/2 (1971) 119-120.
318.“Picturesque Pedagogy from the Tamil Past.” *Saiva Siddhanta* **6**/4 (1971) 219-221. (Reprinted as no. 355.)
319.“Our Lady of the Mount in 1724.” *The Examiner* (Bombay) **122** (Jan. 23, 1971) 60.
320.“Jesus and the Freedom of Man.” *The Call Divine* **19**/11 (1971) 582-583.
321.“Au coeur secret de l’Inde: Quelques activités du Père Richard De Smet, S.J.” *Missi*. Supplément de 8 pages, Édition Belge (November 1971) 2-3, 6.
322.“Une visite à la ville sainte des Madhvas.” *Missi* (December 1971) 4-6.
323.“Some Key Definitions.” *Indian Cultures Quarterly* **27**/1 (1971) 19-23.
324.“Questioning Vedānta.” *Indian Philosophical Annual* 7 (1971) 97-105.
325.“The Problematics of the Knowledge of God.” *Indian Philosophical Annual* 7 (1971) 121-125. (Reprint of nos. 314, 499.)
326.“The Indian Understanding of Man.” *Indian Ecclesiastical Studies* **10**/3 (1971) 169-178. (Reprint of no. 305; cf. nos. 329, 330, 331 and 343.)
327. “Advances in Muslim-Christian Dialogue.” *Indian Ecclesiastical Studies* **10**/4 (1971) 210-217. (Reprinted as nos. 356 and 372.)
328. “Affinities between Guru Nānak and Jesus Christ.” *The Sikh Review* **19** (1971) 5-11. (Reprint of no. 290. Cf. no. 488.)
329. “The Indian Understanding of Man.” *The Call Divine* **19**/5 (1971) 211-223. (Reprint of no. 305; cf. nos. 326, 330, 331 and 343.)
330. “Early Trends in the Indian Understanding of Man.” N.d. 1-8. (Reprint of no. 305; cf. nos. 329, 326, 331 and 343.)
331.“Early Trends in the Indian Understanding of Man.” *The Divine Life* **33**/2 (1971) 60-67. (Reprint of no. 305; cf. nos. 329, 326, 330 and 343.)
332.Review of G. Parrinder, *Avatar and Incarnation. Journal of Religious Studies* (Punjabi University, Patiala, India) **3**/1 (1971) 171-173.
333.Review of *Proceedings of the 26th International Congress of Orientalists. Indian Antiquary* (3rd series) **5**/4 (Oct. 1971) 229-233.
334.Review of Pritibhushan Chatterji, *Philosophy of Josiah Royce*. *Boletin de la Asociaciòn Española de Orientalistas* 7 (1971) 239-240. (Reprint of no. 313.)

1972

335.“From Love to Service.” *Messenger of* the *Sacred Heart* (Feb. 1972) 30-32 and (Mar. 1972) 25-28.
336.“Quiz Time.” *The Herald* (Calcutta) (Jan. 28, 1972) 6.

337."The Stress on Service in Christianity." *Vivekananda Kendra Patrika* **1**/1 (February 1972) 139-143.
338."Three Stages of the Theological Process." *Asian Report* **4**/7 (15 July 1972) 17.
339."Gandhi, the Pursuit of Truth." *Proceedings of the Seminar on Gandhian Thought* (Poona: University of Poona, 1972) 35-37. (Reprint of no. 307.)
340."Hinduism." *The Divine Life* **34**/8 (1972) 289-292. (Cf. no. 341. Probably offprinted in no. 341.)
341."Hinduism." Y.V.F.A. Press, Shivanandanagar. 1-4. (Probably offprint of no. 340.)
342."The Priest as Kalyāṇa Mitra." *The Clergy Monthly* **36**/7 (1972) 299-301.
343."Early Trends in the Indian Understanding of Man." *Philosophy East and West* **22**/3 (1972) 259-268. (Reprint of no. 259; cf. nos. 329, 326, 330 and 331.)
344."Secularization as a Dimension of Christianity." (A summary by D. Rodrigues) *Aumol* **19** (1972) 124-126. (Reprinted as no. 368.)
345."The Philosophy of a Modern Biologist, Jacques Monod." *The Journal of the Indian Academy of Philosophy* **11**/1 (1972) 54-63.
346."L'exégèse dans l'hindouisme." *Axes* **4**/4 (1972) 28-37 (Cf. English translation in no. 614.)
347."Team-Spirit and Team-Work in the Society of Jesus According to Its Constitutions." N.d. 14 pp. Typescript, Collected Papers B, 365-378. (Published as no. 348.)
348."Team-spirit and Team-work in the Constitutions of the Society of Jesus." *Ignis* **1**/3 (1972) 5-18. (Cf. no. 347.)
349.Review of Ruth Reyna, *Introduction to Indian Philosophy: A Simplified Text* (Delhi: Tata-McGraw-Hill, 1971). *Indian Ecclesiastical Studies* **11**/3 (1972) 208-209.
350.Review of R. Balasubramanian, *The Personalistic Existentialism of Berdyaev. Indian Ecclesiastical Studies* **11**/3 (1972) 210-212.
351."Śaṅkara and Aquinas on Creation." *Indian Ecclesiastical Studies* **11**/4 (1972) 235-241. (Reprint of no. 297.)
352."Is the Concept of 'Person' Congenial to Śāṅkara Vedānta?" *Indian Philosophical Annual* **8** (1972) 199-205. (Reprinted as nos. 371 and 376.)
353."Mokṣa." *The Divine Life* **34**/9 (1972) 372-373. (Offprinted as no. 354.)
354."Moksha—Deliverance." N.d. 1-2. (Offprint of no. 353.)
355."Picturesque Pedagogy from the Tamil Past." *The School Teacher* **4**/3 (1972) 124-126. (Reprint of no. 316.)
356."Advances in Muslim-Christian Dialogue." *Islam and the Modern Age* **3**/1 (1972) 47-56. (Reprint of no. 326. Cf. no. 372.)
357.Review of M.V. George, *My Lord and My God. The Clergy Monthly* **36**/6 (July 1972) 263-264. (Reprinted as no. 358.)
358.Review of M. V. George, *My Lord and My God. The Living Word* **78**/5 (Sept. 1972) 376-377. (Reprint of no. 357.)
359."Gita in Time and Beyond Time." *The Bhagavad Gita and the Bible. Proceedings of the Seminar under the Auspices of the Christian Retreat and Study Centre, Rajpur, Dehradun. May 5-9, 1972*. Ed. B. R. Kulkarni. Delhi: Unity Books, 1972. 1-30. (Reprinted as no. 540.)

360. "The Personal God of the Bhagavad-Gītā." N.d. 12 pp. Typescript, Collected Papers B, 479-500. (Published as no. 361.)

1973

361. "Discovery of the Personal God in the Gita." *The Divine Life* **35**/3 (1973) 97-100, 133-136. (Cf. nos. 360 and 362. Reprinted as no. 491 and 584.)
362. "Discovery of the Personal God in the Gita." Printed at the Y.V.F.A. Press, P.O. Shivanandanagar, n.d. 1-8. (Offprint of no. 361.)
363. "Advaitavada and Christianity." *The Divine Life* **35**/6 (1973) 237-239. (Reprinted as nos. 367 and 374, and in Marathi tr. in no. 364.)
364. "Advaita va Khristī Dharma." Tr. into Marathi by M. Lederle and published by him. N.d. (Marathi tr. of no. 363.)
365. "Highlights of the Life of Faith (Śraddhā) in India." *God's Word Among Men; Essays in Honour of J. Putz, S.J.* Ed. G. Gispert-Sauch. Delhi: Vidyajyoti, 1973. 39-58.
366. "Suggestions for an Indian Dialogical Theology." *Bangalore Theological Forum* **5**/1 (1973) 74-80.
367. "Advaitavada and Christianity." *Bulletin of the Secretariate for Non-Christians* **23-24** (1973) 143-146. (Reprint of no. 363.)
368. "Secularization as a Dimension of Christianity." *Ateismo e Dialogo* (Bollettino del Segretariato per i non-credenti) **8**/2 (1973) 24-29. (Reprint of no. 344.)
369. "Necessity and the Principle of Sufficient Reason (I)." *Journal of the Philosophical Association* **14**/45-46 (1973) 77-86.
370. "The Challenge of Secularization." *Present Day Challenges to Religion.* Ed. Thomas Paul. Alwaye: PITP, 1973. 83-98.
371. "Is the Concept of 'Person' Suitable in Vedanta?" *Indian Ecclesiastical Studies* **12**/3 (1973) 155-162. (Reprint of no. 352. Cf. no. 376.)
372. Review of Pritibhushan Chatterji, *Studies in Comparative Religion. Indian Ecclesiastical Studies* **12**/3 (1973) 219-220.
373. "Advances in Christian-Muslim Dialogue." *Service and Salvation.* Ed. J. Pathrapankal. Bangalore: TPI, 1973. 521-529. (Reprint of no. 326. Cf. no. 356.)
374. "Does Christianity Profess Non-Dualism." *The Clergy Monthly* **37**/9 (1973) 354-357. (Reprint of no. 363, with change of title.)
375. "Contemporary Philosophical Anthropology." *New Consciousness* **1**/3 (February 1973).
376. "Is the Concept of 'Person' Congenial to Vedanta?" *Reflection* (Rajpur, Dehradun) **2** (1973) 3-9. (Reprint of nos. 352 and 371.)
377. Review of E. De Meulder, *Renascent Youth of India* and *The Restoration of the Aboriginal Peasantry. The Examiner* (Bombay) **124**/8 (Feb. 24, 1973) 123 (version A). (Reprinted as nos. 378 and 382.)
378. Review of E. De Meulder, *Renascent Youth of India* and *The Restoration of the Aboriginal Peasantry. The Messenger of the Sacred Heart* (Apr. 1973). (Reprint of no. 377.)
379. Review of E. De Meulder, *Renascent Youth of India* and *The Restoration of the Aboriginal Peasantry. Indian Ecclesiastical Studies* **12** (1973) 80-81 (version B). (Reprinted as no. 380.)

380.Review of E. De Meulder, *Renascent Youth of India* and *The Restoration of the Aboriginal Peasantry. The New Leader* (Mar. 4, 1973) (version B). (Reprint of no. 379.)

381.Review of *XLII[e] Semaine de Missiologie de Louvain: Mission au temps des revolutions. Indian Ecclesiastical Studies* **12**/4 (1973) 70.

382.Review of E. De Meulder. *Renascent Youth of India* and *The Restoration of the Aboriginal Peasantry. The Morning Star* **65**/5 (May 1973) 103. (Reprint of 377. Cf. no. 379.)[3]

383."Towards an Indian View of the Person." Typescript bound with articles by various authors from the *Encyclopedia Universalis*. JDV S3/EN19. 1-21. (Published as no. 384.)

1974

384."Towards an Indian View of the Person." *Contemporary Indian Philosophy*. Series II. Muirhead Library of Philosophy. Ed. M. Chatterjee. London: Allen and Unwin, 1974. 51-75. (Cf. no. 383. Reprinted as no. 755.)

385."Prospective de l'Evangelisation en Inde." Lumen Vitae (Brussels) 29 (1974) 257-269. (Cf. English version in no. 386.)

386."Pathways for Evangelization in India." *Lumen Vitae* **29**/3 (1974) 403-417. (English version of no. 385. Shorter version German version in no. 492.)

387."A Bird's-Eye View of Hinduism." *Indian Ecclesiastical Studies* **13**/4 (1974) 299-304.

388."The Witness (*Sākṣin*), Source of Thought and Action." *Philosophy: Theory and Practice (Seminar on World Philosophy, Madras, Dec. 7-17, 1970)*. Ed. T.M.P. Mahadevan. Madras: University CASP, 1974. 176-185. (Reprinted as no. 560.)

389."'Philosophical Theories and Practice': Comments." (Comments on S. K. Saksena's paper.) *Philosophy: Theory and Practice (Seminar on World Philosophy, Madras, Dec. 7-17, 1970)*. Ed. T.M.P. Mahadevan. Madras: University CASP, 1974. 460-461.

390."The Open Person and the Closed Individual." *Journal of the Philosophical Association* **15**/47 (1974). (Reprint of no. 304.)

391."Recent Developments in the Christian Approach to the Hindu." *Lumen Vitae* **29**/4 (1974) 515-520. (Reprinted in no. 498 as a book review.)

392."The Status of the Scriptures in the 'Holy History' of India." *Research Seminar on Non-Biblical Scriptures*. Ed. D.S. Amalorpavadass. Bangalore: NBCLC, 1974. 280-299. (Offprinted as no. 393. Partially reprinted as no. 538.)

393."The Status of the Scriptures in the 'Holy History' of India." *Research Seminar on Non-Biblical Scriptures*. Ed. D. S. Amalorpavadass. Bangalore: NBCLC, 1974. 1-20. (Offprint of no. 392.)

394.Review of Asandas Balchand, *The Salvific Value of Non-Christian Religions according to Asian Christian Theologians. The Indian Journal of Theology* **23**/1-2 (Jan-June 1974) 143-144. (Reprinted as no. 497.)

395.Review of J. Feys, *The Philosophy of Evolution in Shri Aurobindo and Teilhard de Chardin. Indian Philosophical Quarterly* (new series) **1**/3 (April 1974) 267-269. (Reprinted as no. 396.)

396.Review of J. Feys, *The Philosophy of Evolution in Shri Aurobindo and Teilhard de Chardin. Indian Ecclesiastical Studies* **13**/1 (1974) 70-71. (Reprint of no. 395.)
397.Review of A. D'Almeida, *Nyāya Philosophy: Nature and Validity of Knowledge. Indian Ecclesiastical Studies* **13**/1 (1974) 76.
398."Justin (Saint)." Typescript, Collected Papers C, 583. (Published as no. 437.)
399."Clement of Alexandria (Saint)." Typescript, Collected Papers C, 584. (Published as no. 435.)
400."Tertullian." Typescript, Collected Papers C, 585. (Published as no. 440.)
401."Porphyry." Typescript, Collected Papers C, 586. (Published as no. 451.)
402."Augustine (Saint)." Typescript, Collected Papers C, 587-590. (Published as no. 423.)
403."Dionysius the Areopagite (Pseudo)." Typescript, Collected Papers C, 591. (Published as no. 441.)
404."Hugh of St Victor." Typescript, Collected Papers C, 592. (Published as no. 482.)
405."Peter the Lombard." Typescript, Collected Papers C, 593. (Published as no. 453.)
406."Richard of St Victor." Typescript, Collected Papers C, 594. (Published as no. 466.)
407.Albertus Magnus (Saint)." Typescript, Collected Papers C, 595. (Published as no. 422.)
408."Alexander of Hales." Typescript, Collected Papers C, 596. (Published as no. 418.)
409."Peter of Spain." Typescript, Collected Papers C, 597. (Published as no. 452.)
410."Eckhart (Meister)." Typescript, Collected Papers C, 598-599. (Published as no. 433.)
411."Maine de Biran." Typescript, Collected Papers C, 600. (Published as no. 461.)
412."Marechal (Joseph)." Typescript, Collected Papers C, 601-604. (Published as no. 459.)
413."Lavelle (Louis)." Typescript, Collected Papers C, 605. (Published as no. 467.)
414."*Anekeśvarvāda.*" (Polytheism.) *Marāṭhi Tattvajñāna Mahākoṣa.* Ed. D.D. Vadekar. Pune: Marathi Tattvajnana Mahakosa Mandal, 1974. **1**:22.
415."*Avatāra – Siddhānta.*" (Doctrine of Incarnation.) *Marāṭhi Tattvajñāna Mahākoṣa.* Ed. D.D. Vadekar. Pune: Marathi Tattvajnana Mahakosa Mandal, 1974. **1**:43-44.
416."*Antaḥprajñā.*" (Intuition.) *Marāṭhi Tattvajñāna Mahākoṣa.* Ed. D.D. Vadekar. Pune: Marathi Tattvajnana Mahakosa Mandal, 1974. **1**:50.
417."Aquinas, Saint Thomas." *Marāṭhi Tattvajñāna Mahākoṣa.* Ed. D.D. Vadekar. Pune: Marathi Tattvajnana Mahakosa Mandal, 1974. **1**:51-54.
418."Alexander (of Hales)." *Marāṭhi Tattvajñāna Mahākoṣa.* Ed. D.D. Vadekar. Pune: Marathi Tattvajnana Mahakosa Mandal, 1974. **1**:65. (Cf. no. 408.)

419.[With S.H. Dixit.] "*Ātmavāda*." (Doctrine of *Ātman*.) *Marāṭhi Tattvajñāna Mahākoṣa*. Ed. D.D. Vadekar. Pune: Marathi Tattvajnana Mahakosa Mandal, 1974. 1:69-70.

420."*Ātmā – Ihetara Jīvana*." (Soul – Afterlife.) *Marāṭhi Tattvajñāna Mahākoṣa*. Ed. D.D. Vadekar. Pune: Marathi Tattvajnana Mahakosa Mandal, 1974. 1:71-73.

421."Ānanda." (Bliss.) *Marāṭhi Tattvajñāna Mahākoṣa*. Ed. D.D. Vadekar. Pune: Marathi Tattvajnana Mahakosa Mandal, 1974. 1:74.

422."Albertus Magnus." *Marāṭhi Tattvajñāna Mahākoṣa*. Ed. D.D. Vadekar. Pune: Marathi Tattvajnana Mahakosa Mandal, 1974. 1:76-77. (Cf. no. 407.)

423."Augustine, Saint." *Marāṭhi Tattvajñāna Mahākoṣa*. Ed. D.D. Vadekar. Pune: Marathi Tattvajnana Mahakosa Mandal, 1974. 1:81-83. (Cf. no. 402.)

424."Ortega y Gasset, J." *Marāṭhi Tattvajñāna Mahākoṣa*. Ed. D.D. Vadekar. Pune: Marathi Tattvajnana Mahakosa Mandal, 1974. 1:88.

425."*Īśvara*." (God.) *Marāṭhi Tattvajñāna Mahākoṣa*. Ed. D.D. Vadekar. Pune: Marathi Tattvajnana Mahakosa Mandal, 1974. 1:99-101.

426."*Īśvara – Astitva*." (Existence of God.) *Marāṭhi Tattvajñāna Mahākoṣa*. Ed. D.D. Vadekar. Pune: Marathi Tattvajnana Mahakosa Mandal, 1974. 1:101-102.

427."*Īśvara va Jagat*." (God and the World.) *Marāṭhi Tattvajñāna Mahākoṣa*. Ed. D.D. Vadekar. Pune: Marathi Tattvajnana Mahakosa Mandal, 1974. 1:104-105.

428."*Īśvaravāda*." (Theism.) *Marāṭhi Tattvajñāna Mahākoṣa*. Ed. D.D. Vadekar. Pune: Marathi Tattvajnana Mahakosa Mandal, 1974. 1:105-106.

429."*Īśvaraśāstra*." (Theology.) *Marāṭhi Tattvajñāna Mahākoṣa*. Ed. D.D. Vadekar. Pune: Marathi Tattvajnana Mahakosa Mandal, 1974. 1:106-107.

430."*Īśvarasvarūpa*." (God's Nature.) *Marāṭhi Tattvajñāna Mahākoṣa*. Ed. D.D. Vadekar. Pune: Marathi Tattvajnana Mahakosa Mandal, 1974. 1:107-108.

431."*Upāsanā va Upāsanāmārga*." (Worship and Ways of Worship.) *Marāṭhi Tattvajñāna Mahākoṣa*. Ed. D.D. Vadekar. Pune: Marathi Tattvajnana Mahakosa Mandal, 1974. 1:116.

432."*Ekeśvaravāda* (Monotheism)." *Marāṭhi Tattvajñāna Mahākoṣa*. Ed. D.D. Vadekar. Pune: Marathi Tattvajnana Mahakosa Mandal, 1974. 1:121-122.

433."Eckhart, Meister." *Marāṭhi Tattvajñāna Mahākoṣa*. Ed. D.D. Vadekar. Pune: Marathi Tattvajnana Mahakosa Mandal, 1974. 1:122-123. (Cf. no. 410.)

434."*Kutumba*." (Family.) *Marāṭhi Tattvajñāna Mahākoṣa*. Ed. D.D. Vadekar. Pune: Marathi Tattvajnana Mahakosa Mandal, 1974. 1:190-191.

435."Clement (of Alexandria)." *Marāṭhi Tattvajñāna Mahākoṣa*. Ed. D.D. Vadekar. Pune: Marathi Tattvajnana Mahakosa Mandal, 1974. 1:213-214. (Cf. no. 399.)

436."*Gūḍhavāda*." (Mysticism.) *Marāṭhi Tattvajñāna Mahākoṣa*. Ed. D.D. Vadekar. Pune: Marathi Tattvajnana Mahakosa Mandal, 1974. 1:229-230.

437."Justin." *Marāṭhi Tattvajñāna Mahākoṣa*. Ed. D.D. Vadekar. Pune: Marathi Tattvajnana Mahakosa Mandal, 1974. 1:256-257. (Cf. no. 398.)

438."Gilson, E.H." *Marāṭhi Tattvajñāna Mahākoṣa.* Ed. D.D. Vadekar. Pune: Marathi Tattvajnana Mahakosa Mandal, 1974. **1**:262.

439."*Jīva* (*Jīvātman*)." (Individual Ego, Self, Soul.) *Marāṭhi Tattvajñāna Mahākoṣa.* Ed. D.D. Vadekar. Pune: Marathi Tattvajnana Mahakosa Mandal, 1974. **1**:262-263.

440."Tertullian." *Marāṭhi Tattvajñāna Mahākoṣa.* Ed. D.D. Vadekar. Pune: Marathi Tattvajnana Mahakosa Mandal, 1974. **1**:318. (Cf. no. 400.)

441."Dionysius (the Areopagite)." *Marāṭhi Tattvajñāna Mahākoṣa.* Ed. D.D. Vadekar. Pune: Marathi Tattvajnana Mahakosa Mandal, 1974. **1**:328-329. (Cf. no. 403.)

442."Duhem, Pierre." *Marāṭhi Tattvajñāna Mahākoṣa.* Ed. D.D. Vadekar. Pune: Marathi Tattvajnana Mahakosa Mandal, 1974. **1**:335.

443."*Tattvajñāna, Khristī Dharmāntīla.*" (Philosophy, in the Christian Religion.) *Marāṭhi Tattvajñāna Mahākoṣa.* Ed. D.D. Vadekar. Pune: Marathi Tattvajnana Mahakosa Mandal, 1974. **1**:396-399.

444."*Tattvajñāna, Pāścātya – Madhya Kālakhaṇḍa.*" (Western Philosophy, Medieval Period.) *Marāṭhi Tattvajñāna Mahākoṣa.* Ed. D.D. Vadekar. Pune: Marathi Tattvajnana Mahakosa Mandal, 1974. **1**:488-491.

445."*Tattvajñāna, (Bhāratāntīla) Ingrajīntīla.*" (Philosophy in English in India.) *Marāṭhi Tattvajñāna Mahākoṣa.* Ed. D.D. Vadekar. Pune: Marathi Tattvajnana Mahakosa Mandal, 1974. **1**:526-540. (English tr. in no. 279.)

446."*Tattvajñāna, Bhāratīya Dṛṣṭikoṇa.*" (Philosophy, Indian Viewpoint.) *Marāṭhi Tattvajñāna Mahākoṣa.* Ed. D.D. Vadekar. Pune: Marathi Tattvajnana Mahakosa Mandal, 1974. **1**:540-543.

447."*Tattvajñāna, Sarvasāmānya.*" (Philosophy, General.) *Marāṭhi Tattvajñāna Mahākoṣa.* Ed. D.D. Vadekar. Pune: Marathi Tattvajnana Mahakosa Mandal, 1974. **2**:31-34.

448."*Dharmatattvajñāna, Bhāratīya Tattvajñāna.*" (Philosophy of Religion in Indian Philosophy.) *Marāṭhi Tattvajñāna Mahākoṣa.* Ed. D.D. Vadekar. Pune: Marathi Tattvajnana Mahakosa Mandal, 1974. **2**:157-162.

449."*Dharmatattvajñāna, Sarvasāmānya.*" (Philosophy of Religion, General.) *Marāṭhi Tattvajñāna Mahākoṣa.* Ed. D.D. Vadekar. Pune: Marathi Tattvajnana Mahakosa Mandal, 1974. **2**:166-169.

450."*Naitika Sanstha.*" (Ethical Society.) *Marāṭhi Tattvajñāna Mahākoṣa.* Ed. D.D. Vadekar. Pune: Marathi Tattvajnana Mahakosa Mandal, 1974. **2**:243-244.

451."Porphyry." *Marāṭhi Tattvajñāna Mahākoṣa.* Ed. D.D. Vadekar. Pune: Marathi Tattvajnana Mahakosa Mandal, 1974. **2**:280. (Cf. no. 401.)

452."Peter (of Spain)." *Marāṭhi Tattvajñāna Mahākoṣa.* Ed. D.D. Vadekar. Pune: Marathi Tattvajnana Mahakosa Mandal, 1974. **2**:281. (Cf. no. 409.)

453."Peter the Lombard." *Marāṭhi Tattvajñāna Mahākoṣa.* Ed. D.D. Vadekar. Pune: Marathi Tattvajnana Mahakosa Mandal, 1974. **2**:281. (Cf. no. 405.)

454."*Prakaṭatā va sambhāvyatā.*" (Actuality and Potency.) *Marāṭhi Tattvajñāna Mahākoṣa.* Ed. D.D. Vadekar. Pune: Marathi Tattvajnana Mahakosa Mandal, 1974. **2**:295-296.

455."Poincaré, H." *Marāṭhi Tattvajñāna Mahākoṣa.* Ed. D.D. Vadekar. Pune: Marathi Tattvajnana Mahakosa Mandal, 1974. **2**:331.

456."Fabro, C." *Marāṭhi Tattvajñāna Mahākoṣa.* Ed. D.D. Vadekar. Pune: Marathi Tattvajnana Mahakosa Mandal, 1974. **2**:332-333.

457."Farber, M." *Marāṭhi Tattvajñāna Mahākoṣa*. Ed. D.D. Vadekar. Pune: Marathi Tattvajnana Mahakosa Mandal, 1974. **2**:333.
458."Blondel, M." *Marāṭhi Tattvajñāna Mahākoṣa*. Ed. D.D. Vadekar. Pune: Marathi Tattvajnana Mahakosa Mandal, 1974. **2**:387-388.
459."Marechal, J." *Marāṭhi Tattvajñāna Mahākoṣa*. Ed. D.D. Vadekar. Pune: Marathi Tattvajnana Mahakosa Mandal, 1974. **2**:430-431. (Cf. no. 412.)
460."*Mānavavāda*." (Humanism.) *Marāṭhi Tattvajñāna Mahākoṣa*. Ed. D.D. Vadekar. Pune: Marathi Tattvajnana Mahakosa Mandal, 1974. **2**:436-437.
461."Maine de Biran." *Marāṭhi Tattvajñāna Mahākoṣa*. Ed. D.D. Vadekar. Pune: Marathi Tattvajnana Mahakosa Mandal, 1974. **2**:479. (Cf. no. 411.)
462."*Yatitvavāda*." (Asceticism.) *Marāṭhi Tattvajñāna Mahākoṣa*. Ed. D.D. Vadekar. Pune: Marathi Tattvajnana Mahakosa Mandal, 1974. **2**:486-487.
463."*Yuddha – Nītiśāstra*." (Ethics of War.) *Marāṭhi Tattvajñāna Mahākoṣa*. Ed. D.D. Vadekar. Pune: Marathi Tattvajnana Mahakosa Mandal, 1974. **2**:492-493.
464."*Rachanāvāda*." (Structuralism.) *Marāṭhi Tattvajñāna Mahākoṣa*. Ed. D.D. Vadekar. Pune: Marathi Tattvajnana Mahakosa Mandal, 1974. **2**:499.
465."Roy, Raja Ramamohan." *Marāṭhi Tattvajñāna Mahākoṣa*. Ed. D.D. Vadekar. Pune: Marathi Tattvajnana Mahakosa Mandal, 1974. **2**:556-557.
466."Richard (of St Victor)." *Marāṭhi Tattvajñāna Mahākoṣa*. Ed. D.D. Vadekar. Pune: Marathi Tattvajnana Mahakosa Mandal, 1974. **2**:558. (Cf. no. 406.)
467."Lavelle, L." *Marāṭhi Tattvajñāna Mahākoṣa*. Ed. D.D. Vadekar. Pune: Marathi Tattvajnana Mahakosa Mandal, 1974. **2**:571-572. (Cf. no. 413.)
468."Levi-Strauss, C." *Marāṭhi Tattvajñāna Mahākoṣa*. Ed. D.D. Vadekar. Pune: Marathi Tattvajnana Mahakosa Mandal, 1974. **2**:581.
469."Weiss, P." *Marāṭhi Tattvajñāna Mahākoṣa*. Ed. D.D. Vadekar. Pune: Marathi Tattvajnana Mahakosa Mandal, 1974. **2**:597.
470."*Vivāha*." (Marriage.) *Marāṭhi Tattvajñāna Mahākoṣa*. Ed. D.D. Vadekar. Pune: Marathi Tattvajnana Mahakosa Mandal, 1974. **3**:66-67.
471."*Vyakti*." (Person.) *Marāṭhi Tattvajñāna Mahākoṣa*. Ed. D.D. Vadekar. Pune: Marathi Tattvajnana Mahakosa Mandal, 1974. **3**:97-98.
472."*Vyaktitattva*." (Principle of Individuation.) *Marāṭhi Tattvajñāna Mahākoṣa*. Ed. D.D. Vadekar. Pune: Marathi Tattvajnana Mahakosa Mandal, 1974. **3**:98-99.
473."*Vyaktivāda*." (Personalism.) *Marāṭhi Tattvajñāna Mahākoṣa*. Ed. D.D. Vadekar. Pune: Marathi Tattvajnana Mahakosa Mandal, 1974. **3**:99.
474."*Śraddhā*." (Faith.) *Marāṭhi Tattvajñāna Mahākoṣa*. Ed. D.D. Vadekar. Pune: Marathi Tattvajnana Mahakosa Mandal, 1974. **3**:151-152.
475."*Sattāśāstra, Bhāratīya Tattvajñāna*." (Metaphysics in Indian Philosophy.) *Marāṭhi Tattvajñāna Mahākoṣa*. Ed. D.D. Vadekar. Pune: Marathi Tattvajnana Mahakosa Mandal, 1974. **3**:178-185.
476."*Sattāśāstra, Sāmānya*." (Metaphysics, General.) *Marāṭhi Tattvajñāna Mahākoṣa*. Ed. D.D. Vadekar. Pune: Marathi Tattvajnana Mahakosa Mandal, 1974. 3:193-195.
477."*Samā* [sic] *Theologica* (Aquinas)." (Summa Theologica, Aquinas.) *Marāṭhi Tattvajñāna Mahākoṣa*. Ed. D.D. Vadekar. Pune: Marathi Tattvajnana Mahakosa Mandal, 1974. **3**:231.

478."*Sarveśvaravāda*." (Pantheism.) *Marāṭhi Tattvajñāna Mahākoṣa*. Ed. D.D. Vadekar. Pune: Marathi Tattvajnana Mahakosa Mandal, 1974. **3**:233-234.
479."*Sākṣātkāra*." (Direct Illumination.) *Marāṭhi Tattvajñāna Mahākoṣa*. Ed. D.D. Vadekar. Pune: Marathi Tattvajnana Mahakosa Mandal, 1974. **3**:248-249.
480."*Sṛṣṭi* (*Jagat*)." (Creation, World.) *Marāṭhi Tattvajñāna Mahākoṣa*. Ed. D.D. Vadekar. Pune: Marathi Tattvajnana Mahakosa Mandal, 1974. **3**:269-270.
481."Sellars, R.W." *Marāṭhi Tattvajñāna Mahākoṣa*. Ed. D.D. Vadekar. Pune: Marathi Tattvajnana Mahakosa Mandal, 1974. **3**:271.
482."Hugh (of St Victor)." *Marāṭhi Tattvajñāna Mahākoṣa*. Ed. D.D. Vadekar. Pune: Marathi Tattvajnana Mahakosa Mandal, 1974. **3**:323. (Cf. no. 404.)

1975

483."Nāma-japa in Christianity." *The Call Divine* **22** (1975) 181-186.
484."The Nudity of Mahāvīra Jina and of Jesus Christ." *Vidyajyoti: Journal of Theological Reflection* **39** (1975) 131-133. (Reprinted as no. 556.)
485."The Aristotelian-Thomist Conception of Man." *Indian Philosophical Quarterly* **2**/4 (July 1975) 307-318. (Offprinted in no. 514.)
486."Lettre de l'Inde." *Le Pont* (Charleroi) **6**/3 (June 1975) 10-11.
487."Constantine's Legislation and the Religious Transformation of the Roman Empire." *The Modern Review* **137**/6 (1975) 444-448.
488."Affinities between Guru Nanak and Jesus Christ." *Perspectives on Guru Nanak*. Ed. Harbans Singh. Patiala: Punjabi University, 1975. 110-118. (Reprint of nos. 290 and 328.)
489."The Method of Mediaeval Schoolmen in Europe and India." 4 pp. Typescript, Collected Papers C, 606-609.
490."Un document interessant l'histoire de la diffusion du Sanskrit en Europe." 3 pp. Typescript, Collected Papers C, 617-619.
491."Discovery of the Personal God in the Gita." *Indian Spirituality in Action*. Ed. Sr Vandana. Bombay: Asian Trading Corporation, 1975. 152-169. (Reprint of no. 361; cf. no. 584.)
492."Ein Weg zu Christus durch Indiens Religionsgeschichte." *Orientierung* **39**/9 (1975) 105-108. (Shorter version of nos. 385 and 386.)
493.Review of Mario Piantelli, *Śaṅkara e la Rinascita del Brāhmanesimo*. *Indica* **12**/1 (March 1975) 56-61. (Reprinted as nos. 494, 511 and 543.)
494.Review of Mario Piantelli, *Śaṅkara e la Rinascita del Brāhmanesimo*. *Boletin de la Asociaciòn Española de Orientalistas* **11** (1975) 249-254. (Reprint of no. 493; cf. nos. 511 and 543.)
495.Review of S.P. Kanal. *The Ethics of Devātmā*. *Boletin de la Asociaciòn Española de Orientalistas* **11**(1975) 243-246. (Reprinted as nos. 496, 508 and 510.)
496.Review of Satyavan P. Kanal. *The Ethics of Devātmā*. *Indica* **12**/1 (Mar. 1975) 67-70. (Reprint of no. 495; cf. nos. 508 and 510.)
497.Review of Asandas Balchand. *The Salvific Value of Non-Christian Religions according to Asian Christian Theologians writing in Asian-published Theological Journals, 1965-1970*. *Lumen Vitae* **30**/2 (1975) 293-294. (Reprint of no. 394.)

498.Review of M. Braybrooke. *The Undiscovered Christ: A Review of Recent Developments in the Christian Approach to the Hindu. Indian Journal of Theology* **24** (1975) 66-71. (= no. 391.)
499."The Problematics of the Knowledge of God." *Research Journal of Philosophy* (Ranchi University). **6**/1 (March 1975) 142-144. (Reprint of nos. 314, 325.)

1976

500."Arjun Meditates on the Philosophers' Transition from Atheism to Theism from the Fourth to the Tenth Century A.D." *When Two Great Hearts Meet.* Ed. E. De Meulder. Allahabad: St Paul Publications, 1976. 164-191. (Reprinted as no. 554.)
501."Arjun Meets the King: Indian Roots for the Lord-Vassal Relationship in the Spiritual Exercises of St Ignatius." *When Two Great Hearts Meet.* Ed. E. De Meulder. Allahabad: St Paul's Publications, 1976. 192-220. (Reprinted as nos. 619, 716-717.)
502."A Copernican Reversal: The Gitakara's Reformulation of Karma." *Chinmaya Mission Silver Jubilee Volume*. Ed. S. Barlingay. Poona, 1976. 34-41. (Reprinted as no. 512.)
503."Robert de Nobili and Vedānta." *Vidyajyoti: Journal of Theological Reflection* **40**/8 (1976) 363-371.
504."Chinks in the Armour of Avidyā." *Knowledge, Culture and Value. Papers Presented in Plenary Sessions, Panel Discussions and Sectional Meetings of World Philosophy Conference [Golden Jubilee Session of the Indian Philosophical Congress] Delhi, Dec. 28, 1975 – Jan. 3, 1976*. Ed. R.C. Pandeya and S.R. Bhatt. Delhi: Motilal Banarsidass, 1976. 77-84.
505."The Discovery of the Person." *Indian Philosophical Quarterly* **4**/1 (Oct. 1976) 1-9. (Offprinted in no. 514.)
506."The Loss of the Person." *Indian Philosophical Quarterly* **4**/1 (Oct. 1976) 10-23. (Offprinted in no. 514.)
507."The Revelation of God's Love in Christianity." *An Apostle of India's Spiritual Culture*. Ed. N. Ananthanarayan. Shivanandanagar: Divine Life Society Publications, 1976. 189-195.
508."A Hindu Ethical Reformer: Devātmā." *Vidyajyoti: Journal of Theological Reflection* **40** (1976) 325-328. (Reprint of no. 495; cf. nos. 496 and 510.)
509.Review of A. G. Aranjaniyil. *The Absolute of the Upanishads, Personal or Impersonal. Indian Book Chronicle* (July 1976).
510.Review of S.P. Kanal. *The Ethics of Devātmā. International Philosophical Quarterly* **16**/1 (Mar. 1976) 122-125. (Reprint of no. 495; cf. nos. 496 and 508.)

1977

511.Review of Mario Piantelli. *Śaṅkara e la Rinascita del Brāhmanesimo. Indian Philosophical Quarterly* **4**/3 (Apr. 1977) 429-435. (Reprint of nos. 493 and 494.)
512."A Copernican Reversal: The Gītākāra's Reformulation of Karma." *Philosophy East and West* **27**/1 (1977) 53-63. (Reprint of no. 502.)

513. "The Rediscovery of the Person." *Indian Philosophical Quarterly* **4**/3 (Apr. 1977) 413-426. (Offprinted in no. 514.)

514. *A Short History of the Person.* Abstracts from *Indian Philosophical Quarterly* 4/1 (Oct. 1976), 4/2 (Apr. 1977) and 2/4 (July 1975). Poona: University of Poona, 1977. (Offprint of nos. 505, 506, 513 and 485.)

515. "Contemplation in Śaṅkara and Rāmānuja." *The Living Word* (Pontifical Institute, Alwaye) **83**/3 (1977) 199-210. (Reprinted as nos. 557 and 578.)

516. "Amesha Spentas." *Verbo: Enciclopedia Luso-Brasileira de Cultura.* Lisboa: Editorial Verbo, 1977. **1**:1817-1818. (Cf. no. 166. Reprint of no. 167. Reprinted as no. 640.)[4]

517. "Amida." *Verbo: Enciclopedia Luso-Brasileira de Cultura.* Lisboa: Editorial Verbo, 1977. **1**:1823-1824. (Cf. no. 167. Reprint of no. 169. Reprinted as no. 641.)

518. "Anāhitā." *Verbo: Enciclopedia Luso-Brasileira de Cultura.* Lisboa: Editorial Verbo, 1977. **2**:61. (Cf. no. 169. Reprint of no. 208. Reprinted as no. 642.)

519. "Aryo-Samaj." *Verbo: Enciclopedia Luso-Brasileira de Cultura.* Lisboa: Editorial Verbo, 1977. **2**:1467-1468. (Cf. no. 172. Reprint of no. 209. Reprinted as no. 643.)

520. "Āshrama." *Verbo: Enciclopedia Luso-Brasileira de Cultura.* Lisboa: Editorial Verbo, 1977. **2**:1506-1507. (Cf. no. 173. Reprint of no. 210. Reprinted as no. 644.)

521. "Asura." *Verbo: Enciclopedia Luso-Brasileira de Cultura.* Lisboa: Editorial Verbo, 1977. **2**:1697. (Cf. no. 174. Reprint of no. 211. Reprinted as no. 645.)

522. "Ātman." *Verbo: Enciclopedia Luso-Brasileira de Cultura.* Lisboa: Editorial Verbo, 1977. **2**:1754-1755. (Reprint of no. 212. Reprinted as no. 646.)

523. "Avatāra." *Verbo: Enciclopedia Luso-Brasileira de Cultura.* Lisboa: Editorial Verbo, 1977. **3**:98. (Cf. no. 175. Reprint of no. 233. Reprinted as no. 647.)

524. "Avesta." *Verbo: Enciclopedia Luso-Brasileira de Cultura.* Lisboa: Editorial Verbo, 1977. **3**:132, 135. (Cf. no. 176. Reprint of no. 234. Reprinted as no. 648.)

525. "Bhagavadgītā." *Verbo: Enciclopedia Luso-Brasileira de Cultura.* Lisboa: Editorial Verbo, 1977. **3**:1226-1227. (Cf. no. 177. Reprint of no. 235. Reprinted as no. 649.)

526. "Bhakti." *Verbo: Enciclopedia Luso-Brasileira de Cultura.* Lisboa: Editorial Verbo, 1977. **3**:1227. (Cf. no. 178. Reprint of no. 236. Reprinted as no. 650.)

527. "Bhil." *Verbo: Enciclopedia Luso-Brasileira de Cultura.* Lisboa: Editorial Verbo, 1977. **3**:1229. (Cf. no. 179. Reprint of no. 237. Reprinted as no. 651.)

528. "Brama." *Verbo: Enciclopedia Luso-Brasileira de Cultura.* Lisboa: Editorial Verbo, 1977. **3**:1775. (Cf. no. 180. Reprint of no. 238. Reprinted as no. 652.)

529. "Braman." *Verbo: Enciclopedia Luso-Brasileira de Cultura.* Lisboa: Editorial Verbo, 1977. **3**:1775-1776. (Cf. no. 181. Reprint of no. 239. Reprinted as no. 653.)

530.“Bramana.” *Verbo: Enciclopedia Luso-Brasileira de Cultura.* Lisboa: Editorial Verbo, 1977. **3**:1776. (Cf. no. 182. Reprint of no. 240. Reprinted as no. 654.)

531.“Bramanismo.” *Verbo: Enciclopedia Luso-Brasileira de Cultura.* Lisboa: Editorial. Verbo, 1977. **3**:1778-1779. (Cf. no. 183. Reprint of no. 241. Reprinted as no. 655.)

532.“Bramo-Samaj.” *Verbo: Enciclopedia Luso-Brasileira de Cultura.* Lisboa: Editorial Verbo, 1977. **3**:1782-1783. (Cf. no. 184. Reprint of no. 242. Reprinted as no. 656.)

533.“Dharma.” *Verbo: Enciclopedia Luso-Brasileira de Cultura.* Lisboa: Editorial Verbo, 1977. **6**:1213. (Reprint of no. 262. Reprinted as no. 657.)

534.“Dharma-Sastra.” *Verbo: Enciclopedia Luso-Brasileira de Cultura.* Lisboa: Editorial Verbo, 1977. **6**:1213. (Reprint of no. 263. Reprinted as no. 658.)

535.“Dhyana.” *Verbo: Enciclopedia Luso-Brasileira de Cultura.* Lisboa: Editorial Verbo, 1977. **6**:1214-1215. (Reprint of no. 264. Reprinted as no. 659.)

536.“Digha-Nikaya.” *Verbo: Enciclopedia Luso-Brasileira de Cultura.* Lisboa: Editorial Verbo, 1977. **6**:1360. (Reprint of no. 265. Reprinted as no. 660.)

537.“Gandhi.” *Verbo: Enciclopedia Luso-Brasileira de Cultura.* Lisboa: Editorial Verbo, 1977. **9**:151-152. (Reprint of no. 296. Reprinted as no. 661.)[5]

538.“The Status of the Scriptures in the ‘Holy History’ of India.” *The Divine Life* **39** (Apr.-Aug. 1977) 108-110, 146-147, 175-177, 266-268. (Partial reprint of no. 392.)

539.“Preface.” Mohan Singh Uberoy, *Bible and Literature.* 4 pp.

540.“The *Gītā* in Time and Beyond Time.” *The Divine Life* **39** (1977) 108-110, 146-147, 175-177, 266-268. (Reprint of no. 359.)

541.“Rāmānuja, Pantheist or Panentheist?” *Annals of the Bhandarkar Oriental Research Institute (Diamond Jubilee Volume)* (1977-78) 561-571.

542.“Origin: Creation and Emanation.” *Person and God. The International Society for Metaphysics: Studies in Metaphysics*, vol. 3. (Papers of the Jerusalem Session [1977] of the *International Society for Metaphysics.*) Ed. George F. McLean and Hugo Meynell. Lanham, MD: University Press of America, 1988. 209-220; comment by Hugo Meynell, 221-225. (Reprinted as nos. 555 and 676; cf. no. 677.)

543.Review of M. Piantelli. *Śaṅkara e la Rinascita del Brahmanesimo. Indian Philosophical Quarterly* **4**/3 (Apr. 1977) 429-435. (Reprint of nos. 493, 494 and 511.)

544.Review of J. Feys. *A = B, an Enquiry into the Upanishads' Basic Insight. Indian Philosophical Quarterly* **5**/1 (Oct. 1977) 103-104. (Reprinted as nos. 545 and 558.)

545.Review of J. Feys. *A = B, an Enquiry into the Upanishads' Basic Insight. Boletin de la Asociaciòn Española de Orientalistas* **13** (1977) 287-289. (Reprint of no. 544; cf. no. 558.)

546.Review of G. Chemparathy. *An Indian Rational Theology: Introduction to Udayana's Nyāyakusumāñjali. Boletin de la Asociaciòn Española de Orientalistas* **13** (1977) 276-280. (Reprinted as no. 563.)

547.Review of A. Lokhande. *Tukārāma, His Person and his Religion. Boletin de la Asociaciòn Española de Orientalistas* **13** (1977) 281-283. (Reprinted as nos. 548 and 564.)

548.Review of A. Lokhande. *Tukārāma, His Person and his Religion. International Philosophical Quarterly* **17**/4 (Dec. 1977) 491-493. (Reprint of no. 547; cf. no. 564.)

549.Review of J. Feys. *The Life of a Yogi. Boletin de la Asociaciòn Española de Orientalistas* **13** (1977) 283-287. (Reprinted as nos. 550 and 559.)

550.Review of J. Feys. *The Life of a Yogi. International Philosophical Quarterly* **17**/3 Sept. 1977) 363-367. (Reprint of 549; cf. no. 559.)

551.Review of W. Romanowski, ed., *Teoria i Metodyka cwiczen Relaksowo-Koncentrujacych* (Theory and Methods of Relaxation-Concentration Training). *Boletin de la Asociaciòn Española de Orientalistas* **13** (1977) 289-290. (Reprinted as no. 552.)

552.Review of W. Romanowski, ed., *Teoria i Metodyka cwiczen Relaksowo-Koncentrujacych* (Theory and Methods of Relaxation-Concentration Training). *International Philosophical Quarterly* **17**/3 (1977) 369-370. (Reprint of no. 551.)

1978

553.Orthodox Darśanas. Handwritten notes taken by Ivo Coelho, SDB, from course given to Bachelor of Philosophy Students, Pune: Jnana Deepa Vidyapeeth, 1978-79. 70 pp.

554."The Philosophers' Transition from Atheism to Theism from the Fourth to the Eleventh Century A.D." *Challenges of Societies in Transition.* Ed. M. Barnabas, P.S. Jacob and S.K. Hulbe. New Delhi: Macmillan, 1978. 310-338. (Reprint of no. 500).

555."Origin: Creation and Emanation." *Indian Theological Studies* **15**/3 (1978) 266-279. (Reprint of no. 542. Cf. nos. 676 and 677.)

556."The Nudity of Mahāvīra Jina and of Jesus Christ." *The Divine Life* **40**/1 (1978) 19-20. (Reprint of no. 484.)

557."Contemplation in Śaṅkara and Rāmānuja." *The Divine Life* **40**/6-7 (June-July 1978) 176-179, 210-212. (Reprint of no. 515; cf. nos. 578 and 579.)

558.Review of J. Feys. [*A* = *B*:] *An Enquiry into the Upanishads' Basic Insight. Indica* **15**/1 (1978) 60-61. (Reprint of nos. 544 and 545.)

559.Review of J. Feys. *The Life of a Yogi. Indian Philosophical Quarterly* **5**/4 (July 1978) 731-737. (Reprint of nos. 549and 550.)

1979

560."The Witness (Sākṣin), Source of Thought and Action." *The Divine Life*, **41**/2-4 (1979) 48-51, 110-115. (Reprint of no. 388.)

561."Philosophy in English in India." *Philosophy in the Fifteen Modern Indian Languages*. Ed. V.M. Bedekar. Pune: Continental Prakashan for The Council for the Marathi Encyclopaedia of Philosophy, 1979. 39-73. (Tr. of no. 445. Reprint of no. 279.)

562."The Indian Ascertainment of the Godhead (from the Vedas to Udayanācārya)." *Indica* **16**/1 (1979) 59-73.

563.Review of G. Chemparathy. *An Indian Rational Theology: Introduction to Udayana's Nyāyakusumāñjali. Indian Philosophical Quarterly* **6**/2 (Jan. 1979) 357-362. (Reprint of no. 546.)

564.Review of A. Lokhande. *Tukārāma, His Person and his Religion. Indian Philosophical Quarterly* **6**/2 (Jan. 1979) 353-355. (Reprint of nos. 547 and 548.)

565.Cyclostyled letter offering offprints of articles (38 items) to friends. 1 December 1979. 1p.

1980

566."Foreword." E. De Meulder, *All Men Became Brothers*. Allahabad: St Paul Press, 1980. 9-11.

567."Are Mind-Transcending Experiences Self-Interpreting?" *Vidyajyoti: Journal of Theological Reflection* **44** (1980) 528-532. (Reprinted as no. 591.)

568."Assamese Vaiṣṇavism according to the *Ghoṣāratna*." *Boletin de la Asociación Española de Orientalistas* **16** (1980) 127-133. (Reprinted as no. 569.)

569."Assamese Vaisnavism according to the Ghosaratna." *Indian Missiological Review* **2**/3 (1980) 255-263. (Reprint of 568.)

570."Natural Law." *Indian Law Review* **1**/11 (May 1980) 53-63. (Offprinted as no. 571; Reprinted as no. 598, and in an enlarged version in no. 572.)

571."Natural Law." N.d. 1-12. (Offprint of no. 570.)

572."Natural Law." *Indian Theological Studies* **17**/3 (1980) 247-265. (Enlarged version of no. 570.)

573."Śāṁkara Vedānta and Christian Theology." *Review of Darshana* **1**/1 (1980) 33-48.

574."The Sociological Dimension of Buddhism." *Jeevadhara* **59** (1980) 365-374. (Cf. no. 606.)

575."Love versus Identity." *Indian Philosophical Quarterly* **7**/4 (July 1980) 519-526.

576."The Integrative Doctrine of God in the Bhagavad-Gītā." *Prayer and Contemplation*. Ed. C.M. Vadakkekara. Bangalore: Asian Trading Corporation, 1980. 139-158. (Cf. no. 577.)

577."The Integrative Doctrine of God in the Bhagavad-Gītā." *Prayer and Contemplation*. Ed. C.M. Vadakkekara. Bangalore: Asian Trading Corporation, 1980. 1-19. (Probably offprint of no. 576.)

578."Contemplation in Śaṅkara and Rāmānuja." *Prayer and Contemplation*. Ed. C.M. Vadakkekara. Bangalore: Asian Trading Corporation, 1980. 209-220. (Reprint of nos. 515 and 557. Offprinted as no. 579.)

579."Contemplation in Śaṅkara and Rāmānuja." *Prayer and Contemplation*. Ed. C.M. Vadakkekara. Bangalore: Asian Trading Corporation, 1980. 1-12. (Offprint of no. 578.)

580."Stretching Forth to Infinity: The Mystical Doctrine of Gregory of Nyssa." *Prayer and Contemplation*. Ed. C.M. Vadakkekara. Bangalore: Asian Trading Corporation, 1980. 331-348.

581."Foreword." S.M. Michael, SVD. *The Cultural Context of Evangelization in India*. Indore: Satprakashan, 1980. 1-4.

582."The Catholic Church in the Crucible." *Religious Situation in the Present-Day World: Seminar Papers*. Ed. Taran Singh. Patiala: Punjabi University, 1980. 49-57.

583."Fond Memories of our O.I.C. Students." *Spark* (Pune: Bethany Ashram, 1980) 13-15.

584."Discovery of the Personal God in the Gītā, I, II, III." *Bulletin of the North American Board for East-West Dialogue* **7-8-9** (1980) 7-9, 6-7, 7-9. Available at http://monasticdialog.com/bulletins.php. (Reprint of nos. 361 and 491.)

585.Review of Sangam Lal Pandey, *Whither Indian Philosophy? Boletin de la Asociaciòn Española de Orientalistas* **16** (1980) 263-266.

586.Review of Suzanne Siauve, *Hindouisme et Christianisme en dialogue: Suzanne Siauve (1919-1975): Minor Writings of S. Siauve. Boletin de la Asociaciòn Española de Orientalistas* **16** (1980) 266-267. (Reprinted in no. 587.)

587.Review of Suzanne Siauve, *Hindouisme et Christianisme en dialogue: Suzanne Siauve (1919-1975): Minor Writings of S. Siauve. Indian Theological Studies* **17**/1 (1980) 76-78. (Reprint of no. 586.)

588.Review of Paul Hacker, *Kleine Schriften. Boletin de la Asociaciòn Española de Orientalistas* **16** (1980) 267-273.

589.Review of Charles Swain, *People of the Earth: Trans-Traditional Dialogue in Christian Perspective. Indian Missiological Review* **2**/3 (1980) 305-309.

590.Review of S. P. Kanal, *To Be Good. Indian Theological Studies* **17**/4 (1980) 398-399.

1981

591."Are Mind-Transcending Experiences Self-Interpreting?" *The Divine Life* **43**/5 (1981) 154-158. (Reprint of no. 567.)

592."Fleeting Time and Sacrificially Produced Continuity in Vedic Brahmanism and in Early Christianity." *Boletin de la Asociación Española de Orientalistas* **17** (1981) 147-166. (Reprinted as no. 609.)

593."Natural Law and the Dharma of Renascent Hinduism." *Indian Law Review* **2**/3 (1981) 3-19. (Cf. offprint in no. 594. Reprinted as no. 600.)

594."Natural Law and the Dharma of Renascent Hinduism." *Indian Law Review* **2**/3 (1981) 1-17. (Offprint of no. 593.)

595."The Integrative Theology of Prāṇnāth." *Vidyajyoti: Journal of Theological Reflection* **45**/5 (1981) 239-241.

596."Ethics of Swaminarayan and Christianity." *New Dimensions in Vedanta Philosophy, Bhagawan Swaminarayan Bicentenary Commemoration Volume: 1781-1981*. Ahmedabad: Bochasanwasi Shri Aksharpurushottam Samsthā, 1981. Part II:8-18.

597."Le poids du système des castes au Bihar (Inde)." *Axes* **13** (1981) 39-46.

598."Natural Law." *The Divine Life* **43** (1981) 154-158. (Reprint of no. 570.)

599."The Significance of Myth in Comparative Religion." *The Viśva-Bhārati Journal of Philosophy* **11**/1-2 (1981) 48-54.

600."Natural Law and the Dharma of Renascent Hinduism." *Indian Theological Studies* **18**/2 (1981) 105-134. (Reprint of no. 593.)

601.Review of Chacko Valiaveetil, *Liberated Life: Ideal of Jivamukti* [sic] *in Indian Religion especially in Śaiva-Siddhānta. Indian Theological Studies* **18**/3 (Sept. 1981) 304-307. (Reprinted as no. 602.)

602.Review of Chacko Valiaveetil, *Liberated Life: Ideal of* Jīvanmukti *in Indian Religions specially in Śaiva-Siddhānta. Boletin de la Asociaciòn Española de Orientalistas* **17** (1981) 251-253. (Reprint of no. 601.)

603.Review of John K. Locke S.J., *Karuṇāmaya: The Cult of Avalokiteśvara-Matsyendranāth in the Valley of Nepal. Indian Theological Studies* **18**/4 (Dec. 1981) 385-387.

604.Review of Sangam Lal Pandey, *Whither Indian Philosophy: Essays in Western and Indian Epistemology. Review of Darshana* **2**/2 (1981) 57-62.

605.Selected Questions of Metaphysics. Cyclostyled notes for a course given at St Peter's Seminary, Bangalore, February 1981. 16 pp.

606."The Sociological Dimension of the Buddha's Teaching." *Bulletin of Aide Inter-Monastère / North American Board for East-West Dialogue* **11** (May 1981) 3pp. Available at http://monasticdialog.com/bulletins.php. (Cf. no. 574.)

1982

607."The Christian Conception of Man." *Southern Chronicle* (Kottayam) **8**/1 (1982) 21-27. (Reprinted as nos. 687-688.)

608."Hegel on Indian Philosophy." Review of Ignatius Viyagappa, *G.W.F. Hegel's Concept of Indian Philosophy* (Rome, 1980). *Vidyajyoti: Journal of Theological Reflection* **46**/11 (1982) 555-557.

609."Fleeting Time and Sacrificially Produced Continuity in Vedic Brahmanism and in Early Christianity." *Indian Theological Studies* **19**/2 (1982) 1-26. (Reprint of no. 592.)

610.Review of Wilhelm Halbfass, *Indien und Europa: Perspektiven ihrer geistigen Begegnung. Indian Theological Studies* **19**/2 (June 1982) 183-188.

611."The Concept of Man in Thomism and Neo-Thomism." *Indian Philosophical Annual* **15** (1982-83) 1-32. (Reprinted as no. 678.)

1983

612."Ancient Indian Royal Tradition." *The Divine Life* **45**/5-6-7--8 (1983) 188-192; 225-228; 257-260.

613."Probing the Dev Darśana." *Perspectives of the Philosophy of Devātmā.* Ed. K. Mittal. Delhi: Motilal Banarsidass, 1983. 233-249.

1984

614."Hindu and Neo-Hindu Exegesis." *Indian Theological Studies* **21**/3-4 (1984) 225-240. (English translation, rev. and enlarged, of no. 346.)

615."Shri Aurobindo and Hindu Myth." *Southern Chronicle* (Kottayam) **10**/6 (June 1984) 8-11. (Cf. no. 616.)

616."Shri Aurobindo and Hindu Myth." *Southern Chronicle* (Kottayam) **10**/6 (June 1984) 1-4. (Offprint of no. 615.)

617."Jesus and Non-Violence." *Gandhi Jyoti* (Journal of Gandhian Thought, Bhagalpur University) **1**/3 (1984) 155-159.

618."Comments on C.R.B. Menon's 'A Biological Theory of Communal Conflict'." *Southern Chronicle* (Kottayam) **10**/8 (1984) 15-16.

619."Indian Roots for the Lord-Vassal Relationship in the Spiritual Exercises of St Ignatius." *Ignis* 6-7 (1984) 5-39. (Reprint of no. 501. Cf. nos. 716-717.)

620."Christianity and Society." *The Viśva-Bhārati Journal of Philosophy* **21**/1 (1984) 89-99. (Reprinted as no. 626.)

621."Some Characteristics of Buddhist Exegesis." *Indian Theological Studies* **21**/3-4 (1984) 241-249.

622.Review of B. Barzel, *Mystique de l'ineffable dans l'hindouisme et le christianisme: Çankara et Eckart. Indian Theological Studies* **21**/2 (1984) 194-195.

1985

623."Notes on Hinduism versus the Plurality of Religious Traditions." *Boletin de la Asociación Española de Orientalistas* **21** (1985) 289-300. (Reprinted as no. 633.)

624."Man's Integral Dynamism and His Quest for Values." *Reality, Knowledge and Value: Felicitation Volume in Honour of A.G. Javadekar*. Ed. S.R. Bhatt. Delhi: Bharatiya Vidya Prakashan, 1985. 133-142.

625."The Hindu Dharma and its Modern Metamorphosis." *The Southern Chronicle* (Kottayam) **11**/12 (1985) 3-9.

626."Christianity and Society." *Indian Theological Studies* **22**/4 (1985) 325-337. (Reprint of no. 620.)

627.Review of Othmar Gächter, *Hermeneutics and Language in Pūrva Mīmāṃsā: A Study in Śābara Bhāṣya. Indian Theological Studies* **22**/1 (1985) 115-116.

628.Review of W. Halbfass, *Studies in Kumārila and Śaṅkara* (1983). *Journal of the American Oriental Society* **105**/2 (1985) 373-374. (Reprinted as no. 629.)

629.Review of W. Halbfass, *Studies in Kumārila and Śaṅkara* (1983). *Indian Theological Studies* **22**/2 (1985) 205-209. (Reprinted as no. 628.)

630.Review of George Chemparathy, *L'autorité du Véda selon les Nyāya-Vaiśeṣikas. Indian Theological Studies* **22**/1 (1985) 113-114.

631.Review of J. Vattanky, SJ, *Gaṅgeśa's Philosophy of God* (Madras: The Adyar Research Centre, 1984). *Indian Theological Studies* **22**/2 (1985) 209-212. (Reprinted as no. 638.)

632.Review of Noel Sheth, SJ, *The Divinity of Krishna* (Delhi: Manoharlal, 1984). *Indian Theological Studies* **22**/2 (1985) 201-205. (Reprinted as no. 636.)

1986

633."Hinduism versus the Plurality of Religious Traditions." *Indian Theological Studies* **23**/1 (1986) 22-36. (Reprint of no. 623.)

634."Spiritual Values of Advaita Vedanta and Social Life." *Indian Philosophical Annual* **18** (1985-86) 1-15.

635."The Hindu Dharma: Permanence and Change." *E. Ugarte Felicitation Volume: Philosophy and Human Development.* Ed. A. Amaladass, S.L. Raj and J. Elampassery. Madras: Satya Nilayam, 1986. 3-26.

636.Review of Noel Sheth, SJ, *The Divinity of Krishna* (Delhi: Manoharlal, 1984). *Philosophy East and West* **36**/3 (July 1986) 305-307. (Reprint of no. 632.)

637.Review of Chantal van der Plancke, *L'Apocalypse*. *Lumen Vitae* **40** (1985) 236-237.

638.Review of J. Vattanky, SJ, *Gaṅgeśa's Philosophy of God* (Madras: The Adyar Research Centre, 1984). *Philosophy East and West* **36**/4 (1986) 429-430. (Reprint of no. 631.)

639.Review of *Doctrine de la non-dualité (advaita-vāda) et Christianisme* (1982) by 'Un Moine d'Occident' [= Fr Elie, La Trappe]. *Indian Theological Studies* **23**/1 (1986) 65-68.

640."Amesha Spentas." *Verbo: Enciclopedia Luso-Brasileira de Cultura.* Lisboa: Editorial Verbo, 1986. **1**:1817-1818. (Reprint of nos. 167, 516.)

641."Amida." *Verbo: Enciclopedia Luso-Brasileira de Cultura.* Lisboa: Editorial Verbo, 1986. **1**:1823-1824. (Reprint of nos. 169, 517.)

642."Anāhitā (Ardrū Sūrā)." *Verbo: Enciclopedia Luso-Brasileira de Cultura.* Lisboa: Editorial Verbo, 1986. **2**:61. (Reprint of nos. 208, 518.)

643."Aryo-Samaj." *Verbo: Enciclopedia Luso-Brasileira de Cultura.* Lisboa: Editorial Verbo, 1986. **2**:1467-1468. (Reprint of nos. 209, 519.)

644."Āshrama." *Verbo: Enciclopedia Luso-Brasileira de Cultura.* Lisboa: Editorial Verbo, 1986. **2**:1506-1507. (Reprint of nos. 210, 520.)

645."Asura." *Verbo: Enciclopedia Luso-Brasileira de Cultura.* Lisboa: Editorial Verbo, 1986. **2**:1697. (Reprint of nos. 211, 521.)

646."Ātman." *Verbo: Enciclopedia Luso-Brasileira de Cultura.* Lisboa: Editorial Verbo, 1986. **2**:1754-1755. (Reprint of nos. 212, 522.)

647."Avatāra." *Verbo: Enciclopedia Luso-Brasileira de Cultura.* Lisboa: Editorial Verbo, 1986. **3**:98. (Reprint of nos. 233, 523.)

648."Avesta." *Verbo: Enciclopedia Luso-Brasileira de Cultura.* Lisboa: Editorial Verbo, 1986. **3**:132, 135. (Reprint of nos. 234, 524.)

649."Bhagavadgītā." *Verbo: Enciclopedia Luso-Brasileira de Cultura.* Lisboa: Editorial Verbo, 1986. **3**:1226-1227. (Reprint of nos. 235, 525.)

650."Bhakti." *Verbo: Enciclopedia Luso-Brasileira de Cultura.* Lisboa: Editorial Verbo, 1986. **3**:1227. (Reprint of nos. 236, 526.)

651."Bhil." *Verbo: Enciclopedia Luso-Brasileira de Cultura.* Lisboa: Editorial Verbo, 1986. **3**:1229. (Reprint of nos. 237, 527.)

652."Brama." *Verbo: Enciclopedia Luso-Brasileira de Cultura.* Lisboa: Editorial Verbo, 1986. **3**:1775. (Reprint of nos. 238, 528.)

653."Braman." *Verbo: Enciclopedia Luso-Brasileira de Cultura.* Lisboa: Editorial Verbo, 1986. **3**:1775-1776. (Reprint of nos. 239, 529.)

654."Bramana." *Verbo: Enciclopedia Luso-Brasileira de Cultura.* Lisboa: Editorial Verbo, 1986. **3**:1776. (Reprint of nos. 240, 530.)

655."Bramanismo." *Verbo: Enciclopedia Luso-Brasileira de Cultura.* Lisboa: Editorial Verbo, 1986. **3**: 1778-1779. (Reprint of nos. 241, 531.)

656."Bramo-Samaj." *Verbo: Enciclopedia Luso-Brasileira de Cultura.* Lisboa: Editorial Verbo, 1986. **3**:1782-1783. (Reprint of nos. 242, 532.)

657."Dharma." *Verbo: Enciclopedia Luso-Brasileira de Cultura.* Lisboa: Editorial Verbo, 1986. **6**:1213. (Reprint of nos. 262, 533.)

658."Dharma-Sastra." *Verbo: Enciclopedia Luso-Brasileira de Cultura.* Lisboa: Editorial Verbo, 1986. **6**:1213. (Reprint of nos. 263, 534.)

659."Dhyana." *Verbo: Enciclopedia Luso-Brasileira de Cultura.* Lisboa: Editorial Verbo, 1986. **6**:1214-1215. (Reprint of nos. 264, 535.)

660."Digha-Nikaya." *Verbo: Enciclopedia Luso-Brasileira de Cultura.* Lisboa: Editorial Verbo, 1986. **6**:1360. (Reprint of nos. 265, 536.)

661."Gandhi." *Verbo: Enciclopedia Luso-Brasileira de Cultura.* Lisboa: Editorial Verbo, 1986. **9**:151-152. (Reprint of nos. 296, 537.)

1987

662."Forward Steps in Śaṅkara Research." (Pratap Seth Endowment Lecture on Śaṅkara Vedānta: Indian Philosophical Congress, 62nd session, 6-9 June 1987, University of Kashmir, Srinagar.) *Darshana International* (Moradabad, India) **26**/3 (1987) 33-46.

663."The Medieval Inheritance of Dante." *Journal of the Department of English* (University of Calcutta) **23**/1-2 (1986-1987) 37-49.

1988

664."Light from the Christian *Jñāna-Karma-Bhakti Samuccaya*." *Religious Consciousness and Life-Worlds.* Ed. T.S. Rukmani. New Delhi: Indus, 1988. 64-83. (Cf. no. 675.)

665."Dynamics of Hinduism and Hindu-Christian Dialogue." *Communio: International Catholic Review* 15 (Winter 1988) 436-450. [In no. 697, 25, De Smet complains that the title has been unduly changed by the editor, the original being "The Dynamics of Hinduism and a Christian Interpretation."]

666."A Presentation." Sachit Dhar, *Where the Universe Becomes One Nest: On Marxism and India: A Study; Or: On Christianity, India and Marxism: A Study.* Calcutta: Aditi Nath Sarkar / Smt. Monika Devi and Trustees, 1988. vii-xv.

667."The Wide Range of De Nobili's Doctrine." Review of Soosai Arokiasamy, *Dharma, Hindu and Christian, according to Roberto de Nobili* (Rome, 1986). *Vidyajyoti: Journal of Theological Reflection* **52**/3 (1988) 159-164.

668."Swami Narendranand's 'Hindu Spirituality'." *Vidyajyoti: Journal of Theological Reflection* **52**/2 (Feb. 1988) 108-109.

669.Review of Soosai Arokiasamy, SJ, *Dharma, Hindu and Christian, according to Roberto de Nobili* (Documenta Missionalia Series 19. Roma: Editrice Pontificia Università Gregoriana, 1986). *Vidyajyoti: Journal of Theological Reflection* **52**/3 (March 1988) 159-164.

670."Tukaram's God-Experience." Review of Thomas Dabre, *The God-Experience of Tukaram, A Study in Religious Symbolism* (Pune: Jnana

Deepa Vidyapeeṭh, 1987). *Jivan: Jesuits of South Asia: Views and News* **9**/1 (January 1988) 28.

1989

671.“Gītā/Gospel Convergencies.” *Sevartham* **14** (1989) 13-19. (Reprinted as no. 679.)

672.“The Buddha, Meister Eckhart and Śaṅkarācārya on ‘Nothing’.” *Journal of Religious Studies* (Patiala: Punjabi University) **17** (1989) 56-69.

673.“Radhakrishnan’s Interpretation of Śaṅkara.” *Radhakrishnan Centenary Volume*. Ed. G. Parthasarathi and D.P. Chattopadhyaya. Delhi: Oxford University Press, 1989. 53-70.

674.“Radhakrishnan’s Second Presentation of Śaṅkara’s Teaching.” *Prajña: Kashi Hindu Vishvavidyalaya Patrika* (Special issue for S.R.’s Centenary *smṛti*) **34** (1989) 83-96.

675.“Christian Integration of the Three Margas.” *Ignis* **18**/1 (1989) 19-27. (= abstracts from no. 664.)

676.“Origin: Creation and Emanation.” *Wisdom Light* (Shivananandanagar) (January and April 1989) 27-42. (Reprint of nos. 542 and 555. Offprinted as no. 677.)

677.“Origin: Creation and Emanation.” *Wisdom Light* (Shivananandanagar) (1989) 1-20. (Offprint of no. 676.)

678.“The Concept of Man in Thomism and Neo-Thomism.” *Indian Theological Studies* **26** (1989) 336-372. (Reprint of no. 611.)

679.“Gītā/Gospel Convergencies.” *Southern Chronicle* (Kottayam) **15** (1989) 18-21. (Reprint of no. 671.)

680.“Jesus and the Avatāra.” *Dialogue and Syncretism: An Interdisciplinary Approach*. Ed. J.D. Gort, H.M. Vroom, R. Fernhout, A. Wessels. Grand Rapids: W.B. Eerdmans / Amsterdam: Editions Rodopi, 1989. 153-162.

681.Review of Felix Wilfred, *The Emergent Church in a New India* (Tiruchirapalli: St Paul’s Seminary, 1988). *Indian Theological Studies* **26** (1989) 98-99.

682.Review of Zacharias Paranilam, *Christian Openness to the World Religions* (Alwaye: Pontifical Institute Publications, 1989). *Indian Theological Studies* **26** (1989) 187-188.

683. “Pierre Johanns.” *Dictionary of Indian Christian Theology*. Bangalore: United Theological College (Lott), 1989. (Mentioned in no. 697, 24.)

684.“Analogy/*Lakṣaṇā*.” *Dictionary of Indian Christian Theology*. Bangalore: United Theological College (Lott), 1989. (Mentioned in no. 697, 24.)

685.“Aquinas, Thomas.” *Dictionary of Indian Christian Theology*. Bangalore: United Theological College (Lott), 1989. (Mentioned in no. 697, 24.)

686.“Reply (to NBCLC questionnaire regarding the New Universal Catechism) from the Standpoint of Hinduism.” (Mentioned in no. 697, 26.)

1990

687.“The Biblical Concept of a Human Person.” *Ignis* **19** (1990) 59-64. (Reprint of part of no. 607.)

688."The Christian Concept of a Human Person." *Ignis* **19** (1990) 127-130. (Reprint of second part of no. 607.)
689."Technology and the Ethico-Religious Claims." *New Technological Civilization and Indian Society*. Ed. B.D. Nag Chaudhuri. New Delhi / Shimla: Indus, 1990. 61-66.
690."Surrounded by Excellence: An Evocation." *Jivan: Jesuits of South Asia: Views and News* **11**/10 (December 1990) 8, 10-11.
691."Relevant Advice." (Presentation of a letter of St Ignatius on the apostolate in East Africa.) *Ignis* **19** (1990) 163-164.
692.Review of Ignatius Jesudasan, *Gandhian Theology of Liberation* (Anand: Gujarat Sahitya Prakash, 1987). *Indian Theological Studies* **27** (1990) 97-98.
693.Review of Henri de Lubac, *Mémoire sur l'occasion de mes écrits* (Namur: Collection Culture et Verité, 1989). *Indian Theological Studies* **27** (1990) 373-375.
694.Review of N.S. Xavier, *The Two Faces of Religion* (Bangalore: Theological Publications in India, 1989). *Indian Theological Studies* **27** (1990) 375-378.
695.Review of Sylvie Murr, Vol. 1: *Moeurs et Coutumes des Indiens* (1777): Un inédit du Père G.-L. Coeurdoux, S.J. dans la version de N.-J. Desvaulx. Vol. II: *L'Indologie du Père Coeurdoux* (Paris: Ecole Francaise d'Extrême Orient, 1987). *Indian Theological Studies* **27** (1990) 371-373.
696.Review of Parmananda Divarkar, *The Path of Interior Knowledge* (Anand: *Gujarat Sahitya* Prakash, 1990). *Indian Theological Studies* **27** (1990) 378-380.
697.Publications of Dr Richard V. De Smet, PhD, SJ. [1989]. 26 pp. Typescript. [Prepared over the years: up to 1968 (8 pp.); 1969-70 (1 p.); 1968-77 (7 pp.); 1972-75 (1 p.); 1979-81 (2 pp.); 1981-82 (1 p.); 1982-83 (1 p.); 1983-85 (1 p.); 1986-87 (2 pp.); 1988-89 (1 p.); 1989-90 (1 p.).]
698."Beaux compagnons dormant...." *La revue générale* 6 (1990) 111-112. (Mentioned in no. 726, 13.)

1991

699."Robert de Nobili as Forerunner of Hindu-Christian Dialogue." *Hindu-Christian Studies Bulletin* **4** (1991) 1-9.
700."The Exercises in India: An Early Ignatian Revival." *Ignis* **20** (1991) 191-198.
701."A Mirror for Provincials." *Ignis* **20** (1991) 23-24.
702."Christ and the Transforming Growth of Religions." *Vidyajyoti: Journal of Theological Reflection* **55** (1991) 449-457.
703."Interphilosophical and Religious Dialogue in my Life." *Pilgrims of Dialogue*. Ed. A. Pushparajan. Mannar: Sangam Dialogue Centre, 1991. 1-6.
704.Review of John Locke, *Buddhist Monasteries of Nepal* (Kathmandu: Sahayogi Press, 1985). *Indian Theological Studies* **28** (1991) 202-203.
705."The Trajectory of My Dialogical Activity." Autobiographic text for Bradley Malkovsky. 23 April 1991. 13 pp. Typescript.

1992

706.“Dove va l’India?” *La Civiltà Cattolica* Anno **143**/quaderno 3405 (1992) II:301-308.
707.“The Concord Incantation of Atharvaveda III, 30.” *Vidyajyoti: Journal of ‘Theological Reflection* **56** (1992) 616-618.
708.“A Curious Fact of Jesuit Literary History.” *Jivan: Jesuits of South Asia: Views and News* **13**/4 (April 1992) 30.
709.“A Contribution to Ecological Theology.” *Vidyajyoti: Journal of Theological Reflection* **56** (1992) 172-174.
710.“The Creative Word in Śaṅkara Vedānta.” *Divine Life* (1992) 14-20. (Reprinted as no. 732.)
711.[With Saral Jhingram.] “Secularism and the Supernatural.” Exchange of letters between Prof. Mrs Saral Jhingram and De Smet. *Indian Theological Studies* **29** (1992) 55-67.
712.Review of Tord Fornberg, *Jewish-Christian Dialogue and Biblical Exegesis* (Uppsala: Studia Missionalia Uppsaliensa, 1988). *Vidyajyoti: Journal of Theological Reflection* **56** (1992) 240-241.
713.Review of Som Raj Gupta, *The Word Speaks to the Faustian Man: A Translation and Interpretation of the Prasthānatrayī and Śaṅkara's Bhāṣya for the Participation of Contemporary Man*, vol. I: Īśā, Kena, Kaṭha and Praśna Upanisads (Delhi: Motilal Banarsidass, 1991). *Indian Theological Studies* **29** (1992) 274. (Reprinted as no. 714.)
714.Review of Som Raj Gupta, *The Word Speaks to the Faustian Man: A translation and interpretation of the Prasthānatrayī and Śaṅkara's Bhāṣya for the participation of contemporary man*, vol. I: Īśā, Kena, Kaṭha and Praśna Upaniṣads (Delhi: Motilal Banarsidass, 1991). *Boletin de la Asociaciòn Española de Orientalistas* **28** (1992) 282. (Reprint of no. 713.)
715.“Sankara's Perspective on Meaning and Truth.” 25 February 1992. Manuscript. 17pp. (Published as no. 729.)

1993

716.“Indian Roots for the Lord-Vassal Relationship in the Spiritual Exercises of St Ignatius, Part I.” *Indian Journal of Spirituality* **6** (1993) 191-206. (Reprint of nos. 501 and 619.)
717.“Indian Roots for the Lord-Vassal Relationship in the Spiritual Exercises of St Ignatius, Part II.” *Indian Journal of Spirituality* **6** (1993) 294-321. (Reprint of nos. 501 and 619.)
718.“Modernity and Postmodernity.” *Indian Theological Studies* **30** (1993) 5-17.
719.“Sidelights on Segers' Conception of ‘Christ-Bread’.” *Indian Theological Studies* **30** (1993) 343-351.
720.“Introducing Christian Youth to Hindu Spirituality.” *Divyadaan: A Philosophical Annual* **5** (1993-94) 31-40.
721.Review of Moti Lal Pandit, *Towards Transcendence: A Historico-Analytical Study of Yoga as a Method of Liberation* (New Delhi: Intercultural Publications, 1991). *Indian Theological Studies* **30**/1 (1993) 71-72.

722.Review of Jose Thachil, *The Upaniṣads: A Socio-Religious Approach* (New Delhi: Intercultural Publications, 1993). *Indian Theological Studies* **30**/2 (1993) 175-177.

723.Review of John Vattanky, *Development of Nyāya Theism* (New Delhi: Intercultural Publications, 1993). *Indian Theological Studies* **30**/2 (1993) 177-179.

724.Review of Srinivasa Rao, *Advaita: A Critical Investigation* (Bangalore: Indian Philosophical Foundation, 1985). *Indian Theological Studies* **30**/2 (1993) 179-181.

725."L'induità e la nascita della filosofia indiana." *La Civiltà Cattolica* Anno **144**/quaderno 3433 (1993) III:29-36.

726.Bibliography of Fr Richard De Smet, SJ. [Title on next page: R. De Smet: Classified Bibliography (partial).] 9 November 1993. 25 pp. + 1 p. insert entitled Fr Richard De Smet's Bibliography (1993-94). Typescript.

727."What is this Word-Seeder Trying to Say? Acts of the Apostles 17:16-34." *Jivan* **14**/5 (May 1993) 21.

1994

728."Foreword" to Joseph Satyanand, *Nimbārka: A Pre-Śaṁkara Vedāntin and His Philosophy.* Varanasi: Vishwa Jyoti Gurukul, 1994. [13-14.]

729."Śaṇkara's Perspective on Meaning and Truth." *Hermeneutics: Truth and/or Meaning.* Ed. J. Maliekal. Kondadaba: St John's Regional Seminary, 1994. 50-60. (Cf. no. 715.)

730."The Presuppositions of Jaimini and the Vedāntins." *Journal of Indian Council of Philosophical Research* **11**/2 (1994) 77-87.

731."Job's 'Insufferable Comforters' and the Law of Karma." *Vidyajyoti: Journal of Theological Reflection* **58**/5 (1994) 308-318.

732."The Creative Word in Śaṅkara-Vedānta." *La parola creatrice in India e nel Medio Oriente. Atti del Seminario della Facoltà di Lettere dell'Università di Pisa, 29-31 maggio 1991.* Ed. Catarina Conio. Pisa: Giardini, 1994. 91-99. (Reprint of no. 710.)

733."Hindu Eschatology and Assistance to the Dying." *L'assistenza al morente.* Ed. E. Sgreccia et al. Milan: Vita e Pensiero, 1994. 298-307.

734."From Catholic Theology to Sankara Vedanta and Return with Fr F.X. Clooney." Review Article, Francis X. Clooney, *Theology after Vedānta: An Experiment in Comparative Theology* (Albany: State University of New York, 1993). *Vidyajyoti: Journal of Theological Reflection* **58** (1994) 795-807.

735."The Spiritual Completeness of Our Priestly Studies." *Indian Journal of Spirituality* **7**/2 (1994) 201-212.

736."From the Vedas to Radhakrishnan." A Paper for the Symposium on the Contribution to 'Indian Philosophy' by Contemporary Christian Thinkers of India. Madras: Satyanilayam, 1-3 March 1994. 6 pp. Typescript.

1995

737."The Dynamics of Contemplation according to Shankaracharya." *Atti del Congresso Internazionale di Semiotica del Testo Mistico*, 1991. Ed. G. de

Gennaro. L'Aquila: Edizioni del Gallo Cedrone, 1995. 666-674.
738."The Origin and Reach of Prayer to the One God." *Shabda, Shakti, Sangam*. Ed. Vandana Mataji. Rishikesh: Jeevan-Dhara Sadhana Kutir, 1995. 79-82.
739."Towards a Real-Life Indian Theology, 1. In the Beginning was Oṁ." *Vidyajyoti: Journal of Theological Reflection* **59** (1995) 333-337.
740."Towards a Real-Life Indian Theology: 2. The Advaita of Christianity." *Vidyajyoti: Journal of Theological Reflection* **59** (1995) 405-409.
741.Review of B.N.K. Sharma, *In Defence of Dvaita against Advaita: Advaitasiddhi vs. Nyāyāmṛta: An Up to Date Critical Reappraisal.* Part I. *Indian Theological Studies* **32** (1995) 181-184.
742.Review of George Panthanmackel, *One in Many: An Investigation into the Metaphysical Vision of Karl Rahner* (Bangalore: Indian Institute of Spirituality, 1993). *Journal of Indian Council of Philosophical Research* **13** (1995) 189-191.

1996

743."Materials toward an Indo-Western Understanding of the Dignity of the Human Person." *Journal of Dharma* **21** (1996) 39-46.
744."Origins and Problems of Bioethics in India." *Vidyajyoti: Journal of Theological Reflection* **60** (1996) 654-662.

1997

745.[Editor and contributor, with J. Neuner.] *Religious Hinduism*. 4th rev. ed. Mumbai: St Pauls, 1997. (Reprint of nos. 185 and 266.)
746."Foreword." *Religious Hinduism: A Presentation and Appraisal*. Ed. R. De Smet and J. Neuner. 4th rev. ed. Mumbai: St Pauls, 1997. 15-20. (Rev. of no. 267.)
747."The Religious Discoveries of the Vedic Indians." Chapter 3. *Religious Hinduism: A Presentation and Appraisal*. Ed. R. De Smet and J. Neuner. 4th rev. ed. Mumbai: St Pauls, 1997. 65-79.
748."Śaṅkara's Non-Dualism (Advaita-Vāda)." Chapter 4. *Religious Hinduism: A Presentation and Appraisal*. Ed. R. De Smet and J. Neuner. 4th rev. ed. Mumbai: St Pauls, 1997. 80-96. (Rev. of no. 270.)
749."Rāmānuja and Madhva." Chapter 5. *Religious Hinduism: A Presentation and Appraisal*. Ed. R. De Smet and J. Neuner. 4th rev. ed. Mumbai: St Pauls, 1997. 97-107. (Reprint of no. 271.)
750."Sin and Its Removal." Chapter 11. *Religious Hinduism: A Presentation and Appraisal*. Ed. R. De Smet and J. Neuner. 4th rev. ed. Mumbai: St Pauls, 1997. 170-181. (Rev. of no. 272.)
751.[With J. Gonsalves.] "Śaivism." Chapter 24. *Religious Hinduism: A Presentation and Appraisal*. Ed. R. De Smet and J. Neuner. 4th rev. ed. Mumbai: St Pauls, 1997. 314-330.
752."The Present Situation." Chapter 29. *Religious Hinduism: A Presentation and Appraisal*. Ed. R. De Smet and J. Neuner. 4th rev. ed. Mumbai: St Pauls, 1997. 388-401.

753."Nyāya Philosophy of Language." Review of John Vattanky, SJ, *Nyāya Philosophy of Language: Analysis, Text, Translation and Interpretation of* Upamana *and* Sabda *sections of* Karikāvali, Muktāvali *and* Dinākari (Delhi: Sri Satguru Publications, 1995). *Vidyajyoti: Journal of Theological Reflection* **61** (1997) 57-58.

1998

754."From Tamil Shaivism to Saint Paul with Jaswant Raj." Review of Joseph Jaswant Raj, SDB, *Grace in the* Saiva Siddhāntam *and in St Paul: A Contribution in Inter-Faith Cross-Cultural Understanding* (Madras: South Indian Salesian Society, 1989). *Indian Theological Studies* **55** (1998) 74-84.

755."Towards and Indian View of the Person." *Contemporary Indian Philosophy. Second Series*. Ed. M. Chatterjee (Delhi: Motilal Banarsidass, 1998) 51-75. (Reprint of no. 384.)

756. "The Significance of the Resurrection for the Hindu-Christian Dialogue, with Special Reference to the Soul-Body Relationship." N.d. (Mentioned in no. 697, p. 8.)

757."The Vedāntins' Diverse Conceptions of Vākya (Sentence) as Responsible for the Diversity of their Interpretations of the Same Scriptures." N.d. (Mentioned in no. 726, 4.)

II. Secondary Sources

Amalraj, Paulraj. The Concept of *Tadaṭmya* in Sankaracarya as Interpreted by Richard De Smet and Sara Grant. M.Ph. dissertation. Director: Albano Fernandes, SDB. Nashik: Divyadaan – Salesian Institute of Philosophy, 2003. Unpublished.

Amalraj, Paulraj. Review of Sara Grant, *Sankara's Concept of Relation. Divyadaan: Journal of Philosophy and Education* **16** (2005) 100-103.

Clooney, Francis X. "Śaṃkara's Theological Realism: The Meaning and Usefulness of Gods (*Devatā*) in the *Uttara Mīmāṃsā Sūtra Bhāṣya.*" *New Perspectives in Advaita Vedānta: Essays in Commemoration of Professor Richard De Smet, SJ.* Ed. Bradley J. Malkovsky. Leiden / Boston / Köln: Brill, 2000. 30-50.

Coelho, Ivo. "Fr. Richard V. De Smet (1916-97): Reminiscences." *Divyadaan: Journal of Philosophy and Education* **8**/1 (1997) 3-15.

Coelho, Ivo. Review of Bradley J. Malkovsky, ed., *New Perspectives on Advaita Vedanta: Essays in Commemoration of Professor Richard De Smet, SJ. Divyadaan: Journal of Philosophy and Education* **18**/1 (2007) 127-133.

D'Souza, Joseph A. "Father Richard De Smet: A Personal Appreciation." *Calcutta Jesuit Newsletter* (April 1997).

De Marneffe, Jean. "Richard De Smet, S.J." *Interrelations and Interpretation: Philosophical Reflections on Science, Religion and Hermeneutics in Honour of Richard De Smet, S.J. and Jean de Marneffe, S.J.* Ed. Job Kozhamthadam. New Delhi: Intercultural Publications, 1997. xvii-xx.

Fernandes, Albano. A Glimpse into the Understanding of Sankara's Philosophy of Non-Dualism (*Advaita*). Class notes. Nashik: Divyaaan – Salesian Institute of Philosophy, 2001.

Fernandes, Albano. *The Hindu Mystical Experience: A Comparative Philosophical Study of the Approaches of R.C. Zaehner and Bede Griffiths.* New Delhi: Intercultural Publications, 2004.

Gandhi, Herbert Amos. "The Concept of Maya in Shankara." *Jnanodaya: Journal of Philosophy* (Yercaud, India) **15** (June 2008) 75-85.

Grant, Sara. *Towards an Alternative Theology: Confessions of a Non-Dualist Christian.* Bangalore: Asian Trading Corporation, 1991.

Grant, Sara. *Śaṅkarācārya's Concept of Relation.* Delhi: Motilal Banarsidass, 1999.

Grant, Sara. "The Contemporary Relevance of the Advaita of Śaṇkarācārya." *New Perspectives in Advaita Vedānta: Essays in Commemoration of Professor Richard De Smet, SJ.* Ed. Bradley J. Malkovsky. Leiden / Boston / Köln: Brill, 2000. 148-163.

Kozhamthadam, Job. "Writings of Richard De Smet, S.J.: A Select Bibliography." *Interrelations and Interpretation: Philosophical Reflections on Science, Religion and Hermeneutics in Honour of Richard De Smet, S.J. and Jean de Marneffe, S.J.* Ed. Job Kozhamthadam. New Delhi: Intercultural Publications, 1997. 265-284.

Lipner, Julius. "Śaṁkara on Metaphor with reference to *Gītā* 13.12-18." *Indian Philosophy of Religion.* Ed. R.W. Perrett. Kluwer Academic Publishers, 1989.

Lipner, Julius. "Śaṃkara on satyaṃ jñānam anantaṃ brahma (TaiUp. 2.1.1)." *Relativism, Suffering and Beyond: Essays in Memory of Bimal K. Matilal.* Ed. P. Bilimoria and J.N. Mohanty. Delhi: Oxford University Press, 1997.

Lipner, Julius J. "The Self of Being and the Being of Self: Śaṁkara on 'That You Are' (*tat tvam asi*)." *New Perspectives in Advaita Vedānta: Essays in Commemoration of Professor Richard De Smet, SJ.* Ed. Bradley J. Malkovsky. Leiden / Boston / Köln: Brill, 2000. 51-69.

Lipner, Julius. "Richard V. De Smet, S.J.—An Appreciation by Julius Lipner." *Hindu-Christian Studies Bulletin* **11** (1998) 51-54.

Malkovsky, Bradley J. The Role of Divine Grace in the Soteriology of Srī Śaṅkarācārya. Ph.D. dissertation. University of Tübingen, 1993.

Malkovsky, Bradley J. "A Bibliography of the Publications of Richard V. De Smet, S.J." *New Perspectives in Advaita Vedānta: Essays in Commemoration of Professor Richard De Smet, SJ.* Ed. Bradley J. Malkovsky. Leiden / Boston / Köln: Brill, 2000. 165-178.

Malkovsky, Bradley J. "Advaita Vedānta and Christian Faith." *Journal of Ecumenical Studies* **36**/3-4 (1999) 397-422.

Malkovsky, Bradley J. "In Memoriam: Richard De Smet, S.J. (1916-1997)." *Hindu-Christian Studies Bulletin* **10** (1997) 3-4.

Malkovsky, Bradley J. "Introduction: The Life and Work of Richard V. De Smet, S.J." *New Perspectives in Advaita Vedānta: Essays in Commemoration of Professor Richard De Smet, SJ.* Ed. Bradley J. Malkovsky. Leiden / Boston / Köln: Brill, 2000. 1-17.

Malkovsky, Bradley J. "Preface." *New Perspectives in Advaita Vedānta: Essays in Commemoration of Professor Richard De Smet, SJ.* Ed. Bradley J. Malkovsky. Leiden / Boston / Köln: Brill, 2000. vii-viii.

Malkovsky, Bradley J. "Śaṁkara on Divine Grace." *New Perspectives in Advaita Vedānta: Essays in Commemoration of Professor Richard De Smet, SJ.* Ed. Bradley J. Malkovsky. Leiden / Boston / Köln: Brill, 2000. 70-83.

Malkovsky, Bradley J. "The Personhood of Śaṃkara's *Para Brahman.*" *The Journal of Religion* 77 (1997) 541-562.

Malkovsky, Bradley J., ed. *New Perspectives in Advaita Vedanta: Essays in Commemoration of Professor Richard De Smet, SJ.* Leiden / Boston / Köln: Brill, 2000.

Mattapallil, Sunil Jose. "De Smet's Interpretation of Creation in Sankara." *Jnanodaya: Journal of Philosophy* (Yercaud, India) no. **15** (June 2008) 127-132.

Mattapallil, Sunil. The Concept of Creation in Sankara as Interpreted by Richard V. De Smet, SJ. M.Ph. dissertation. Director Ivo Coelho, SDB. Nashik: Divyadaan – Salesian Institute of Philosophy, 2006. Unpublished.

Mukhia, Terence. A Defence of Sankara's Non-Dualism as Interpreted by Richard De Smet. M.Ph. dissertation. Director Albano Fernandes, SDB. Nashik: Divyadaan – Salesian Institute of Philosophy, 1998. Unpublished.

Palaparambil, Jacob. "Creation in Sankara as Interpreted by Richard V. De Smet." *Jnanodaya: Journal of Philosophy* (Yercaud, India) no. **15** (June 2008) 161-168.

Rao, S.N. "Śaṅkara in Contemporary Inter-Religious Dialogue: A Brāhmin's Perspective." *New Perspectives in Advaita Vedanta: Essays in Commemoration of Professor Richard De Smet, SJ.* Ed. Bradley J. Malkovsky. Leiden / Boston / Köln: Brill, 2000. 122-147.

Rukmani, T.S. "Dr Richard De Smet and Sankara's Advaita." *Hindu-Christian Studies Bulletin* **16** (2003) 12-21.

Satyanand, Joseph. *Nimbārka: A Pre-Śaṁkara Vedāntin and His Philosophy.* New Delhi: Munshiram Manoharlal, 1997.

Thayil, James (Joy Chacko). Essential Teachings of *Sāṃkhyakārikā*: A Comparative Study of *Tattva-Kaumudi* of Vācaspati Miśra and notes of *Sāṃkhyakārika* of Richard V. De Smet. M.Ph. dissertation. Director Richard V. De Smet. Pune: Jnana Deepa Vidyapeeth, 1993. Unpublished. JDV S21/T34.

Thiyagarajan, Satish Kumar. "De Smet's Re-Interpretation of the Classical Advaidic [sic] Reading of *Mahavakyas.*" *Jnanodaya: Journal of Philosophy* (Yercaud, India) no. **15** (June 2008) 169-179.

Vattanky, John. "Fr Richard De Smet, S.J.: Friend, Scholar, Man of Dialogue." *Vidyajyoti: Journal of Theological Reflection* 71/4 (April 2007) 245-261.

Vincent, Patrick. "Friend, Scholar and Man of Dialogue: Father Richard De Smet, SJ." *Calcutta Jesuit Newsletter* (1997).

Vincent, Patrick. "Friend, Scholar and Man of Dialogue: Father Richard De Smet, SJ. 14 April 1916 – 2 March 1997." *Jivan: Jesuits of South Asia: Views and News* **18/5** (May-June 1997) 23-24.

Notes

[1] In no. 697, 7, De Smet lists 27 contributions (art. 131-157) to the *Enciclopedia Verbo*, without indicating a date. However, in a handwritten note he indicates a total of 129 contributions. This is confirmed by no. 726, 6b, where he indicates 129 contributions to the encyclopedia, 1963-1976.

[2] Kozhamthadam lists this as a book published by Herder, Freiburg. In no. 697, 7, however, De Smet, lists it as an article, without any other publishing data except 'Herder.'

[3] In no. 697, BR 282, De Smet lists this item as [a review of] M.V. George, *My Lord and My God, The Morning Star* **65**/5 (May 1973) 103.

[4] In no. 697, 16, De Smet lists 82 contributions (art. 396-477) to the *Enciclopedia Verbo*, 1977.

[5] Following De Smet in no. 697, 7, Kozhamthadam and Malkovsky list also the entries "Ganesha" and "Gandharva"; in the 1977 edition at least, however, these are not by De Smet.

INDEX

empirical limits, 121; as opposed to genus, 157; renouncer as quasi-modern, 107; replaced by singular, 86
Individual spirit, in Sāṁkhya, 128
Individual, as first substance, 46; as paragon of reality, 46
Individualism, 215; and personalism, 81, 94; consequences of atomic, 67; in Descartes, 63, 88
Individuality: from self-awareness, 50; most imperfect degree of singularity, 27-28; not holistic in ancient India, 51; of God, of pure forms, of members of species, 157; of man, 190; of *nous*, Aristotelian denial of, 169; open to supreme *Ātman*, 50-51
Individuals, unmediated polarity of, 72
Individuation, principle of, 157-8
Indologists, Jesuit, 8
Indwelling, of God in creatures, 204
Inner man, Neoplatonic insistence on, 178-9
Intellect: active, 193; and natural appetite for truth, 199
Intellective soul: capacity for complete reflection, 207; end-in-itself, 207-8; not a self-luminous essence, 194-5. *See also*: Human soul.
Intellectual dynamism, 212, 224
Intellectual, replaces rational, 12
Intellectuality, and holistic character of person, 86-87
Intelligere, 193, 194
Interpersonal relationships, 180, 206
Introspection, philosophical, 195
Intuition of God's essence, supreme end of man, 208
Intuition, 193, 194; intellectual, 86, 164-5
Intus legere, 193, 194
Iqbal, M., 149
Iṣṭa, 107
Īśvara, 120; anthropomorphic conception of God, 13
I-Thou relationship, 152; between God and man, 105, 175; beyond highest transcendence, 107
Iyer, K. Sundarama, 139
Jacobi, F.H., 120, 155; influence on German Protestant thinkers, 76; restriction of person to human beings, 13, 75-76
Jaga asaki vastuprabhā, 144
Jagad-andhakāra-prasaṅgaḥ, 143
Jahad-ajahal-lakṣaṇā, 14, 23 n 34
Jainism, 101, 148, 149, 151, 153; and Ātmavāda, 38-39; and unity of man, 38; idea of man, 38-39; idea of person, 16; real connection of *jīvas* with bodies, 17; realist epistemology, 38; seven *tattvas* of, 102
James, William, 145, 153, 154; and redintegration of the person, 76
Jana, and person, 15
Jews, immortality and resurrection, 146
Jijñāsa, 104, 170
Jina, Buddha, Kṛṣṇa, comparison between, 132
Jīva, 149-52; and *jīvātman*, 142; and person, 15, 119; consubstantial with bodies, 17, 18; connected with bodies, 17; experienced 'I', 142; Godlike, 128; in Jainism, 127, 128; object of knowledge, 142; similar to Aristotelian souls, in Jainism, 17; ultimate subject of attribution in man, 113
Jīvātman, 145, 149-52, 150, 152; and rebirth, 19; as projection / reflection, 151; as reflection of supreme *Ātman*, 114, 115; as superimposition (*upādhi*), 151; as ultimate subject of attribution in man, 113autonomous, 114; contingent on supreme *Ātman*, 114; different from and co-existent with *īśvara*, 151; in